Praise for

Members of One Another:
How to build a biblical ethos into your church

What should a real Christian community look like? What should its ethos be, and how in particular should it function? What should its leadership structure be like, and how does one discern God's vision for such a body of believers? If you are interested in these kind of questions, and you've been curious about how house churches or in fact any sort of body of believers can and ought to work, then Dennis McCallum's *Members of One Another: How to Build a Biblical Ethos into any local Body* is the book for you.

—**Dr. Ben Witherington, III**, Amos Professor of NT for Doctoral Studies
Asbury Theological Seminary
Doctoral Faculty St. Mary's College, St. Andrews University, Scotland

———

For all of these past 7+ years, I have regularly mourned that there was not a book that summarized the biblical principles and practical applications that I have discovered both through observing Xenos and continuing my own study of the New Testament. Praise God, now we have the book!!! In this book, Dennis has done a tremendous job unpacking the Scriptures, shedding light on some of the perils of our modern culture, and inspiring our hearts to truly live out the reality that we are members of one another in Christ. Our church and my home group are teaching and seeking to live out the principles outlined in this book within our context. Lives are changing! People are coming to Christ! Sleepy Christians are waking up and engaging in Christ's mission! Cynical Christians are stepping down from their seats of judgment and getting in the game! New leaders are developing! Home groups are growing and beginning to multiply!

Finally, two words of warning are in order. First, this book is not about the latest greatest church growth model. Xenos is not trying to build a worldwide "Xenos Church Association" full of churches that simply copy their every move.

Rather, these principles are grounded in the New Testament and must be fleshed out in your particular ministry context. Second, if you take these principles seriously and begin to apply them they really will change your life and your church. However, this will not be without tremendous cost and sacrifice.

I challenge you to do what I and several of our church leaders are doing – Read this book with one eye. Read the New Testament (especially the book of Acts) with the other. And then let your mind and heart dream of what God could do through you as you live as members of one another advancing the Gospel in your context and to the very ends of the earth.

—**Todd Stewart,** Pastor of New Hope Church

Not since Ray Stedman wrote the book *Body Life* nearly fifty years ago has a book on the church caused me to lose as much sleep as this book. Dennis McCallum has brought a living picture of the struggle to release the people to be the true body of Christ. As one who has visited Xenos a number of times, I know they actually practice the principles in this book. People there are excited about their home church rather than the big building. As an outsider, I see Xenos as biblically and theologically correct, and they have struggled to live that out.

—**Dr. John M. Perkins,** Author, *Let Justice Roll Down* and *Beyond Charity*

Dennis McCallum's most recent book, *Members of One Another,* is not a pharisaical firebomb being thrown at the church. It reflects a pastor's heart that doesn't want to beat up the church, but rather, wants to see the church built up. As a pastor, I was both challenged and convicted. This is a must read for the church and for every church leader.

—**Patrick Schwenk,** Teaching Pastor, NorthPoint Church

Members of One Another isn't like most books on the church because its author keeps together what too many of us put asunder these days - a faithful biblical theology of the church and loads of church experience. Dennis McCallum studies like a scholar and serves as a shepherd. If you've spent time at his church, Xenos Christian Fellowship, you've seen the fruit of his work: authentic and passionate followers of Christ. Read this book and go to the Xenos Summer Institute for your next church conference. The Lord will encourage you that New Testament church *is possible,* and He'll give you biblical and practical ideas for building a biblical ethos into your church.

—**Pastor Ken MacGillivray,** Hopevale Church

—*ᴕᴕᴕ*—

Finally! To the best of my knowledge, there has not been a strong book written on what it really means to be members together in decades. Now there is. Thanks Dennis for putting it all down for us in a way we can apply it.

—**Dr. Dave Earley,** Director of the Lovett Center for Ministry Training
　　Director and Chair of Pastoral Leadership and Church Planting
　　Liberty Baptist Theological Seminary

—*ᴕᴕᴕ*—

"If you're serious about being an agent of change for the Kingdom of God, this book will provide you with the practical insight and wisdom of a community of Jesus followers who have been engaged in disciple-making — not for months, but for several decades. A truly unique and valuable perspective."

—**Craig A. Steffen,** Elder Apex Community Church

Members of One Another

How to build a biblical ethos into your church

Dennis McCallum

International Standard Book Number: 978-1-935920-06-5

All scripture citations are from New American Standard Bible:
1995 Update (LaHabra, CA: The Lockman Foundation, 1995),
unless otherwise indicated.

For more information and author access, go to
membersofoneanother.com

NEW PARADIGM

New Paradigm Publishing

Contents

Introduction ix

Section 1: Grasping the Core Issues 1

    Chapter 1. An Awesome Church 3

    Chapter 2. Jesus Launches His Body 13

    Chapter 3. Living Out Our Unity: Koinonia 25

    Chapter 4. Relationships: How Deep? 33

Section 2: 7 Pictures of the Church.....................................45

    Chapter 5. Pictures: The Body of Christ 47

    Chapter 6. Pictures: God's Army...................................61

    Chapter 7. Pictures: God's Building 67

    Chapter 8. Pictures: God's Family.................................75

    Chapter 9. Pictures: God's Field 81

    Chapter 10. Pictures: Jesus' Bride 91

    Chapter 11. Pictures: God's Flock................................101

Section 3: Lessons From Stories and Letters 113

    Chapter 12. Of Wine and Wineskins..........................115

    Chapter 13. The New Testament Pattern of Ministry...........123

    Chapter 14. Equipping God's People 133

    Chapter 15. The New Testament Pattern of Worship...........147

    Chapter 16. The Ministry of the Word.........................157

    Chapter 17. Other Lessons on Leadership 165

    Chapter 18. Outreach in the Church 181

Chapter 19. Church Finance 195

Chapter 20. Church discipline 203

Chapter 21. Student Ministry 223

Chapter 22. Ministry to the Poor 247

Chapter 23. Missions 255

Section 4: Practical Ideas for Change 261

Chapter 24. Pastors or Elders Seeking Change 263

Chapter 25. Home Group Leaders and

Average Members Seeking Change 287

Chapter 26. Planting a New Church 297

Chapter 27. The Key to a Quality Church 309

Appendix 1 Character Qualifications for Elders 315

Appendix 2 Qualifications for Deacons..................................321

Introduction

What would an awesome church look like?

That's what I wondered.

In 1969 I was arrested and jailed for drug trafficking. There, I surrendered my life to Christ and promised to follow him from then on. When they released me unexpectedly to probation, I was left alone on the campus of a large university trying to recover from several years of addiction and lawless living. My probation terms required that I abstain from all drugs, attend college with passing grades, and live at my parents' house. I had a curfew of 9:00 every night and I wasn't allowed to drive. Walking the streets of the university that fall, I spent most days alone and rode the bus to my parent's house at night.

Someone told me about a Bible study at the student union on Tuesday evenings and I began to attend. I didn't know anyone there, and they didn't seem too interested in getting to know me. They seemed nervous around me, probably because of my appearance and my scowling, cynical, and maybe even hostile demeanor. I didn't care though, because I was prejudiced against church kids, having grown up in the church myself. These very straight-laced students didn't look to me like likely friends.

The teacher, however, was very interesting—a former Campus Crusade staffer who had left Crusade and gone into some alliance of people (long-since disbanded) seeking out an experience of the early church described in the book of Acts. In fact, he was expositing Acts when I went to the group, so that was the first book of the Bible I heard taught as a walking Christian. I think the Holy Spirit immediately began to work on my mind and heart through that study series.

The conventional church

I didn't know much at this point in my Christian life, but one thing stood out: I was certain that whatever I did, it wasn't going to be the conventional church. I was sure there must be another answer.

I had been raised in a Christian Reformed church, and then a conservative Methodist church, which changed into a liberal Methodist church while we attended there (because they replaced the believing pastor with a liberal one). At some point, my parents left that church, although I had already checked out of Christianity by that time. After my arrest some years later, my probation agreement required me to do what my parents wanted, which included attending church again, now at a Baptist church.

Looking back now, I realize these four types of church were very different from one another in doctrine. But at the time they didn't seem different at all; in fact, to my eye they seemed almost identical. All four were traditional churches; all four behaved the same way, they all met on Sunday mornings, all had similar services, all sang many of the same songs, all had the same *feel* and largely the same *outlook*—at least so it seemed. I had a feeling from day one that my future lay somewhere different from this traditional version of "church."

My negative feeling toward churches was partly based on personal taste—a feeling that this "wasn't for me." It wasn't my music, my dress, my language, or my time of day. But I also sensed with certainty that it wasn't for my friends. My strong sense that it would be a big mistake to bring any of my non-Christian counter-cultural friends to one of these churches was a big barrier; one that demanded an alternative.

I think that's why the campus lectures on the book of Acts meant so much to me. It began to dawn on me that the church hadn't always been what I was seeing. What I read about in the early church seemed to have little similarity to what I saw in the conventional modern church. When some of my friends became Christians later that year, we often talked about this difference. We all saw it. Viewed from the outside, the contemporary church was different in a thousand ways from the one described in the pages of the New Testament.

I raised this observation with Christians I knew who were loyal to the traditional church. They all reacted differently, but one thought was common: Why should today's church be the same as it was in the primitive period? Our culture is different from theirs, we aren't under persecution like they were, and two thousand years have passed. Where does the Bible say the church should stay the same as it was in the early period?

Such questions confused me, but I remained at least partially unconvinced that it was okay for the church to be so different from the New Testament church. I was definitely uncomfortable with some ways the church had changed since the days of Jesus, although I could see that some change was appropriate, and even evident within the New Testament itself (like the way Paul spent longer periods in one place in his later journeys, or the way gentile churches discontinued temple-based practices). I had no coherent way to view the whole question of change in the church.

Studying the church

During the forty years since then, I have eagerly studied the church. I studied church history and theology as an undergraduate and in seminary. Since then, I have continued to study both in books and in the laboratory of life. My friends and I have tried scores of ideas over a period of several decades.

During those years we've gone through times of powerful renewal and times of intense struggle and defeat. I've learned just as much from our many mistakes as from our victories. I've also traveled widely, studying what others are doing. I have personally visited multiple examples of every significant pattern of church that people are pursuing in America, as well as many others around the world. During these study visits, I usually spend time with the leadership and often have a sizeable research team with me to interview good numbers of members and staff. We typically visit not only the large services but also various home groups, classes, or villages to get a broad picture. I've learned from working with others who are planting new churches, as well as leaders of existing churches who want to change direction.

One thing becomes clear: as the old saying goes, "there is more than one way to skin a cat." I'm not sure why people are interested in skinning cats, but I agree with several experts on the church who have described highly spiritual and effective churches using very different models. People err when they conclude that one particular model is the key. I'm convinced there is no one way to do church. But I have also felt a growing certainty that some things are biblical and necessary. If these required aspects are missing, trouble always follows. These biblically mandated features of the church are the subject of this study.

Let me be clear: This is a Bible study. It's not a study of the church I'm in, or of other specific churches. I'm not interested in advancing my group as a model. Our church has so many problems and weaknesses I feel reluctant to even write on the subject of the church—I worry people will think I'm saying our church has it together; we've figured it all out. Well, we don't have it together and we haven't figured it out. I'm as agonized about the deficiencies in our church today as at any time in our history.

The real point isn't what we do or what the other group does or whether those things work. The point is what God teaches in his word. As a Bible teacher, that's what I'm interested in teaching: What can we fairly conclude from the Bible about God's will for his church? In Columbus, I teach a class on the church (the fancy term is ecclesiology) from a 'simple' or biblical point of view. That class is the basis for this book. The chapters in this book make up the different areas one must consider in a full picture of the church as God reveals it.

Theology and ethos

A local church's ethos is the collection of beliefs and values that animate people's view of church life and ministry. Here is where people's theology and their values system intersect to form the outlook and attitudes of a group. Ethos is a broader concept than theology. It includes theology, but has less to do with the group's formal statement of faith, and more to do with underlying judgment calls involving expectations and application of truth.

In most churches, people seem to buy into certain assumptions about what is appropriate and what should be expected from one's self, from others, from groups, and from meetings. Many of these assumptions include a combination of theological and attitudinal content. Consider different possible answers for the following examples:

- How much time should people devote to fellowship, discipleship, and evangelism? What should be the balance between time devoted to the things of God and time devoted to career, sports, entertainment, etc.? These questions have no exact answer in scripture, even though we could argue for some general conclusions like those in this book.

- What does it mean to be adequately equipped for the work of ministry (Ephesians 4:12)? That's a judgment call. We will see that churches answer this question in wildly differing ways.

- What makes for a good Christian meeting? Different believers would answer that so differently that they would find it difficult to tolerate each other's versions.

- What is the proper balance between politeness and honesty in the body of Christ? What about confidentiality (or privacy) versus transparency? In other words, should believers talk about others' lives and problems, or not? How deeply should Christians be involved in each other's lives? When would a group be considered disengaged? When are they enmeshed, or lacking boundaries?

- Where do ministry results fit in? How should we interpret poor results? Are good results always necessarily compatible with faithful theology? Will faithful theology necessarily lead to good results?

- What elements should we see in those we consider leaders?

- How responsible should individuals in any meeting feel for the quality of that meeting?

- How responsible should members feel for the spiritual well-being of other members of their church?

- What goes into a good time of corporate prayer? Anyone who has spent time in different groups knows how differently people answer a question like this.

- How should Christians show love to one another? What constitutes a loving community? Here is a good example that demonstrates the importance of priority—many people might agree on most items we could assemble in a list of answers to this question. But what are the priorities? Which ways of loving are more important and which are less so? Should real love include discipline?

- What should church leaders emphasize in their discourse? What should they teach, but not really emphasize as much? The issue of emphasis often accounts for the vast difference we see between different churches.

- What kind of shortcomings and foibles in people should we largely ignore and forgive? What behaviors or attitudes are so negative something should be said?

- How much should we depend on celebrity personalities, or complex organizational structures for advancement toward our mission goals? How much should we look to every-member ministry as the key to healthy growth?

- What is the balance between efforts expended bringing people to Christ versus building them up in the faith?

- What should be the balance between expending time and effort on things that benefit people in our group versus those outside our group?

You can see that these questions (and many others we could

mention) contain theology, and that's important. A church won't have good ethos without a careful study and teaching of the theology of the church. But these questions also contain subjective values that vary greatly from group to group. Sometimes we find ourselves unable to even state the reply to such questions in words—the answers are too subjective for that. Yet, people in a given group will often look at a case in point and share a similar opinion: "That group is too soft," or "those people are disengaged." "That group is too man-centered," or "that group expects too much from its members."

Sources of group ethos
Theology
A group's assumptions may have a basis in scripture, but many people can't articulate that basis, or at least haven't analyzed where biblical instruction leaves off and application and opinion begin.

Leaders, on the other hand (whether formal leaders, or just opinion leaders) need to think through how theology affects a group's outlook and expectations. Studying theology and teaching biblical concepts to the church can have a potent effect on people's outlook and expectations. But other things count as well.

Modeling
Values can be transmitted from person to person when people model those values. When a respected leader consistently expresses passion for certain values, people tend to adopt those values themselves. But other people can model as well. Members in a group affect each other as they talk and react to situations, both negatively and positively.

This is one of the dangers of leaving negative comments and behaviors un-refuted in the church. Negative models can pull down the ethos in a group if enough of them are left to express their views and actions without correction. No wonder Paul told Timothy to reprove and rebuke people as needed—he had to protect the ethos of the group. You see the same concern in the Thessalonian correspondence where Paul was worried that lazy members who refused to work might become the norm unless the group took a stand against unruly lifestyles (2 Thessalonians 3:6-15).

Persuasion

People can affect ethos by arguing a case. When you persuade people to a point of view, they tend to act accordingly. Here, leaders are at an advantage because they get more "airtime" than other members do, and usually have training and gifting that make them more persuasive. Leaders regularly have to persuade people using theology, scripture, and arguments (pragmatic, common sense, and emotional) to show that a certain direction will take people where they need to go. Strangely, this potent source of church ethos (persuasion) gets relatively little coverage in church leadership literature.

A group's unspoken ethos grows up with the group, and lodges in people's minds with tenacity. In some cases, original church planters stamp the group with an ethos that continues for decades. In other cases, the church's history and tradition tend to perpetuate similar views and attitudes to those of earlier players.

Mission, vision, and ethos

Group ethos may partly grow out of a group's view of their mission or their vision, but is different from either of these. Both terms, "mission" and "vision" refer to what the church is *supposed to do* or *the way things should be*. Ethos, on the other hand, describes what *is* in the church, not what *ought to be*. What leaders articulate when they cast vision for a group is part of what ends up in the group's ethos. But many other features will also contribute. The overall expectations and sense of appropriateness that govern people's attitudes and actions in a group could derive from many sources, and leadership vision-casting would be only one of them.

Since ethos, refers to *what already is* in a church, it includes the negative as well as the positive. For instance, people in one group might have little interest in learning the Bible, and instead focus mostly on experiences. Another group might be quite bookish but rarely practice the things they learn. Some groups have little interest in deep involvement with one another. Others enjoy building into each others' lives. Any of these constitute aspects of ethos, but include positive as well as negative features.

A group's ethos can develop unintentionally. Leaders may not realize certain habits of thought and action are developing, and would never approve if they did realize it. A regular tug-of-war probably surges just under the surface during the life of any group as people pull for their views and values in different areas.

Altering ethos

The most important point is this: a group's ethos can be altered.

Just as rocks roll down hills rather than up them, a church's ethos tends to slide downward unless it is carefully nurtured and even re-inserted at times. Maintaining good ethos isn't easy—both during "in season" and "out of season" times. Leaders and members have to watch sensitively for shifts in people's attitudes and outlooks and be ready to reassert truth. Otherwise, they may find themselves in a group that is nothing like the one they used to belong to or lead.

Changing a group's ethos from something negative or inadequate to something exciting and biblical is a major project, involving a lot of work and time—maybe even a fight. But the payoff is awesome! On their own, people in a group with a healthy ethos will take upon themselves the tasks involved in building up the church. Initiative will replace inertia. Generous outgiving love can become so commonplace that people can't imagine a group without it. Instead of leaders endlessly pleading to heedless members, they will find themselves scrambling just to keep up with the rapid movement of events and the urgent need for equipping.

The Bible and ethos

Since a group's ethos includes both objective beliefs (truths that stand whether we believe them or not) and subjective values or interpretations, we cannot easily turn to passages in the Bible that set us straight in these areas. However, the Bible is not silent on the subject. We will see that New Testament churches had an ethos of their own, and some of that is embodied in explicit precepts or instructions we should follow. We can detect, by careful reading, other aspects not explicitly taught but demonstrated by example, and we should seriously consider trying to incorporate those as well.

Careful readers notice that the ethos was different in various New Testament local churches. Compare the ethos in Corinth with that in Jerusalem in Acts 2-7 and you see a striking difference. Notice how a strong group like that in Philippi, developed an unusual giving ethos from the beginning and never lost it (Philippians 4:10-19), while each church addressed in Revelations two and three seem to have a different ethos.

When we see how ethos shapes every aspect of behavior and outlook in a group, the question quickly becomes, "How do we get this healthy ethos in our group?" That's where this book comes in. To build healthy group ethos, you have to have a clear picture of where you're heading. Carefully studying what the Bible says about the church is the most important step you can take toward that goal.

Unhappiness with the church today

Today, abundant evidence suggests the church in America is losing ground. Several major studies just completed confirm that the evangelical church in America has stopped growing and is declining relative to population, especially since 2000.[1] Even those churches

---

[1] Thom Rainer says, "Perhaps most startling is the gravity of how many exit the church and the pace at which this exodus is occurring. Each generation that passes loses more than the previous generation. Shock does not begin to describe how we felt after reading the research results. The church is losing the generational battle. Not only are we losing our nation to the ways of the world, but we are not winning our own children in Christian families. Multitudes are dropping out of church. But many are also not claiming the faith of their parents." Thom S. Rainer, and Sam S. Rainer *Essential Church: Reclaiming a Generation of Dropouts,* (Nashville: B&H Publishing Group, 2008) 14. The chorus of voices on this subject is sizeable and beyond doubt. Some examples are: Julia Duin, *Quitting Church: Why the Faithful are Fleeing and What to Do about It,* (Grand Rapids: Baker Books, 2008); Dave Olson, *The American Church in Crisis: Groundbreaking Research Based on a National Database of over 200,000 Churches,* (Grand Rapids: Zondervan, 2008); Alvin Reid, *Radically Unchurched: Who they are and how to reach them,* (Grand Rapids, Kregel Academic, 2002); and Christine Wicker, *The Fall of the Evangelical Nation: The Surprising Crisis Inside the Church,* (New York: HarperOne, 2008). Bradey Wright has recently written a book intending to refute all these claims called *Christians Are Hate-Filled Hypocrites ...and Other Lies You've Been Told,* (Bethany House, 2010). In my opinion, he fails because his views rest mainly on the ambiguous notion of "affiliation" which indicates that 80% of Americans are Christians. He also shows the same data as the others for the most part, but simply doesn't interpret them as alarming.

that are growing do so almost entirely by winning people away from other churches.[2] The fastest growing faith group in America is unbelievers.[3] While many of the young say they have no problem with Jesus or the church, the massive National Study of Youth and Religion shows that they are no longer a part of anything that could be called Christianity. As Smith and Denton put it, "Christianity is either degenerating into a pathetic version of itself or, more significantly, Christianity is actively being colonized and displaced by quite a different religious faith."[4] According to some authorities, they are leaving the church in unprecedented numbers, in most cases never to return.[5]

How much of this discontent is the result of our culture trending toward increased hostility toward God? How much is the result of compromise or lack of spirituality in the church? Is the church losing people because of its message or its practice? Or is it both?

Where are we to turn? Is it possible that a reconsideration of biblical teaching on the church could reverse this negative trend? I think this is exactly where we must turn.

---

[2] "Of the 350,000 churches in the U.S... less than 1 percent is growing by conversion growth." (Alvin Reid, *Radically Unchurched*. 23). Also see our research demonstrating over 90% of all growth in American churches is by transfer in Dennis McCallum, *Satan and his Kingdom: What the Bible Says and How it Matters to You* (Minneapolis: Bethany House, 2009) 271-272.

[3] Christine Wicker, *The Fall of the Evangelical Nation*, 53, citing studies by Barna and The American Religious Identification Survey.

[4] They call the religion of American teenagers, "moralistic therapeutic Deism." Cited in Kendra Greasy Dean, *Almost Christian: What the Faith of Our Teenagers Is Telling the American Church*, (Oxford: Oxford University Press, 2010) 3.

[5] "It has been estimated that between 69 and 94 percent of churched youth are leaving the traditional church after high school, and very few are returning." Josh McDowell and David H. Bellis, *The Last Christian Generation*, (Green Key Books, 2006) "More than two-thirds of young churchgoing adults in America drop out of church between the ages of eighteen and twenty-two." Thom S. Rainer, and Sam S. Rainer *Essential Church*, 75.

Grasping the Core Issues

Before getting down to the specifics of biblical teaching on the church, this section is for getting the big picture. What is the church, and what should it be like? What kind of things should we be looking for?

Chapter One

An Awesome Church

Luke tells us of one awesome church beginning in Acts 2:42. This is a good place to start considering the whole question: What does a vital church look like? Luke is at pains to stress how wonderful this period was. What components do we see?

Truth

We read that the members of this group were "continually devoting themselves to the apostles' teaching" (v. 42a). So this group of Christians was clearly "contentful." In other words, this was no ignorant group based purely on subjective feelings and hysteria. These people valued, studied, and learned truth. The ministry of the word was strong in this group.

The expression "continually devoting themselves" is strong. This was not just something they did once in awhile. This group didn't trust their leaders to do the learning: the whole group felt they needed to know truth at a deep level. Happily, we have this same teaching from the apostles in our New Testament. So while we can't go down some evenings and listen to Peter or John lecture, we can read and study their books. Understood properly, the church is a community of truth. We don't come together based mainly on social need or affinity, but based on the great truths of God and especially his work in Jesus Christ. We also shouldn't compromise the truth on the theory that we will be more popular if we do so. Any suggestion that truth isn't important, isn't knowable, or doesn't need to be learned flies into the face of this New Testament example.

Koinonia

Luke says people in this awesome church also continually devoted themselves "to fellowship" (v. 42b). The word translated "fellowship" is *koinonia*. This important word means "to have in common" or "to share." *Koinonia* became the early church's favorite word for their practice when they gathered. They taught that assembling Christians could exchange the life of Christ between one another through serving love. It's such an important concept that we'll devote a later chapter to it. For now, we should notice that these people thought it was so important that they "continually devoted themselves" to it.

A later verse expands on this point. "Day by day continuing with one mind in the temple, and breaking bread from house to house, they were taking their meals together with gladness and sincerity of heart" (v. 46). The expression "day by day" means more or less daily (See NIV "every day"). It sounds like these people found time for being with each other in one way or another *most days*.[6] How different is our contemporary church, where people often have a "Sunday-go-to-meeting" mentality—they try to find an hour or two per week for attending church. This ancient group apparently invested extensive time each week into relationship building and fellowship.

Reflection and prayer

We also read that they continually devoted themselves "to the breaking of bread and to prayer" (v. 42c). These activities likely happened in house meetings, because verse 46 mentions breaking bread "from house to house." Breaking bread probably refers to celebrating the Lord's Supper, because verse 46 also mentions, "taking their meals together," and that would be redundant if breaking bread just meant eating meals. On the other hand, evidence

---

[6] The NLT translates, "They worshipped together at the temple each day." But no word for "worship" appears in this verse. In fact, as we will see later, the New Testament never refers to any meeting of the early church as a worship service. This is a plain case of reading modern concepts back into the New Testament. See the chapter on Worship for a full explanation.

is good that they did both together back then, so this difference is a moot point.

Celebrating the Lord's Supper shows that this community was reflective and reverent, not wanting to forget or take for granted the grace of God and the breathtaking price so recently paid by Jesus. In the Lord's Supper and prayer, we see a strong God-centeredness in the mindset of this group.

Verse 47 adds that they were "praising God," which naturally flows from God-centeredness in prayer. Christians in this group believed that the key to effectiveness, growth, and even survival was the power of God. So prayer and thanksgiving were not peripheral, but central in the ministry of the church.

Supernatural

Luke goes on, "A deep sense of awe came over them all, and the apostles performed many miraculous signs and wonders" (v. 43). These people knew that what was happening could not be explained by human ingenuity or manipulation. These were real miracles—the New Testament kind. Unlike some modern miracle workers, these miracles were so real that even enemies of Christianity said of them, "We can't deny that they have performed a miraculous sign, and everybody in Jerusalem knows about it" (Acts 4:16). They never had to fake anything.

As believers in this group saw God working in mighty ways, they naturally felt "a deep sense of awe." Anyone who has been part of a church where God begins to work powerfully to win the lost, heal, and change lives, knows this feeling. When I was young, the only awe I could remember was what you said to your mom on Sunday morning: "Aw, do we have to go to church?" For many today, awe is the furthest thing imaginable from what they feel when in church—boredom would be closer.

Generosity

Luke goes on to point out that these people's behavior grew quite extreme: "And all those who had believed were together and had all things in common; and they began selling their property and possessions and were sharing them with all, as anyone might have need" (vs. 44, 45). [7] This part is quite a shock to individualistic Americans! Selling your real estate? A community of goods? Are you kidding?

Yes, these people lost track of where the line should be drawn— the line that says God's interests can encroach this far into my life, but no farther. These people gave themselves over to God and his people without limit. They had a poverty problem: Many out-of-towners had come for Pentecost and decided to stay after meeting Christ; they probably had no way to earn a living. They were under occupation by Rome and had to pay high taxes. It was a poor culture anyway. They had no social security for widows or orphans, no welfare for the poor.

Later groups in the New Testament period apparently didn't practice a community of goods like this group. But they probably would have if the need had been as acute. We see evidence for this when even poor Christians were eager to give way more than seemed reasonable to help these same poor people in later years (2 Corinthians 8:1-4). Remarkably, materialistic greed had no hold on this group. In its place, raw, self-giving love predominated.

Outward

Finally, we read that they were "enjoying the goodwill of all the people. And each day the Lord added to their fellowship those who were being saved" (v. 47). This whole description would read so differently without the last comment. Without this verse, this group might be nothing more than what Ralph Winter called a "self-actualizing cult." Sure, people would be giving out, but only to each other. They might be like a circle of people scratching each other's backs. That's not good enough. A healthy organism grows, and God wills growth for his church—not always the same amount for every local group, but always reconciling people to God. Notice, not a single person came in through transfer growth. Each and every new person came through conversion.

---

[7] The fact that participation in this self-divestiture was voluntary does nothing to diminish the force (c. f. Acts 5:4).

The fact that this group had the goodwill of the people shows that they weren't withdrawn to themselves. These people were out in the community doing good and living out their faith in a way people admired even when they weren't persuaded.

What should we make of it?

Okay, maybe this church was awesome; maybe it would have been fun to be a part of that experience. But what are we saying for today? Certainly some of the features in this group might be true of quality local churches today, but come on: people disowning their real estate and giving the money to the poor? People gathering virtually *every day*? Are you kidding? That would be completely insane! As modern people, we have lives to live, things to do. Any group like this that showed up today would be rejected as a cult. Pure fanaticism. This is downright weird! It's bizarre!

Or is it?

Maybe *our* lives are bizarre. In western cities, many think it's normal for people to spend whole series of days and nights without any meaningful human relating. Their "conversations" may never go beyond the superficial; rarely or never connecting on a personal level. Modern people see nothing strange about living in a sea of people who have no idea what's really going on in their lives, and their closest relationship may be with their dog.

Many in the modern west see nothing strange about a life where we have never experienced actual intimacy with a community of people. Western city dwellers usually don't know who their neighbors are. They may remember a time when they were on a sports team or had some dorm roommates with a special closeness, but they've grown up now. For many American adults, superficial banter with people they barely know or "tweeting" on a white screen is called "being friends." At best, the nuclear family involves some personal relating, but we know how well that's going!

We live in a culture where millions choose a video-based entertainment stupor over deep human relationships. Going out several nights a week to Bible studies or "hang-outs" with Christian friends sounds far-out and unreasonable to us. But sitting night after night slack-jawed in front of an LCD screen, watching something we can't quite remember, or playing the same video game over and over, makes perfect sense.

We in the modern west think a life spent earning money all day and enjoying spending it all night is a life of success—even though we know perfectly well we'll have to walk away from all of our riches soon. On the other hand, investing in spiritual riches that will never fade has to be "kept in perspective;" we wouldn't want to get carried away! Missing time with the people of God is often unavoidable, but not missing a workout at the gym.

What prevents us?

As twenty first century western Christians, we have to realize we are products of our culture. Why would so many Christians in the modern west look at a picture like that in Acts 2 and shake their heads skeptically? Why do so many feel it just isn't realistic? What barrier holds us back from living like they did?

It's not the Holy Spirit; we have the same Holy Spirit they did.

Could it be that God no longer wants people in the body of Christ to live this way? Not if we can believe our New Testament. We will see overwhelming evidence that this picture is not just a curious example, but reflects direct, moral imperatives; instructions that are not optional for Bible believing Christians.

Our problems as modern people are severe. We are cynical; we simply don't believe that a picture like that in Acts 2 is possible today. Such unbelief will effectively block what God wants for us. Cynical Christians will never even try something they believe is nonsense.

Then too, we have prior loyalties that cannot be interfered with. If a New Testament church experience happened within our existing schedule and priorities, we wouldn't object. But if experiencing real body life means changing our entertainment schedule or our furious pursuit of sports leagues, driving our kids to excel in ten different ways (all based on the values of the world), or even turning down a promotion that would take us away from fellowship, that's really too much! The goals of the world-system too often trump the things of God.

If we lived like these people in Acts, we would be completely different than any of our neighbors—real oddballs. That doesn't appeal to people who derive their sense of well-being from how similar they are to everyone else. Our need to conform to others' expectations and standards can block us from experiencing radical body life.

Yet an array of data suggests that we aren't happy with our driven, materialistic, and impersonal lives.[8] Neither are we happy with our churches. Something is missing. What is it?

Only one way out

As Bible believing Christians, we should know exactly what the answer is. Jesus taught that God made us for love. Adding more inches to the screen size of our HD TV's won't scratch the itch inside, any more than booze, drugs, or power would. God made us for love, and we have to connect the dots between our pursuit of alternatives to real love and the emptiness we feel.

Of course, western people welcome love, but usually not the love of God. We want romance, we want hot love affairs, and maybe some family love too. But that's it. One problem is that these pursuits could all be self-serving. We might appreciate self-gratifying love and still miss the point. Jesus said we need to love one another as he loved us—the sacrificial way. He specified that just loving those who love us is not good enough; that even nonbelievers do that (Matthew 5:46). So people who didn't know God back then also embraced this narrow band of self-gratifying love.

Sacrificial love. Love where I surrender my life up to the project of serving others. Radical love. Love without limits. This is what Jesus was beckoning us toward when he referred to those who lose their lives but will ultimately save them (Luke 9:24). And then he gave us the body of Christ as the ultimate venue for living this out.

---

[8] Robert E. Lane, *The Loss of Happiness in Market Democracies*, (New Haven CN: Yale University Press, 2000). Juliet Shor, *The Overspent American: Why We Want What We Don't Need*, (San Francisco: Harper Paperbacks, 1999). John de Graaf, David Wann, David Wann , Thomas H Naylor, David Horsey, Vicki Robin, *Affluenza: The All-Consuming Epidemic*, (Berrett-Koehler Publishers; 2nd edition, 2005). Tim Kassel, *The High Price of Materialism*, (Cambridge, MA; The MIT Press, 2003).

Until we accept that the relational and spiritual side of life—love with God and with others—is where our fulfillment and satisfaction lie, we will continue to feel that other things are more important. We will refuse to let God and his people encroach into our time and affections beyond minimal levels.

American Christians sense an awful vacuum in western Christianity, but are frankly confused on what to do about it. Spirituality and devotional books fly off the shelves (and many are quite good), but as we read the contemporary literature on how to fix your ailing Christian walk, and compare it with the New Testament, one big difference comes across again and again: The body of Christ. Even when contemporary writers mention the people of God as part of the solution, their discussions often become vague at that point. Many people today frankly wonder what this part means.

In the New Testament, the context and content for every book is the same—the close community of God's people. These are all communities, rather like the one in Jerusalem we just considered. We *never* see a version of Christianity in the New Testament that envisions the individual with his or her God. It's *always, always, always* the people of God growing together at a deep level. Without this, much of the content of the New Testament simply makes no sense. Entire swaths of scripture become nothing but a dead letter, to be reinterpreted in the most superficial and ultimately silly ways.

Confusion mixes with frustration for modern westerners. On one level, so many see a tantalizing picture in the New Testament that they would love to experience today. But on another level, it all just seems so impossible.

Often, young, idealistic Bible students are ardent for change and reality in the church. Then, after ten or twenty years, those same people feel a low-level sadness that comes from compromising God's picture. They feel that they were young then; realities have since caught up with them. For some reason, people in western churches feel that conditions in our culture make the early picture impractical.

But the New Testament picture of church life is definitely possible today. We are not talking here about something exotic that God reserves for the few. This lifestyle is the will of God for all of us.

If we don't have it, that's probably because we've departed from his teaching, or have accepted definitions and values that come from our modern, individualistic culture.

Consumer Christianity

The definition we most likely have imbibed (often without realizing it) is a consumer version of Christianity.

When you go to the store, you're a consumer. You're looking for something. You know you'll have to pay for what you get, but the point is you want some things and they had better be good. If the products are lacking or over-priced, you'll probably go to the competitor's store next time. The store is there to provide things you want.

When the consumer mentality goes to church, nothing changes. The question for the Christian consumer is always the same: What's in it for me? A church might "meet my needs," or maybe we hear rumors that a different church down the road is better. Church leaders realize they have to compete—who will provide the biggest blessing? Who can make people feel most satisfied with the weekend's program? Who will put on the most impressive performance?

The New Testament picture of the church is incompatible with this consumer perspective. God declares in his word that the community of God is a gathering where I go intending to give out, not to receive. To the extent I do receive blessing, that's only so I'll be better equipped to serve. Instead of existing to "meet my needs," the body of Christ exists to equip me to meet others' needs. Ironically, according to Jesus, I will probably feel better in an out-giving, ministry-oriented church, but that's incidental. My focus needs to be on self-sacrifice, as Jesus explains:

> If anyone wishes to come after Me, he must deny himself, and take up his cross daily and follow Me.
> For whoever wishes to save his life will lose it, but whoever loses his life for My sake, he is the one who will save it (Luke 9:23-24).

This passage and its many parallels in scripture may well be one of the least understood concepts in western Christianity today. Nothing could be further from the consumer concept. Experiencing what Jesus describes will be very costly. There will be sacrifice. Taking up a cross is something you do when you're getting ready to die. A cross is a place of agony. Ease and comfort are incompatible with this picture.

If you're a modern western Christian, you may have some things to unlearn. Your whole view of Christianity and the church may be at odds with what God teaches in some very serious ways. In the pages to follow, we will examine biblical images and teaching that paint a picture of the community of God, and that picture may contradict what you have assumed so far. If you just want reassurance that all is well with the church as it is today in the west, you probably won't enjoy this book. But if your heart longs for something deeper, this could be a good first step toward actually experiencing what God has in mind for you.

Chapter Two

Jesus Launches His Body

Before we can do and be the body of Christ, we have to understand what it is according to God. This is one of the biggest barriers to successful body life today: failure to understand what the body of Christ is. It would be a huge mistake to skip this section of the book. Author Mark Driscoll recently commented that at a pastors' conference on the church he found that none of the pastors in his group could give a coherent definition of what the church is! My experience is similar. People want to bypass this part and get to the question of methods. But trying to implement organic church principles without understanding what God teaches about the body of Christ will result in confusion, frustration, and probably failure.

Our mystical union with Jesus

In the book of Romans, Paul explains that we are identified with Jesus' death and resurrection, and therefore we should present ourselves to God as those alive from the dead (Romans 6:13). This union with Jesus, this new position we have in Christ, is one of the most important, but often poorly understood, teachings in the New Testament.

Theologians call it the "mystical union" of believers with Christ. Our mystical union is very profound—not just a metaphor or a picture. It refers to something real; in some ways it's *more real* than our temporal lives here. To be "in Christ" is to be united with him now and forever. Paul says, "The person who is joined to the Lord is one spirit with him" (1 Corinthians 6:17 See also Romans 8:1, 9; 16:11; Galatians 2:20; Ephesians 2:13; 5:30; 2 Peter 1:4). As theologian Charles Hodge said, "No doctrine of the Bible, relating to the plan of salvation, is more plainly taught or more wide reaching than that which concerns the union between Christ and his people."[9]

Our oneness with Jesus describes how God looks at us: he sees us in his Son. That means what is true of Jesus becomes true of us in the eyes of God. God directly links many of his most important New Testament promises to this spiritual union with Jesus. Notice how the authors of the New Testament use the term "in Christ," "in the beloved," "in him," or similar expressions in this partial list drawn from the nearly 200 uses in the New Testament:

Things we get from our mystical union with Jesus	
Passages	**What is Promised**
Romans 8:1 There is therefore now no condemnation for those who are *in Christ Jesus*.	Freedom from condemnation
Romans 8:2 For the law of the Spirit of life *in Christ Jesus* has set you free from the law of sin and of death.	Freedom from the law of sin
Romans 8:39 [Neither] height, nor depth, nor any other created thing, shall be able to separate us from the love of God, which is *in Christ Jesus* our Lord.	Security and permanence in God's love
1 Corinthians 1:30 But by His doing you are *in Christ Jesus*, who became to us wisdom from God, and righteousness and sanctification, and redemption,	God's wisdom, goodness, etc. imparted to us
2 Corinthians 2:14 But thanks be to God, who always leads us in His triumph *in Christ*, and manifests through us the sweet aroma of the knowledge of Him in every place.	Triumph in spiritual war

---

[9] Charles Hodge, Systematic Theology, (Oak Harbor, WA: Logos Research Systems, Inc., 1997), 2:520.

Ephesians 1:3 Blessed be the God and Father of our Lord Jesus Christ, who has blessed us with every spiritual blessing in the heavenly places *in Christ*,	Every blessing, note the past tense
Philippians 3:9 [I want to gain Christ that I] may be found *in Him*, not having a righteousness of my own derived from the Law, but that which is through faith in Christ, the righteousness which comes from God on the basis of faith,	Righteousness imparted to us
Philippians 4:7 And the peace of God, which surpasses all comprehension, shall guard your hearts and your minds *in Christ Jesus*.	Inner peace of mind
Colossians 3:3,4 For you have died and your life is hidden with Christ in God. When Christ, who is our life, is revealed, then you also will be revealed with Him in glory.	Future inheritance and eternal life
1 John 5:20 And we know that the Son of God has come, and has given us understanding, in order that we might know Him who is true, and we are *in Him* who is true, *in His Son Jesus Christ*. This is the true God and eternal life.	Truth and understanding
2 Corinthians 5:21 He made Him who knew no sin to be sin on our behalf, that we might become the righteousness of God *in Him*.	The righteousness of God
1 Corinthians 1:5 In everything you were enriched *in Him*, in all speech and all knowledge,	Spiritual gifts

You can see from this partial list that those who fail to comprehend our mystical union with Christ miss one of the most important teachings in the New Testament. This is like the center of the web of New Testament teaching; the strands going out from our mystical union with Jesus touch all areas.

What does this have to do with the church?

In Romans 12 we learn that the mystical union not only affects our identity as individuals, but also corporately, as the people of God:

> For just as we have many members in one body and
> all the members do not have the same function, so
> we, who are many, are one body *in Christ*, and
> individually members one of another (v. 4-5)

This passage, like others, says that the same mystical union that makes us one with Jesus also makes us one with each other, or "members one of another." The mystical union operates horizontally as well as vertically. This is why the New Testament calls believers "the body of Christ." It's much more than an illustration. The mystical union of believers is a divine fact: we are individually members, not only of Christ, but also of one another.

Why does Paul, in this same context, urge all-out commitment to Jesus, like when he says a couple of verses earlier, "present your bodies a living and holy sacrifice, acceptable to God, which is your spiritual service of worship" (12:1)? What does that have to do with verses 4 and 5? Just this:

Commitment to Jesus *is* commitment to his body!

These are not two separate things, but one and the same. We are not just members of Christ. We are also *members of one another.* We cannot commit our lives to Jesus without also committing to the people of God. If we think we are totally committed to Jesus, we had better plan on all-out commitment to his body as well.

Anyone who truly understands the mystical union realizes that each of our lives has been joined to the body of Christ in a very profound way. Whether we live that truth out in any visible or tangible way here on earth is another question. But God has already settled the issue: "We are one body in Christ, and individually members one of another."

Over and over throughout the New Testament, this mystical union appears, either explicitly or by implication.

John

Jesus was the first to hint at the mystical union. When he cleansed the temple in John 2, people were amazed that he claimed he could rebuild the temple in three days. But John explains, "when Jesus said 'this temple,' he meant his own body" (John 2:21). John had the benefit of Jesus' later teaching to make this connection. While on earth, Jesus' body was the dwelling place of God, just as the temple symbolized the dwelling place of God in the Old Testament. After Pentecost, believers became the body of Christ and the new temple. Both Paul and Peter also later connected the Old Testament temple to the body of Christ. The temple symbolized the dwelling place of God, which became true of the people of God in the New Testament—not just symbolically, but *literally*. Through the indwelling Spirit and our mystical union, we are God's dwelling place on earth.

At the last supper, Jesus unveiled the mystical union more than ever before. He began to explain the new ministries of the Holy Spirit that God would unleash after his ascension. He taught that the Spirit would indwell believers:

> If anyone loves Me, he will keep My word; and My Father will love him, and We will come to him and make Our abode with him (John 14:23).

He taught the picture of the vine and the branches in Chapter 15, urging his disciples, "Abide in me and I in you..." (v. 4). So it wasn't just that the Spirit would indwell them. It was also that they were 'in Christ.'

Then Jesus said to the Father of those who believe in him, "I pray that they will all be one, just as you and I are one—as you are in me, Father, and I am in you. And may they be in us so that the world will believe you sent me" (John 17:21). Here it is—the mystical union, clearly stated. We see from this important statement that the union of believers is so profound that Jesus makes it analogous to the union between the Father and the Son.

Jesus also revealed throughout this section that the mystical union of believers still lay in the future and depended on his departure. He said, "But I tell you the truth, it is to your advantage that I go away; for if I do not go away, the Helper will not come to you; but if I go, I will send Him to you" (John 16:7). As you can see, this union did not exist before Jesus, during the period of the Old Testament. Both those who refer to the people of God in the Old Testament as "the church" and those who think the church began at

Pentecost generally agree that this was a big change found only after Jesus' life.

Acts

Paul may have originally glimpsed the mystical union the first time he met Jesus. When the risen Christ confronted Saul on the road to Damascus he asked, "Saul! Saul! Why are you persecuting me?" How odd! Paul had never met Jesus. As he lay blinded in Damascus, he must have wondered why Jesus said "me" instead of "my people." Why did he repeat it, "I am Jesus, the one you are persecuting" (Acts 9:4-5)?

Paul said he received his "message from no human source, and no one taught me. Instead, I received it by direct revelation from Jesus Christ" (Galatians 1:12 NLT). He could well have inferred most of the main points in his teaching just from the vision of Jesus on the road, as he lay blind for three days before Ananias and the other Christians made contact. You can imagine Paul turning over and pondering every word he had heard in amazement. One of the themes he probably grasped at this time was the mystical union and the body of Christ. He saw that, although he had only attacked Jesus' followers, Jesus considered that the same as persecuting himself.

1 Corinthians

The church in Corinth was a divided church. That may be why Paul gave several of his clearest teachings about the mystical union in that book. He explains that the formation of the body of Christ is the result of spiritual baptism:

> Some of us are Jews, some are Gentiles, some are slaves, and some are free. But we have all been baptized into one body by one Spirit, and we all share the same Spirit (1 Corinthians 12:13 NLT).

To be "baptized into one body by one Spirit;" what does that mean? Remember, baptism often refers to a "putting into" something

---

[10] For instance, John the Baptist referred to baptism into water, fire, or the Holy Spirit (Matthew 3:11, 12). Jesus referred to his "baptism" as his suffering at the cross (Mark 10:38). It's a mistake to think that all uses of the word baptize mean water baptism.

other than water.[10] This passage is not referring to water baptism but to spiritual baptism into the body of Christ. Earlier, Paul said, "by God's doing you are in Christ" (1 Corinthians 1:30). God places *all* believers into Jesus' body when he spiritually unites them with Christ. Notice how Paul says "we all have been baptized" in 12:13. This is not just true of some Christians.

Paul comes back to this mystical union repeatedly. He explains that because of our union, our actions affect the whole group. For instance, the sinning brother in Chapter 5 defiled the whole church (vs. 5:6-8). He challenges the fornicators in the group, "Do you not know that your bodies are members of Christ? Shall I then take away the members of Christ and make them members of a prostitute? May it never be!" (6:15). They must not understand that, "the one who joins himself to the Lord is one spirit with Him." (6:17). In both of these cases we see the actions of individual members impacting the other members (negatively) even though that was never their intent.

The same applies to positive actions. In 1 Corinthians 12:26 Paul explains, "if one member suffers, all the members suffer with it; if one member is honored, all the members rejoice with it." Notice, this is not an imperative, or an instruction (like a similar verse in Romans 12:15). Here, Paul is not calling on them to empathize, but is simply stating that because of the mystical union, our lives are intertwined. That's why "the eye cannot say to the hand, 'I have no need of you'; or again the head to the feet, 'I have no need of you.'" (12:21).

Think about this last statement. Paul's illustration is a human body. What happens to an eyeball removed from its body and placed on a shelf? Death, and quickly! If we follow the logic of Paul's illustration, we see that we have as much chance of spiritual life apart from the body as would a plucked-out eyeball.

Notice also that Paul is not just saying we need the *presence* of the other members, but that we need their *function*. The reason the eye needs the hand is because eyes are fine when it comes to vision, but pitiful for doing work. Eyes and hands have to work together, and they do work together in our bodies, because of their organic linkage.

This organic inter-connectivity in the body of Christ flies in the face of modern notions of "going to church." Christians who think they need to "attend" church have missed the point. Simply being around other members of the body falls woefully short of Paul's picture in this chapter. Instead, like organs in a living, functioning body, we are supposed to supply what others need while receiving from them things we could never do for ourselves.

The mystical union of believers is an awesome concept that can revolutionize our understanding of the church. Understood correctly, this union constitutes our *corporate* identity, as opposed to our *individual* identities. Think about these provocative words by one author on the church:

> This [corporate unity] is the very opposite of man's condition by nature. In Adam, I have the life of Adam, but that is essentially individual. There is no union, no fellowship in sin, but only self-interest and distrust of others....
>
> Yes, the Cross must do its work here, reminding me that in Christ I have died to that old life of independence which I inherited from Adam, and that in resurrection I have become not just an individual believer in Christ but a member of his Body. There is a vast difference between the two. When I see this, I shall at once have done with independence and shall seek fellowship. The life of Christ in me will gravitate to the life of Christ in others. I can no longer take an individual line. Jealousy will go. Competition will go. Private work will go. My interests, my ambitions, my preferences, all will go. It will no longer matter which of us does the work. All that will matter will be that the Body grows. I said: "When I see this..." That is the great need: to see the Body of Christ as another great divine fact; to have it break in upon our spirits by heavenly revelation that "we, who are many, are

one body in Christ." Only the Holy Spirit can bring
this home to us in all its meaning, but when he does,
it will revolutionize our life and work.[11]

Seeing the body of Christ for what it is will indeed change our
perspective. Even the Lord's supper is intended to remind us, not
only of the death of Jesus, but our mystical union with him. Paul
explains in 1 Corinthians 10, "when we break the bread, aren't we
sharing in the body of Christ? And though we are many, we all eat
from one loaf of bread, showing that we are one body (v. 16, 17 NLT).

Do American Christians grasp their corporate identity in Christ?
I have my doubts. Today, church is something you go to on Sunday,
not something that you *are*. I know the church has to assemble, so
maybe I'm being too fussy, but I don't think so. I think we view the
church as something external to ourselves, something I might go to
if I have the time, something 'over there.' We tend to see churches as
things we attend or join, or even as a building. Instead, we should see
the church as something I'm a part of, and whether I'm assembling
with one group or another, or even if I haven't been assembling at all,
doesn't change anything. Christians who fully grasp the mystical
union see things in a fundamentally different light. All that we expect
and all that we do in the church grows out of our understanding of
what the church is.

Universal or local?

We have been discussing the church as God sees it—covering
the whole world and throughout time, all those joined to Jesus make
up his body. But theologians point out that most letters in the New
Testament are addressed to "local churches"—the church in Corinth,
in Philippi, etc. Most theology texts argue that local churches operate
under different rules and principles than the universal church.

For instance, they ask, "What constitutes a local church?"
Traditional theologians argue that a few people gathering for
fellowship is not enough. You need appropriate church government

---

[11] Watchman Nee, *The Normal Christian Life*, (Hong Kong: Christian Literature Crusade, 1971) 218-219.

along with other "marks of the true church" such as discipline, the sacraments, the ministry of the word, etc. Most argue that people can join the local church, even if they aren't authentic Christians.[12]

The problem with this account is that scripture supplies no such definition of a local church. All such efforts result in creating something unknown in biblical usage. In the Bible, the body of Christ is based on the mystical union, and local churches are any part of that body that is somehow local, including "two or three gathered in my name" (Matthew 18:20—The fact that Jesus was discussing church discipline in this context doesn't change anything). Compare

Colossians 1:18 He is also head of the body, the church...	The universal church
Acts 9: 31 So the church throughout all Judea and Galilee and Samaria enjoyed peace, being built up...	The church throughout a region
1 Corinthians 1: 2 To the church of God which is at Corinth...	The church throughout a city
1 Corinthians 14:34 The women are to keep silent in the churches...	Multiple house churches within a city

the use of the word "church" in the singular in these verses:

You can see from these and similar passages that "church" is a flexible term that can apply in the singular to any size the context demands.

This points to the fallacy of any Christian saying "I'm not in a

---

[12] These attempts to add additional essential elements that must be present before a group can be considered a local church fail the test of faithful exegesis. For instance, theologians from Calvin on have argued that having an appropriate church government is required before a group is a church. But in Acts 14:23 we read that Paul "...appointed elders for them *in every church...*" (emphasis mine). You can see from the language that these were already considered churches *before* elders were appointed. This is true in other areas as well. Some protestant theologians argue that a group isn't a church unless they practice church discipline properly. But Corinth was not practicing discipline and received a rebuke from Paul for that (1 Corinthians 5). However, he didn't say they had ceased to be a church because of their error! (1 Corinthians 1:2). These additional features should be part of a *healthy* church, but I believe the theologians are confusing the *being* of the church with the *well-being* of the church. Such confusion becomes dangerous because it points people to external features for the definition of the church instead of the definition God gives in 1 Corinthians 12:13.

church right now." Yes you are! If you are a believer, you are in a church—really in *the* church. The problem is that you aren't in fellowship with the church.

I'm not going to get finicky about the use of the word "church" in this book; sometimes it refers to a local church (however we define that) and sometimes to the universal church, just like most English speakers use it.[13] The important thing to see is that you, the Christian are one with the body of Christ, and there's nothing you can do to change that. If you live in contradiction to what you are, you will feel tension and inner unhappiness. If you move into your new identity, including your corporate identity, and live out of that, you will see real life change and find your ultimate role in God's plan.

Practical outworking of the mystical union

Few theological teachings have more impact on our view of the church than that about our mystical union with Jesus. If people come to view their church the way God views it, the other points raised in the New Testament follow naturally. As we will see, an organic ethos depends on an organic definition of the church rather than an institutional, structural, or corporate definition. In a word, the essence of the church is spiritual and inward, not external.

Some readers may think this is too abstract and theological to make a difference. Wrong! It does make a difference and a huge one. What the church *does* grows directly out of what the church *is*. For instance, why would Christians in a healthy church consider other member's lives to be their business? Shouldn't they focus on their own lives and let others live theirs? Why would we conclude that every single member in the church should develop a personal ministry? Why think that if one member is built up, all of us will improve? The answer to all these and many others is the same—"we are individually members of one another."

---

[13] The Greek word for church is *ecclesia*. This word is a fusion of the preposition of source (ek= "out") and the verb *kaleo* ("to call"). A literal translation would be "the called out ones." The Greeks used the word to refer to an assembly of people, because most assemblies, such as town meetings, would be announced by a crier, or herald, who would go through the town calling people out to the meeting. The resulting assembly were the called out ones. This is the word Jesus and the other New Testament authors picked to refer to gatherings of the body of Christ.

Chapter Three

Living Out Our Unity: Koinonia

The unity of the body of Christ, based on our mystical union with Jesus, is not something we need to bring about or make happen. Instead, it is an accomplished fact. But just as in other areas, we have a part in living out what God has already accomplished. I think one of the most majestic discussions of the body of Christ is in the book of Ephesians. Here again, Paul begins with a lengthy discussion of the nature and importance of our mystical union with Christ and each other. For three chapters he argues that God's vast plan of the ages has been building toward this outcome.

Two pillars of unity in practice

Finally, in Chapter 4, he pleads with his readers to live out what God has already done:

> Therefore I, the prisoner of the Lord, implore you to walk in a manner worthy of [or "suitable to"] the calling with which you have been called, with all humility and gentleness, with patience, showing tolerance for one another in love, being diligent to preserve the unity of the Spirit in the bond of peace (vs. 1-3).

Notice that Paul extols the "unity of the Spirit" in this passage. This is not an organizational unity. It's not an outward, structural unity where we all share the same church government. People have made huge mistakes during the history of the church by concluding that the key is a single, over-arching church structure or a single leadership entity. Paul is referring to a unity that is spiritual and mystical. It's the unity we studied in the previous chapter—the one that comes from our mystical union with Jesus.

Notice also that the last phrase urges us to "*preserve* the unity of the Spirit," not to *create* unity. Paul is teaching that God has already built real unity into his body, by virtue of the mystical union. But how will this inner, spiritual unity ever come out into the light of day where people can see and experience it?

Relationship

The first clue is in verse two. Showing "humility, gentleness, patience and tolerance in love"—all these are referring to things found in *relationships between people*. Living out our unity in the body of Christ is not to be some strange or far-out thing, like a spell or a feeling that comes over people. Instead, we work out our unity by developing loving, deep, personal relationships between the people of God. Wouldn't that be something—Christian people who deeply loved the others in their spiritual community? It would be very impressive if these relationships reached the level called for in the New Testament writings.

At the deepest level, then, is the unseen, but real, mystical union. But over that and because of it, we are to build relationships that are deep, loving, impressive, maybe even amazing to the watching world. Jesus prayed that the unity between believers would be so profound and unusual that it would convince the world that he was authentic (John 17:23, c.f. 14:34-35).

Truth

But relationships aren't all. Consider verses 4 through 6:
For there is one body and one Spirit, just as you have

been called to one glorious hope for the future. There is one Lord, one faith, one baptism, and one God and Father, who is over all and in all and living through all.

Here again, we see unity. But these seven bases for unity all lie outside our doings with each other. They are truths, or facts, that we did not create and cannot alter. Truth, as well as love, is a key basis for unity. In fact, truth and love have a dynamic relationship that forms the basis for what we should be doing. Paul calls us to bring these two pillars together in verse 15:

But speaking the *truth* in *love*, we are to grow up in all aspects into Him who is the head, even Christ

To speak the truth in love; what does it mean? And how does that result in spiritual growth to maturity?

Sharing

In the New Testament, Christians gathered to share or exchange the life of Christ with each other. The New Testament authors often express this sharing, or having in common, with the Greek word *koinonia. Koinonia* comes from a stem meaning "common," and so means to share or to have in common—to exchange something. The term is a rich one and has many applications, including the one here in Ephesians 4, when Paul refers to "speaking the truth in love."

To develop true *koinonia*—or "body life" as some have called it—is not that easy. We must develop several background features if we expect to practice body life at the New Testament level. Paul explains in Ephesians 4:

Now these are the gifts Christ gave to the church: the apostles, the prophets, the evangelists, and the pastors and teachers. Their responsibility is to equip God's people to do his work and build up the church, the body of Christ (v. 11-12).

Equipping

The process of establishing quality *koinonia* begins with the leadership, according to these verses.[14] Those with spiritual gifts and roles associated with leadership in the local church have the task of "equipping" God's people to do his work, or his ministry. One of the central parts of equipping members in the body is teaching them truth. Paul describes this work in Colossians 1:28: "We proclaim Him, admonishing every man and teaching every man with all wisdom, so that we may present every man complete in Christ" (NASB). If we are serious about "speaking the truth in love" to one another, we will all have to learn the truth from God's word at a much deeper level than most Christians in America have so far, as we will see in chapter 14. Any church that takes this piece seriously is going to have to devote much more energy and resources to the project of equipping people with the truth than today's typical church.

Ministry

Why should God's people be equipped? For "the work of service" (NASB) or "the work of ministry" (RSV). The last word in the phrase, *diakonia*, is translated both service and ministry in our English Bibles. That's because ministry *is* serving people in love.[15] Serving others is the business of the people of God, and properly understood, ministry is the active component in biblical love. Love in the Bible is not selfish love, but serving love, or sacrificial love. Ministry comes in different forms—word ministries, service ministries, and prayer-related ministries. A full understanding of the New Testament concept of ministry takes some time, so we will devote a later chapter to it.

---

[14] Many Charismatic, Pentecostal, "New Apostolic" and "Simple Church" theologians refer to this verse as "the five-fold ministry"—a more or less technical term, signaling the belief that these are offices operating outside or instead of the authority of any local church eldership. At the other extreme are traditions claiming that gifts like apostleship and prophecy ceased around the end of the first century. I don't accept that this verse is about a different form of church government (instead of elders and deacons) or that spiritual gifts have ceased. The original apostles with their specific authority to declare Christian doctrine are now gone, although missionaries or church planters are "send ones" in the secondary sense. The common ground for most evangelicals (and my view) is that this verse refers in a general way to the role of various leaders in the church.

[15] Few translations choose "ministry" in this passage, probably because in western Christianity, "the ministry" is for professional "ministers," not for everyone. The NIV seems to be at pains to render this verse in a way that suggests merely doing good deeds. They translate the singular "work" as plural: "works of service," which could be misleading. I think the RSV has done the best job—"the work of ministry."

Most ministries in the local church involve relationship building.

The fruit of ministry

People's characters need to be transformed before they can be what God wants those who serve him to be. Paul tells us where the trajectory of building up the body leads:

> [We are to grow]...until we all attain to the unity of the faith, and of the knowledge of the Son of God, to a mature man, to the measure of the stature which belongs to the fullness of Christ (Ephesians 4:13).

If this is what God envisions as the result of ministry, it gives us an idea of what will be needed in the way of equipping.

First, notice the words, "we all" (*hoi pantes*). What this passage describes is not for the few or the elite. God calls *each and every one of us* in the body of Christ attain to the level of maturity described. This is also important because as the passage continues, Paul repeatedly uses the word "we" as the subject. In other words, every one of us is to be a recipient as well as a powerful minister in the process of *koinonia*.[16]

Next, he mentions that we are to attain to "the unity of the faith, and the knowledge of the Son of God." For this reason alone, equipping God's people will be an enormous task in modern America, where most new Christians begin in almost complete biblical illiteracy. Attaining to the "knowledge of the Son of God" (v. 13) probably means a lengthy time of study and personal discipleship. Even those raised in the church usually have only a Bible-story knowledge that is practically unusable in ministry situations.

Our characters also need formation. Paul envisions people reaching the level of "a mature man, to the measure of the stature which belongs to the fullness of Christ" (v. 13). Only those who have

---

[16] Every member ministry is assumed or directly taught in scores of passages in the New Testament, as we will see. Notice 1 Thessalonians 5:14 where Paul calls all the "brothers" (and implied, sisters) to ministries of warning, admonishing, and encouraging from, not just the leadership. Then, he calls them to have the letter read to the whole church (v. 27), thus showing that his intended audience is everyone.

been significantly transformed by the Lord themselves can foster such character change. Those lacking the ability to build lasting love relationships are not ready to play their parts as ministers in the body of Christ. Love-takers are not ready to give out in ministry. Self-absorbed or materialistic people are not ready. Addicts of all types are not ready. Immoral people are not ready.

Members in the church have to seek character transformation in each other's lives, if they are to effectively give out in ministry. If we have a church full of passive listeners who aren't growing spiritually, this whole picture breaks down; *Koinonia* becomes an unreal concept. For this reason alone, we see that much more will be needed than what we see in many modern churches. How would the leadership of any sizeable church even know whether or not people in the church are growing? How are leaders supposed to match counseling, admonition, training, and help to people's needs? Vast swaths of our modern understanding of the church will have to be massively revised if the New Testament picture of the church is to be more than a perplexing mystery to our people.

Truth in love

As people become equipped in the truth and see substantial character change, new possibilities open. Such people are in position to do what Paul calls, "speaking the truth in love" in verse 15:

>...but speaking the truth in love, we are to grow up in
>all aspects into Him who is the head.

But what does "speaking the truth in love" mean? Does it mean that we tell people true things in a "lovey" tone of voice? Does it mean that we try to project loving feelings and a friendly demeanor when we tell people the truth?

No.

In the context of New Testament teaching, only one understanding of this phrase makes sense: Paul is teaching that we should speak God's truth (based on his word) to each other in the context of *love relationships*. This is what transforms lives, according to this and other passages.

In the New Testament, love is not a smiling face or tone of voice we show people in the lobby at church. Neither is it just a feeling or demeanor we project toward someone. Jesus' call to love others is far more costly than many modern understandings. Such superficial understandings of love—that it is nothing more than a friendly demeanor—come from the world, not from the Bible.

When Jesus calls his followers to love one another as he loved them, he explains that this means laying down our lives for them (John 15:12-13). He means we should build friendships with others and love them sacrificially as he did. Then, in that context, we need to teach, admonish, and encourage each other, based on the truth as taught in God's word.

Here comes the time commitment. Here comes the interference with worldly goals and values. This means getting outside of my interests, my family, my aspirations, and getting into other people's lives. No wonder the early church devoted extensive time to fellowship. They were taking the concept of speaking the truth in love seriously!

Koinonia and church values

Have you ever wondered why some groups seem to assume that people in the body of Christ should invest deeply into relationships and develop closeness, while other groups assume that you go to church and go home afterward and that's it? This is a perfect example of an area where our theology and our values intersect to form a different ethos. Under some patterns of teaching, people never even try to experience real *koinonia*—they don't even know what it is. But if we expound this concept regularly and deeply, people may begin to aspire to a new level of body life never known before.

Simply knowing what the Bible teaches on koinonia won't be adequate; much more will be needed, as we shall see. On the other hand, failure to teach this area strongly will almost certainly short-circuit any hopes for a New Testament-style church. Ask yourself: Why would people in a church assume they should pursue in-depth equipping? Why would they think they won't be complete until they develop a meaningful ministry? Only deeply held biblical convictions that ministry is the birthright of every Christian, combined with the encouragement of the community will likely result in this outcome. Quality community requires that people understanding and believe at a deep level what the New Testament teaches on *koinonia*.

Chapter Four

Relationships: How Deep?

How do we know what the New Testament means when it calls on God's people to love one-another? Is our modern understanding necessarily deficient or superficial? How could we ever know what the inner lives of people in the New Testament church were like? Maybe their experience in church wasn't much different from ours.

Here is where objective teaching meets interpretation and application to form a group's ethos. We could take the call to speak the truth in love in a number of ways, some of them quite superficial. But New Testament teaching won't let us do that if we face it honestly.

The "one-another" passages

One of the clearest ways to look at this question involves the so-called "one-another" passages in the New Testament. These passages, found scattered all over the New Testament form a baseline for what we should expect when it comes to relationship building and *koinonia*.[17] Because the apostles repeat these calls in dozens of diverse contexts, they must be universal imperatives. Look at these selected examples and consider, in each case, what would be necessary before that passage could be any more than a dead letter.

---

[17] Here is a fairly full list of the one-another passages for further study: John 13:34-35; 15:12, 17; Romans 5:14; 12:10, 16, 18; 13:8; 14:13, 19; 15:5, 7, 14; 16:16; 1 Corinthians 1:10; 16:20; 2 Corinthians 13:12; Galatians 5:13, 14-15, 21, 26; 6:2; Ephesians 4:2, 32; 5: 19, 21; Philippians 2:3, 4; Colossians 3:9, 13, 16; 1 Thessalonians 3:12; 4:9; 2; 5:11, 13; 2 Thessalonians 1:3; Hebrews 3:13; 10:24-25; Col. 3:16; James 4:11; 5:9, 16; 1 Peter 1:22; 4:9; 5:5; 1 John 1:7; 3:11, 16, 22; 4:8; 23; 4:7, 11-12; 2 John 1: 5.

Passage	Needed conditions
Galatians 5:13 For you were called to freedom, brethren; only do not turn your freedom into an opportunity for the flesh, but through love serve one another.	Serving is the concept of ministry. This passage is a plain call for serving love in the body of Christ. How could we possibly accomplish this if our only context for knowing people is a large worship service on a Sunday morning? Those who think the Bible never calls on Christians to become involved in smaller group fellowship are mistaken. Fulfilling these commands is inconceivable apart from some kind of small group involvement.
1 Thessalonians 5:11 Therefore encourage one another, and build up one another, just as you also are doing.	To encourage others effectively, you need to know what's going on in their lives. You would have to be aware of their progress in various areas in order to know what to encourage. Likewise with the notion of building others up—how are we to do this unless we know each other's needs and progress? Unless we have a reasonably good idea of where others are in different areas of their lives, any attempt to build them up would be pure guesswork. Those who have worked to help people grow spiritually know that the transforming power of love and truth doesn't work at arm's length. This imperative assumes people have built good relationships with each other.
Colossians 3:16 Let the word of Christ richly dwell within you, with all wisdom teaching and admonishing one another	If we are to speak the truth in a life-giving way, we first have to let that word "richly dwell within" us. This suggests extensive learning—way more than the average western Christian today. But we would also have to know each other's lives well in order to not only teach doctrine, but to "admonish" (*nutheteo*)—a term related to our concept of counseling. This passage envisions Christians who are knowledgeable in God's word, wise in its application, and engaged enough with each other to counsel one another's lives. Doing

	this with relative strangers or acquaintances is unrealistic. Would you accept admonition from someone who didn't know you or understand your life situation?
James 5:16 Therefore, confess your sins to one another, and pray for one another, so that you may be healed.	Some churches have arranged to have people confess their sins through a screen to priests who barely know them. But this can hardly be what James has in mind. In the context of the New Testament church, this verse refers to something normal Christians do with each other. Most of us would find it difficult to open up about our sin problems with anyone unless we felt significant trust. To be as vulnerable as this verse suggests would take lengthy personal investment to build trusting relationships where people feel safe opening up to one another.
Ephesians 4:32 And be kind to one another, tenderhearted, forgiving each other, just as God in Christ also has forgiven you. Ephesians 4:2 ...with all humility and gentleness, with patience, showing forbearance to one another in love	Conflict and alienation are constant threats, preventing us from building a community of trust and grace. Many people come to Christ with obstinate habits such as hostility, insensitivity, suspicion, and judging others. Many lack the ability to forgive offenses and need extensive training in grace. Every local church would love to see their people acting like these verses describe. But any group that has tried, knows how difficult it is to get a group to move from fleshly selfishness to forgiving love. Close-in modeling, counseling, and admonition are essential to such a transformation. Teaching people how to practice grace with each other must happen in community, just as surely as teaching people to swim needs to happen in water. Too often, modern churches aren't sure whether they have a problem here for one simple reason: their people are so disengaged and distant they rarely interact enough to take offense at each other—not exactly what Paul had in mind.

Romans 15:7 Therefore, accept each other just as Christ has accepted you so that God will be given glory. Romans 12:16 Be of the same mind toward one another; do not be haughty in mind, but associate with the lowly.	These verses aren't just telling us to accept people we like. In the body of Christ, *all* are welcome. This is a tall order for any sizeable group of people. It doesn't mean we can't admonish unruly people, but it does mean we must learn to love them. Every healthy church has significant numbers of hard-to-love people, people with serious problems, including annoying relational dysfunctions. Obeying these passages will test the maturity and graciousness of everyone in the group, especially when people spend time and build close community. In healthy churches, difficult people are not only included, but often become unrecognizable compared to their former selves, and stand as powerful examples of God's life-changing grace. Proper understanding of these passages rules out merely saying, "I have a friend I love and try to build up." That's not good enough. This passage is referring to the body of Christ, not to someone we already love. Two people who love each other is a nice start, but we are called to form Christian community with everyone.
Galatians 6:2 Bear one another's burdens, and thus fulfill the law of Christ.	To bear other people's burdens, you have to know what those burdens are and how to help. Neither of these is easy, and neither will happen in relationally disengaged groups. Discernment, wisdom, initiative in love giving, and perseverance—all are implied in this statement. Anyone who thinks it's easy to practice this imperative in community probably never seriously tried it.
Romans 12:10 Be devoted to one another in brotherly love	The language of these verses and others like them simply cannot be understood as a superficial definition of love too often accepted in western churches. To "fervently love one another from the heart" has to mean deeply committed and

1 Peter 1:22 Since you have in obedience to the truth purified your souls for a sincere love of the brethren, fervently love one another from the heart.	involved *relationships*. This is not describing simply a friendly demeanor toward others we see at church. Love like this is going to take time. Love like this will mean sacrifice.

Before deciding what you think these passages mean for the church today, remember:

- These passages are all moral imperatives direct from God to us, and are *not optional* for serious Christians.
- These commands are not linked to any particular cultural setting, like the first century Greco-Roman world (unlike, for example, women wearing veils, or greeting one another with a holy kiss). They apply directly to twenty-first century America.
- The content of these imperatives applies to all Christians except perhaps those who are severely impaired. The "one-another" language makes it clear that carrying out these actions is not the responsibility of leaders or an elite group, but of all ordinary Christians. The leadership is responsible only to equip members so they can succeed.
- These passages, in context, are not describing how we should relate to our families. Although we should certainly love our families, these passages are about the much more difficult setting of the church. Switching the intended venue from the church to our families would be another example of radical reinterpretation intended to reduce God's call to something we are already doing (Matthew 5:46).
- Disregarding any of these instructions would be sin— just as serious, and even more serious, than stealing,

swearing, getting drunk, or watching pornography. After all, Jesus put loving others at the very top level of importance, second only to loving God. As James says, "Remember, it is sin to know what you ought to do and then not do it" (James 4:17)

Some western Christians become unhappy when studying the one-another passages because they already have set priorities in their lives that make obeying these impractical. While following these instructions from God may be difficult, and may be different from what we are used to, we must accept that *this is biblical Christianity*. We cannot claim Christianity is a livable teaching unless we substantially carry out these oft-repeated instructions.

Think about it: deleting from the New Testament every call for Christians to pray would fatally distort the Christian message, and it would leave Christians in an unspiritual, miserable state. So too, deleting the "one another" passages from the New Testament would destroy the spiritual vitality of the church and everyone in it. While we can always find churches that excuse us from following these instructions, we would only be fooling ourselves about true Christianity.

Honesty

As a Bible teacher, I'm aware every time I teach this area that some people in my audience begin to bristle in anger or uncomfortable resistance. Facing God's word is often uncomfortable, and it should be. Strangely, even some Christians who take a hard line on a wide range of moral issues ignore and disobey these very important moral instructions.

The first step in reforming our situation in the church today is to admit where we stand. Are we doing what God tells us to do? Have we developed the kind of dynamic, health-giving community of love described in these passages, where everyone is being equipped, is loving, is ministering to each other? Or have we accepted a version of the church where most people just watch and listen; a picture that comes nowhere near what God describes in the New Testament?

Again, if we have a problem, the best thing to do is admit it. We can rely on the grace of God to forgive and to help us change. But nothing will happen if we choose to justify a western version of church life that safeguards our right to be individualistic consumer Christians.

The Growth of the Body

Returning to Paul's thought in Ephesians 4, he continues, "speaking the truth in love, we are to grow up in all aspects into Him who is the head, even Christ." (v. 15). Healthy, living organisms grow. Here Paul is teaching that the body of Christ will grow in all aspects if we speak the truth in love.

What are these aspects?

One has already been mentioned in verse 14: "As a result, we are no longer to be children, tossed here and there by waves and carried about by every wind of doctrine, by the trickery of men, by craftiness in deceitful scheming." So maturity in God's word and a well considered Christian worldview is one kind of growth Christians should experience in a healthy body. In place of gullibility and naiveté, the people of God should become more sophisticated in their understanding of him. Several of the most embarrassing aberrations in the church during recent decades never would have happened if Christians had matured in the truth enough to recognize false teaching when they heard it.

Another aspect of growth would be the ability to speak the truth in love to one another, as we argued earlier.

Finally, a local church isn't healthy unless it grows in new people won to faith. We remember reading in Acts 2 that "the Lord was adding to their number day by day those who were being saved" (v. 47). When a local body is living out real *koinonia*, people in the area should find it highly attractive. Friends, neighbors, and relatives will marvel at the life change they see in people who join the group. And of course, healthy, growing Christians care enough about those outside the group to share their faith regularly. Real, New Testament style churches grow, and they grow by reaching new people for Christ.

There could be exceptions to this rule of thumb. Churches in some countries face such difficult ministry fields that growth by conversion has become very difficult and slow. God could also call a halt to growth in some groups for a time in order to let them catch up in other areas of growth. We also live in a situation different from that in the New Testament, because people can quickly decide to go to other nearby churches if they hear something they don't like, so even if we win significant numbers of new people, the church may not get larger.

The Result

Paul finishes his thought in Ephesians 4:

...we are to grow up in all aspects into Him who is the head, even Christ, from whom the whole body, being fitted and held together by what every joint supplies, according to the proper working of each individual part, causes the growth of the body for the building up of itself in love (v. 15, 16).

Here is the goal, the outcome. Let's carefully consider this passage.

First, who is to grow up in all aspects? "We." This is the same "we" that has been the subject throughout the passage—namely, "we all" (v. 13). Again, this passage applies to every one of us.

Next, we notice that the power for growth comes from the head, Jesus. This is a supernatural outcome that no amount of fussing, cajoling, and pressure could ever attain. Nothing less than the raw power of God will change lives at the level suggested here.

At the same time, Jesus exerts his power through human agency. The wording is very explicit: "by what every joint supplies," and "the proper working of each individual part." Both of these phrases mean that our goal is to see *each and every member* of the body of Christ giving out to build up the church. Yes, the power comes from God, but the proper working of every part is also important. God wants to use each one of us to build up his people.

So many church leaders in the west today have abandoned this concept. They believe the key to a successful church is hiring the most charismatic preacher, or having the most inspiring music ministry. Others think a special array of programs or a better building is the answer. None of these appears in this passage, and none of these would occur to Paul or other New Testament authors. If we suggested such things to those in the New Testament church, we would only see quizzical stares—"What are you talking about?.," the look on their faces would say.

Barriers to body life

In Ephesians 4 we have a stirring and exciting picture of what church life is and how it works. Why don't we see more of this in our own day? If the New Testament is so clear about what God calls us to in the church, shouldn't we be seeing more credible examples of communities practicing what we read there? Reporting on the massive flow of people leaving the evangelical church today, Julia Duin says,

> One of the top reasons people give for their leaving church is loneliness: the feeling—especially in large congregations—that no one knows or cares whether they are there.
>
> Many churches have become like supermarkets or gas stations: totally depersonalized arenas where most people no longer feel a responsibility to be hospitable to the person standing next to them... As for those who drop out, no one notices.[18]

What an astonishing claim! But if you're in touch with the state of the church in America, you know it's true all too often. Something that should *never* happen goes on all the time. At the same time, she found that people love and desire real community:

> The people I talk with who have found true community and then must leave it, due to family or job reasons, pine for it for the rest of their lives.[19]

---

[18] Julia, Duin, Quitting Church: Why the Faithful are Fleeing and What to Do about It (Grand Rapids: Baker Books, 2008) 50,

[19] Julia, Duin, *Quitting Church*, 50.

I've seen this as well. Once people actually experience real fellowship and community, they are haunted by that experience even many years later. Yet even when those same people spend time with the people of God seeking to recapture their earlier experience, they can't find what they're looking for. How could the church miss this opportunity? *Why* would we miss it?

The answers to these questions have puzzled observers of the western church for decades, partly because there are multiple factors. The modern church is being constrained from living out a biblical vision by multiple problems. The leading killers of quality community, in my opinion, are accommodation to western time priorities, to a Christian "consumer" mentality, and to postmodern expectations that churches never discipline anyone.[20] Other groups fail because of legalism—an instant killer of closeness and authenticity. Although we could dissect this problem for many pages, the result would be depressing and of questionable value. Instead, we need to consider how to turn the situation around, and it's never too late to turn a church around.

The big picture

Ephesians 4 and the one-another passages powerfully challenge our modern preoccupation with individualism and materialism. In a spiritually healthy church, people would read this chapter nodding their heads all the way: "Of course! How else would the church be?" At the same time, people from pathological groups would feel inward resentment and anger toward the whole concept, and most in the group would agree that these ideas are outdated, hopeless, and in fact ridiculous. "We've got lives to live, things to do," would be the plea of many preoccupied, modern Christians. Like the rich young ruler, these would have to turn away from Jesus in sorrow.

---

[20] According to Leadership Network's 2009 mega church study, involvement in church today is "less about creating an idealized plan to move someone toward commitment and more about providing many ways by which people could craft their unique, customized spiritual experience to meet their needs." Scott Thumma and Warren Bird, *Not Who You Think They Are: The Real Story of People Who Attend America's Megachurches*, (Hartford, CN: Hartford Institute for Religious Research, 2009) 9. This was based in part on their finding that although 90 percent of the sample attend worship regularly, "Nearly 45% say they never volunteer... 32% of megachurch attenders give nothing financially." 7. At the same time they found that megachurches were no worse than other churches on these measures.

Your next move

Suppose you read this chapter, and recognize one or even several of these barriers in your own local church: What's your move?

The starting place should be clear: the heart of one Christian— you. What the church needs today is not complainers or finger-waggers, but examples. Are you ready to model what you think the rest of the church needs to be? Have you had dealings with God on each of these issues and heard from him that you're in the clear? Have you at least formed the intention to change?

Once we have brought our own issues honestly before God, we are in a position to begin to share. But for God's sake, communicate your convictions in a spirit of grace and sensitivity. I've so often seen situations where those who believed most passionately in the values of the early church were the biggest gadflies and accusers in their churches. That's not the way to win people over to a more biblical view. Instead, read the rest of this book and learn to argue the case for organic principles biblically and lovingly.

7 Pictures of the Church

Biblical teaching doesn't come in outline form, all sorted out by subject. Instead, it usually gives us stories and pictures. These pictures can carry us into the heart of the spiritual essence of the church in a way bare statements of truth never could. By reflecting on each of seven key pictures used to describe the church, we can sense the essence of God's vision for his people. These are not the only pictures used in the New Testament, but they are some of the most vivid.

Chapter Five

Pictures: The Body of Christ

When the New Testament portrays the church as the body of Christ, Jesus' human body stands for the collection of his people. Jesus first hinted at this picture (John 2:19-22; Acts 9:5), but Paul used it most often. The church as the body of Christ stresses the way God organically links believers together through the mystical union, just as different parts of our bodies are linked organically and functionally. This was Paul's point in Romans 12:4-5, as we have seen.[21]

Body principles

Paul also uses this picture of the body to teach other aspects of church life. His most extensive teaching using this picture is in 1 Corinthians 12. This passage makes several key points based on the analogy of a living human body:

- **Participation** – After pointing out that, "we have all been baptized into one body by one Spirit" (v. 13, NLT), Paul says, "the body has many different parts, not just one part" (v. 14, NLT). This statement argues against a man-centered church. The key is not to get the best preacher, but to get all the parts of the body to play their roles.

---

[21] Paul teaches on the picture of the body of Christ in other passages as well, including Colossians 1:24, 2:19, and 3:15, Ephesians 1:22, 23, 2:14-16, 4:4, 4:11-16, and 5:23-32.

While having a high-powered charismatic leader can bring people in, the effort should constantly be to raise others up to share leadership and ministry.

- **Every member** – Next he adds, "If the foot says, 'I am not a part of the body because I am not a hand,' that does not make it any less a part of the body. And if the ear says, 'I am not part of the body because I am not an eye,' would that make it any less a part of the body?" (v. 15-16, NLT). In other words, everyone's contribution is important. Those who downplay their own capabilities are misunderstanding how the body works. Suppose someone asked you, "Which is more important, hands or feet?" How could you answer? Clearly, such a comparison makes no sense. Feet are just as important as hands. Why can't we have both hands *and* feet? The Christian who thinks, "I'm not gifted like that person" is often lining up to justify a sin of omission. At other times, he may be envying another's role. Either way, he's missed the point Paul makes next.

- **Diversity** – "If the whole body were an eye, how would you hear? Or if your whole body were an ear, how would you smell anything?" (v. 17, NLT). While the integration of the body teaches unity, this verse teaches the importance of diversity. God can't use cookie-cutter Christians. He has set up the body so that we have to depend on each other for the part we are lacking. This picture directly confronts humanity's longing for autonomy and independence (especially in modern America). This verse again rebukes celebrity approaches to church life. Basing the whole church on a single, famous person is like having an immense eyeball for a body. Pastors who become famous have a special challenge; they must convince their people that their own ministries matter just as much as that of their famous pastor.

- **Sovereignty** – Next comes the important claim, "But now God has placed the members, each one of them, in the body, just as He desired" (v. 18). This means God sovereignly determines your makeup, your gifting, and your spiritual history. God knows your make up exactly. He knows what you can do and what you should do. This passage matches a number of others in the New Testament that say God plans our ministries beforehand.[22]

- **Interdependence** – Verse 21 says, "The eye can never say to the hand, 'I don't need you.' The head can't say to the feet, 'I don't need you'" (NLT). Again, this passage shatters autonomy and individualism for anyone who believes it. Notice, the eye needs not just the *presence* of the hand, but its *function*. Eyes are helpless to do work. Only hands can do that. This is why we need each other. God has blocked any possibility of spiritual health apart from the body. Christians who feel they have no need to engage with the body of Christ—who feel they can do fine on their own—are ignoring or disobeying this verse.

- **All are welcome** – Finally, Paul teaches how to treat weaker members: "In fact, some parts of the body that seem weakest and least important are actually the most necessary. And the parts we regard as less honorable are those we clothe with the greatest care. So we carefully protect those parts that should not be seen, while the more honorable parts do not require this special care. So God has put the body together such that extra honor and care are given to those parts that have less dignity. This makes for harmony among the members, so that all the members care for each other" (v. 22-25, NLT).[23] This

---

[22] Ephesians 2:10; 2 Timothy 4:5, 7.

[23] Many commentators think Paul is referring here to our genitals! Although modern Christians don't like to mention genitals, the Bible consistently shows no such squeamishness. It's an interesting proposition. While we may want to keep our private parts covered in public, most of us would not be happy if they went missing.

passage stresses that every member must be included and cared for. The hard cases whom the world rejects cost us extra. But if we understand God's will for his church, we'll pay that price. In healthy churches, where love is gentle but firm, hard-to-love people are nurtured and usually transformed. They still have problems, but are nothing like they were when they came. They become likeable trophies of the transforming power of God's grace.

- **Organic linkage** – In verse 26 Paul says, "If one part suffers, all the parts suffer with it, and if one part is honored, all the parts are glad." He made a similar statement in Romans 12:15, but there he was giving an instruction; not here. This is not an imperative, but a *statement of fact*. Because of the mystical union, the spiritual state of others in the body of Christ directly affects all of us, just like having a bad liver would mess up your whole body. Again, individualism is shattered if you believe this verse of scripture. Building yourself up isn't good enough. If your fellow believers are fleshly, it will drag you down. If they remain unhealed, it will drag us all down. Their immaturity will impact everyone. So the answer is obvious: don't leave the other members in the group suffering. Build all of them up, and we will all benefit.

In the picture of the body, we see both organic linkage and diversity of function. How true this picture is in a well-formed local church, where people actively live out these statements.

Spiritual gifts

In the metaphor of the body of Christ, the different organs' bodily functions stand for different roles people play in the church. These different functions correspond to the "manifestations of the Spirit" (1 Corinthians 12:7) or to spiritual gifts (1 Corinthians 12:4). The language makes it clear that each and every member of the body has spiritual gifts (The phrase "to each one is given" in verse 7 means "each and every"). Properly understood, the purpose of most spiritual gifts is to serve others in love.[24]

Although many who read 1 Corinthians 12 conclude that the most important thing is to discover your spiritual gifts, Paul never says that. He says we have different spiritual gifts, but he doesn't call us to find out what our gifts are. Neither does he explain how we would do that. Instead, he seems to assume that people will know. The same is true in all other passages discussing spiritual gifts. The New Testament contains no call to discover our spiritual gifts.

Although this flies in the face of so much contemporary teaching, it matches my experience perfectly. I never took a test or went on some search for my spiritual gifts. I just made friends and tried to make myself useful in service wherever I could. People began to observe that they thought I was gifted in certain areas. When we practice love with Christian and non-Christian friends and try to help wherever we can in the church, our gifts will usually emerge quite naturally. We ourselves and other people will notice that we show strength in certain areas, and those are likely areas of gifting.

So discovering our spiritual gifting is probably good, but really unnecessary. At the same time, knowing your spiritual gifts may not change your life as much as you think. We should still try to minister wherever we get a chance, regardless of our gifting. For instance, I may not have a gift of evangelism, but that doesn't mean I shouldn't try to share my faith. I may not have a gift of faith, but I certainly need to believe, and I need to nurture and build such faith as I have. Of course, it makes sense to spend some extra effort in areas where you're gifted, but we all should minister to any need we see to the best of our ability.

Unfortunately, we often see spiritual gifts used as excuses: "Oh, I'm not gifted in that" means "I'm not even going to try to serve in that area." In one church our team visited, almost every small group had multiple members explaining why they never try to witness: that

---

[24] The gift of tongues is apparently an exception according to 1 Corinthians 14:4, where Paul says this gift is for edifying one's self. But even this gift can be for others if interpreted (1 Corinthians 13:12-13).

wasn't their gifting. This is a complete misunderstanding of spiritual gifts. Gifts aren't limitations to ministry, but areas of strength.

The real point

If knowing your gifts isn't the point of this and related passages, what is the point? The point is that we need to know that we are all differently gifted. That should keep us from feeling we have to be like other members of the body. Realizing you can't witness like she does, or teach like he does, is unimportant. Your view should be toward the positive—what *are* you able to do?

Comparing our giftedness to others is pointless, and actually foolish, according to 2 Corinthians 10:12: "When they measure themselves by themselves and compare themselves with themselves, they are without understanding." Trying to compare an eye to a foot is a nonsense project—a category mistake. Comparisons between people are meaningless because our architecture and backgrounds are so different. God made each different person to be just that—different.

If we know how to build quality relationships and we seek chances to serve (minister to) others in those relationships as well as in meetings, everything will work out organically. The key is not to take a spiritual gift assessment (which would have been unthinkable in the early church) but to seek out ministry opportunities.

Remember, we often appear ungifted in certain areas, even though with perseverance we later end up finding gifting there after all. This is especially true with gifts like teaching, counseling (exhortation), or leadership, which require learning and experience before they come to light.

Finally, if knowing our spiritual gifts were important, we would have a statement to that effect in the Bible.[25] Being ministry-minded

---

[25] It's also clear that none of the passages mentioning spiritual gifts has the same list as any of the others (compare 1 Corinthians 12 and 14; Romans 12; Ephesians 4; and 1 Peter 3). This implies that none of these lists is exhaustive, but instead are representative, or suggestive. This in turn suggests that the purpose is not to help us discover our gifts—surely Paul would have listed all the options if that was his intent. The fact that these lists are incomplete suggests Paul is interested in a *way of thinking*, not specific conclusions about our giftedness. Ironically, the modern fixation on the question, "What are my spiritual gifts?" is rather individualistic. The concern here is too much on "me" rather than on how the body of Christ works.

and building relationships is far more important than being able to itemize one's spiritual gifts. Probably God will reveal our gifts as we serve, and we should always remain open to new gifting.

The flow of life

The picture of the church as Jesus' body teaches that the parts of the body (which stand for individual members) are to be joined both in the sense of giving and receiving life. God uses the interaction of the different parts to deliver growth. As we saw in Ephesians 4:16, "Christ, from whom the whole body, being fitted and held together by what every joint supplies, according to the proper working of each individual part, causes the growth of the body for the building up of itself in love." See also Colossians 2:19, where Paul points out the need to hold "fast to the head, from whom the entire body, being supplied and held together by the joints and ligaments, grows with a growth which is from God." The phrases "what every joint supplies" and "the proper working of each individual part" stress how each of us has a contribution that God wants to use to promote growth—in either quality or quantity. Jesus is the one growing the body, but he does this through the various members in this picture, not directly.

No picture of the church is as explicit about the need for every-member ministry as that of the body. No organ in your body exists merely to be nurtured by the rest of the body. All of them have a function, something they contribute. Christians should approach every gathering of the body as an opportunity to serve. Between meetings, we should be looking for ways to invest in others and build them up. When our people begin to grasp the picture of the body, they have reason to change from being takers to being givers. A group where most members grasp this is bound to become an awesome group to be a part of. People's needs are met, new people show up, and the climate is spiritual and others-centered.

Organism vs. Institution

From the body metaphor we also get the notion that bodies are linked and interact organically, not institutionally. What does this distinction mean?

First, we've already discussed how the parts of an organism draw life, nutrition, and healing from the other parts. The flows of fluids, electrolytes, hormones, and special cells in our bodies are *dynamic*. These different building blocks of life and health don't move in predictable, uninterrupted ways. Instead, organisms continually exchange signals and feedback throughout the different systems. All in turn respond differently to internal and external changes in environment, whether heat and cold, availability of food, water, rest, exertion, etc.

Vast, complex systems, like our immune system, are finely attuned to sense things like invasion by a foreign microbe or trauma suffered in a wound. Special blood compounds sense the presence of an organism that doesn't belong and immediately send out a chemical signal that results in the production of antibodies, white blood cells, or other compounds needed for protection.

Internal changes (like the process of growth or invasion by a microbe) and external changes (like temperature, or danger) dictate different supplies from other organs, tissues, and systems in the body. These, in turn, all have a remarkable ability to sense and respond to the present situation. Living organisms possess a fascinating flexibility and adaptability. This process of reading and responding to needs is continual; it never stops. Electrical impulses travel the length of living organisms, bringing information to the brain or other systems to effect response. The more we study living organisms, the more fascinating and astonishing these processes appear.

Because this feedback and response is so dynamic, it becomes impossible to write out a schedule of rules for how any particular part of a body will act at any time. It all depends on the needs of the moment. Of course, there are rules underlying all that happens, but they come into play differently depending on the situation. With all our ingenuity and genius, humans have never come close to building a machine that approaches living organisms in adaptability.

Paul wouldn't have known what we do about biology, but many

of these features would have been obvious even in his day. Anyone notices how when our bodies heat up from exertion, the skin spontaneously excretes cooling sweat. Anyone can watch a wound heal and see the effect of nutrition, sleep, or stress on the body. In a thousand ways, living organisms exhibit adaptability and creative response.

These features seem to be uppermost in Paul's mind as he refers to the "proper working of each individual part." Paul sees individual people interacting like parts of a body—organically.

Institutions are not organic. Institutions are organizations constructed using a set of rules. Most obligations and benefits for different players in institutions are written down somewhere. Changing the way an institution operates usually requires a deliberation process and permissions from a number of committees or individuals. As a result, institutions are notoriously difficult to change. While they tend to have durability, and can be tough to destroy, institutions tend to get out of step with changing circumstances and lose effectiveness. Because they are impersonal, they don't inspire love.

In the picture of the church as the body, Paul is teaching that we should function more like an organism and less like an institution. An organic approach means helping people use their gifting to build their own ministries without unnecessary interference from a centralized bureaucracy. Leaders infusing a group with an organic ethos create an environment where the Spirit can direct the church rather than having lists of rules do the leading. In organic environments, every member plays a role, creatively responding to changing needs and opportunities. An organic ethos means the church recognizes people as being used by God, rather than choosing people to lead according to institutional criteria like degrees or seniority.

But being organic doesn't mean anarchy. Some visions of organic Christianity today imply that only when leaders, structures, and rules are completely absent can the church live out organic principles. But mob action doesn't resemble living organisms any more than do institutions. Organisms operate under rules, but they are more general and still allow for initiative and improvisation. We will see that the same author who taught on the body of Christ also set up limits to what is permissible, and called for leadership offices. He laid down rules for how meetings should be conducted. The teaching that organic body life only appears in a setting where each man "does what is right in his own eyes" is alien to the New Testament, as the next picture shows.

Organic leadership

Churches with organic ethos have leadership and rules, just like the church in the New Testament. But the leaders see themselves trying to discern the mind of the Spirit and preserving Jesus' leadership, not arbitrarily decreeing what they think should be done or worrying about "how we've always done it." They look for indications of the Spirit's ordering of relationships and ministries and try to respect that. Organic leaders assume that God is selecting people for certain roles (1 Corinthians 12:18), and are reluctant to interfere—either by disrupting people's ministries or by thrusting them into ministries they did not develop. Instead, organic leaders act as facilitators, trying to help people develop their own ministries.

There are exceptions. Someone who develops a ministry but discredits him or herself through serious sin may have to be removed from that role (1 Tim. 1:20). At other times, someone who didn't build a ministry may be brought in to lead it, like when Barnabas brought in Paul to help with the surging movement in Antioch (Acts 11:23-26). This might happen because a ministry has lost its leader, or because a ministry grows so rapidly that they are unable to develop natural, organic leadership fast enough to keep up (which probably happened in the case of Antioch). Groups, on the other hand, that consistently bring in outsiders are demonstrating a weak equipping ministry. Some groups actually prefer to hire workers away from other groups to training up their own.

Rules

Leaders who understand the organic nature of the body are also reluctant to multiply rules. They realize that any effort to define how things should go by using rules will likely end up with a Talmud full of regulations that chokes out creativity and initiative. They will devise rules only when the situation dictates that things are going to go seriously wrong unless they put in a restriction. They also review rules from earlier and delete them whenever possible.

For example, in our church we saw that when house churches planted unhealthy daughter groups, the impact on numerous people's lives was serious. Therefore, the elders felt we needed to approve new church plants. By holding out for healthier plants, we believe we have avoided much chaos and suffering in the church. Other rules come from the pages of scripture, and leaders should enforce those. So, while leaders trying to develop an organic ethos do create rules at times, they have a strong bias against having extra-biblical rules of any kind in the church.

Organic growth

Another parallel between organisms and the body of Christ comes from the way organisms grow. When organisms grow, they self-replicate. Even in Paul's day, it was obvious that all organisms reproduce and form new organisms. Today, we realize this process begins at the cellular level. Each cell grows, builds, and then divides, creating a new cell. When ready, the multi-celled organism reproduces as well.

In a church based on organic principles, individuals receive nourishment for personal growth. But they also look for others they can nourish. By leading others to Christ and discipling them into maturity, one individual becomes two. As this happens all over the church, larger groups grow and plant off new groups. The church expands, permeating different neighborhoods and subcultures.

This is different than an approach that seeks growth mainly through a central conduit and later processed through an office or bureau. The biggest difference is whether growth arises across the whole church through the actions of members, or whether the church counts on a famous preacher or magnificent music program to draw people in. Organic groups may have famous leaders or good music, but may also have nothing of the sort, and growth comes anyway, because everyone in the church is mobilized to play their part.

Relationships

Finally, as we saw in the logic of Ephesians 4, groups with an organic ethos are knit together through deep, personal relationships. This is different from institutions. To know people deeply—and to sense need or potential based on relationship—brings in a number of features not found in institutions. Knowing another deeply enables you to feel where that person is, based on an intuitive sensing of subtle differences in demeanor or behavior. With close friends, you can sense even slight differences from the way they usually are. That's why your spouse can always tell when something's wrong. In a healthy, organic body, people should know and be known at this level.

Relationships also enable us to engage with others' needs and to meet those needs in a way we never could when working at a distance relationally. My awareness of my friends' tendencies may enable me to even anticipate need beforehand. Such closeness results in a level of responsiveness no impersonal organization could hope to see.

The trust that grows out of relationships becomes the lifeblood of healthy local bodies. People can listen to criticism from those with whom they have good relationships. Large, relatively impersonal groups simply cannot deliver life change at this level.

The big picture

Communities of people linked together spiritually are more like organisms than institutions. When people see the church this way and act accordingly, organic DNA is the result. New people coming into the group will sense the relatedness, the warmth, the freedom, and the wholesomeness that God intends. Groups that lack the organic ethos feel impersonal, no matter how nice people try to be.

In groups operating on an institutional ethos, people are always wondering why things aren't happening, and who is supposed to be doing them. They wonder what rules govern the present situation.

Under an organic frame of mind, people assume that any need they see was shown them so they could engage it creatively. In institutionally minded groups, people tend to sit around and watch to see what happens next. They see themselves as recipients of a service, not as personally empowered, vitally needed organs, like in a body. Institutionally minded groups should take in hand to introduce major change—a paradigm shift. Opinion leaders will have to gradually lead people through a process of realization of biblical truth.

Chapter Six

Pictures: God's Army

Have you ever noticed how many times New Testament authors use military language when discussing the church? Spiritual warfare is a regular backdrop for much of their thinking about the church. Look through some of these examples:[26]

Matthew 16:18 "...On this rock I will build my church, and the gates of Hades will not withstand it." This verse pictures the church assaulting Satan's kingdom and battering down the gates.

Acts 15:36-38 "Barnabas wanted to take John, also called Mark, with them, but Paul did not think it wise to take him, because he had deserted them in Pamphylia." Paul viewed John Mark's unscheduled departure during the first journey as "desertion."

Romans 13:12 "Let us put aside the deeds of darkness and put on the armor of light..."

1 Corinthians 16:13 "Be on your guard; stand firm in the faith; be men of courage; be strong." These are all military commands for those who are in the heat of battle.

2 Corinthians 2:14-16 "But thanks be to God, who always leads us in triumphal procession in Christ." Triumphal

---

[26] I am indebted to my colleague, Gary DeLashmutt for some of the material in this chapter.

processions were held after military victories, like the victory Jesus won over Satan at the cross (see also Colossians 2:15).

2 Corinthians 6:7 "...in truthful speech and in the power of God; with weapons of righteousness in the right hand and in the left..."

2 Corinthians 10:3-4 "For though we walk in the flesh, we do not war according to the flesh, for the weapons of our warfare are not of the flesh, but divinely powerful for the destruction of fortresses."

Ephesians 6:10-18 "Put on the full armor of God, so that you will be able to stand firm against the schemes of the devil. For our struggle is not against flesh and blood, but against the rulers, against the powers, against the world forces of this darkness, against the spiritual forces of wickedness in the heavenly places. Therefore, take up the full armor of God, so that you will be able to resist in the evil day..."

Philippians 1:27-30 "...I will know that you stand firm in one spirit, contending as one man for the faith of the gospel...." The word translated here "contending" means to fight.

Philippians 2:25 "...Epaphroditus, my brother, fellow worker and fellow soldier...." Paul calls other Christian workers, "fellow-soldiers" (e.g. Philemon 1:2).

Colossians 2:5 "I am with you in spirit, rejoicing to see your good discipline and the stability." These terms translated "good discipline" or "orderly ranks" and "stability" were originally military terms.

1 Thessalonians 5:8 "But since we are of the day, let us be sober, having put on the breastplate of faith and love, and as a helmet, the hope of salvation."

1 Timothy 6:12-14 "Fight the good fight of the faith..."

2 Timothy 2:3-4 "Endure hardship with us like a good soldier of Christ Jesus..."

As you can see, military allusions are frequent, and this list is only partial. It's unmistakable; the church is like God's army. Of course, there are differences between human armies and the body of Christ. We don't have a rigid command hierarchy like they do. We never kill people like they do. Our battle is "not with flesh and blood, but with spiritual wickedness in the heavenly places."[27]

On the other hand, there should be some important similarities between the ethos of a local church and an army at war. Paul's main military themes include conquest, discipline, hardship, and struggle.

Conquest

Our posture in spiritual warfare is offensive. We are the attackers, intent on reclaiming ground from the evil one and freeing his captives. As Jesus put it to Paul, "I am sending you, to open their eyes so that they may turn from darkness to light and from the dominion of Satan to God, that they may receive forgiveness of sins" (Acts 26:17-18). Jesus invaded the world system "for this purpose, to destroy the works of the devil" (1 John 3:8).

The church is not to form a fortress to withstand attack. A defensive mentality is alien to the New Testament and will sicken the church. It leads to self-preservation thinking, to paranoia, to fear, to alienation from our own culture, and to failure in our mission. Instead, we are to cooperate with God as he builds his kingdom, progressively eroding Satan's kingdom—the world-system. We attack his strongholds, releasing the captives within (2 Corinthians 10:4). As the kingdom of God grows, Satan's kingdom diminishes.

Discipline

When Paul reminds Timothy, "No soldier in active service entangles himself in the affairs of everyday life, so that he may please the one who enlisted him as a soldier" (2 Tim 2:4), he is calling Timothy's attention to the need for *focus*. When people fail to grasp the urgency and danger of spiritual warfare their groups are

---

[27]For a full discussion of spiritual warfare and the church, see Dennis McCallum, *Satan and His Kingdom: What the Bible Says and How It Matters to You*, (Minneapolis: Bethany House, 2008)

weakened by their preoccupation with mundane, worldly matters. Groups where people don't understand that we are at war with a dangerous enemy develop what we could call a "soft" ethos. People there can't see why they should turn aside from worldly entanglements to serve Christ. Talk of radical living for Jesus sounds "over the top." Such slack, undisciplined groups cannot win victories for God, and become boring even to their own people.

Soldiers in human armies have to submit to discipline. They can't do what they want when on duty. They "suffer hardship." Training is rigorous and painful work. This is not how many Americans view church. Consumer Christians expect time at church to be a pleasant, soothing experience. Where do these passages fit into that picture?

People who fail to understand that the church is God's army give themselves too much liberty. They see nothing wrong with wrangling and feuding with others in the body of Christ. They feel free to talk down their leaders and grouse. But the military picture calls for solidarity and the ability to stay in formation. Soldiers expect their comrades to do their jobs, and the success of the whole depends on everyone carrying out his or her part. That's why Paul says to "admonish the unruly" (1 Thessalonians 5:14), but rejoices in the Colossians' "good discipline" (Colossians 2:5).

When a group has a militant ethos, people regularly brace themselves for battle. They develop a toughness that baffles weaker groups. Consider prayer as an example. If we see the church as a social club, prayer becomes something we do when we feel like it. But under the army metaphor, disciplined prayer becomes essential. We have a reason to work at prayer, or "struggle in prayer" as Paul puts it (Colossians 4:12; Romans 15:30). People in this kind of group realize they need to make regular times to gather for intercessory prayer, and God answers their prayers.

People who understand the militant images in the New Testament no longer view assembling together as an option for weeks when they're not busy, but instead view it as an important responsibility. Likewise, hard work at becoming equipped makes sense to soldiers, but not to civilians.

Hardship and Struggle

American Civil War General Sherman said, "War is hell." Nobody who knows war could see it any other way. War is harsh, and warriors have to withstand intense suffering and deprivation. Wounds and death are common.

Spiritual war is also harsh, especially if we let ourselves care about others. We can plan on heartache and grief when we see fellow-believers carried away into personal destruction by the evil one and his world-system. Personal sacrifice will be essential to any military victory. While others zone out in front of their entertainment centers, Christian workers agonize in prayer, study, and concern for endangered fellow believers. They suffer the disappointments of personal defeat and failure. They may have to withstand wounds inflicted by their own friends, as well as those from the world.

Alertness is essential in war, and it's costly. Christians who believe what God reveals about military aspects of the body of Christ realize we can't afford to let down our guard. Peter and Paul both stress watchfulness in connection with spiritual war (1 Peter 5:8; Ephesians 6:18). This rules out the apathetic and self-centered stupor typical of those entangled with the world. Engaged Christians should be able to articulate all the key struggles going on in their own home groups as well as in the larger community, and in many cases, should have ideas for how to improve the situation.

Christians in the army of God have to manage their own expectations. They realize this is not going to be easy. There will be blood. Christianity is not a game we play; it's a desperate life-and-death struggle with the eternal life of many at stake. How pitifully soft consumer Christianity is compared with this picture!

The big picture

To some readers, the picture of the church as an army is a jarring contradiction to the picture of the church as a body or a family. But all these pictures point to valid aspects of the church as it should be. The militant aspect of the church must be built into members' and leaders' thinking and action if they are to resist a consumer mentality. Weak, slack, undisciplined, and self-serving groups are far from the New Testament ethos. The militant part of the church's ethos is just as vital to her health as the more nurturing pictures, and leaving any of these pictures out distorts God's intentions for the church. We may be peace loving in secular life, but in the church real love must include a struggle as long as millions are dying without Christ all around us, and God's enemy continues hunting human souls.

Chapter Seven

Pictures: God's Building

Several passages compare the church to a building—specifically, the temple (1 Peter 2: 5; 1 Corinthians 3:9b-17; Ephesians 2:20-22).

Old Testament people called the temple "the house of God," even though they were well aware from the beginning that God didn't literally live there. When he dedicated the temple Solomon said, "But will God really live on earth? Why, even the highest heavens cannot contain you. How much less this Temple I have built!" (1 Kings 8:27, NLT). The temple wasn't the actual house of God, but it *symbolized* God's dwelling for teaching purposes. Still, God got behind that picture by sending the cloud of his glory into the temple. He insisted that people reverence the picture created by the temple.

When God established the mystical union and the universal indwelling of the Holy Spirit, the body of Christ became the *literal* dwelling place of God. As such, the body of Christ replaced the temple and superseded it. Instead of a physical temple, God now builds people together into his dwelling place like "living stones." The New Testament authors call attention to several fascinating points in the picture of the church as God's building.

The Foundation or Cornerstone

Paul and Peter referred back to Jesus' own cue that the temple was related to his body (John 2:19-22). When they discuss the church as a temple, they generally agree on the symbolism with some minor differences.

In 1 Corinthians, Jesus is the foundation. But in Ephesians 2 and 1 Peter 2 he is the cornerstone.[28] The picture of the cornerstone is particularly interesting when considering how they built large official buildings like the temple in those days. Builders didn't have laser levels like we do, but they did have plumb lines (a weight hanging on a string) and levels they could use to get good, true walls. A key part of their technique was the cornerstone. Stonemasons would carefully select this stone and cut it extra-accurately. Once in place, the cornerstone became the standard used to plumb the vertical and horizontal angles of the walls.

You can see why they would compare Jesus to the cornerstone. He is the first, he is perfectly shaped, and we are to base all our actions and standards on him. Jesus, as revealed in the gospels and other apostolic writings, is the be-all and end-all standard for the church.

In Ephesians 2:20, Paul sees Jesus as the cornerstone and adds that the foundation is the "apostles and prophets." Prophets were the agents of communication and the authors of the Old Testament. Apostles did the same thing for the New Testament. This is probably a way of referring to the Bible. But it could also refer to other aspects of their work. God's servants through the centuries laid an historical foundation for his work in Christ.

The Other Stones

Peter and Paul both say the members of the body are like the stones in the temple. First, remember that stone masonry in the ancient world was different than most of our building today. We usually use uniform blocks, whether brick, block, or stone. Not so back then. In most excavated ancient buildings, the stones are of

---

[28]Of course, these passages were written years apart and to different audiences. Paul changes how he conceives of the building project, but that's not surprising because these pictures are not rigid or wooden in application. In 1 Corinthians Paul is viewing human work in building the church. In Ephesians, he is viewing God's work. The main picture still comes across similarly, even if he handles some details differently.

different size, as you can see by comparing the circled stones in this picture from Corinth.
Hand-cutting stone from quarries without the use of explosives or modern stone-saws was time consuming and expensive. They didn't want to waste material in an effort to make every stone identical (an idea that probably had no attraction in this pre-modern setting).

Instead, they used careful artisanship to fit stones together so the walls came out right, even though they were made up of different sized stones.

These are the buildings Paul and Peter have in mind when they use this picture. Like human master builders, God fits different people into the right relationship to other stones, so that the wall is true and the fit is tight. Paul says, "But now God has placed the members, each one of them, in the body, just as He desired" (1 Corinthians 12:18) That's a different picture, but the same point. With each new person who comes into the body of Christ, God carefully places them in the wall where they belong. In other words, where you are, what you are, and who you are with are no accident.

In the original context, this doesn't refer to which local church we attend, but to our gifting and ministry contributions. Our relational network in the local church is probably also in view. But first century Christians had no choice of different local churches, so our situation is different. Most of us live in cities where we can choose which church we serve in. Some are not Bible believing and others are very legalistic or aberrant. In this setting, we can't automatically assume that we belong in the church we currently attend. Arguably, we should select the best Bible-believing church we can find, and then build into others' lives there. Another alternative is starting a new church from scratch. But the picture of the building definitely speaks against hopping from group to group.

Here is why: Consider the difference between a wall and a pile of stone blocks.

In a pile of stones, the stones have no specific relationship to each other. Their random configuration means

that even if a block disappeared, one would hardly notice.

Such random relationships are the antithesis of what we see in

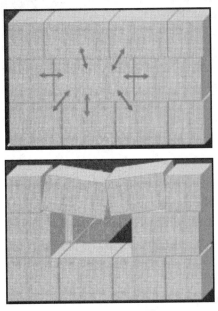

the picture of the wall. In a wall, each stone has a stable relationship to other stones on all sides. Here a missing stone would stick out like a sore thumb and would damage the wall immediately. This is what we should see in these passages. When God builds us into the wall of the temple, he places us into a specific relational and functional setting with the other stones in that wall. God wants us to grow deeply in one setting. Those who hop around from group to group often do so for self-serving reasons. When we are intent on serving and developing ministry, we quickly realize we need to stay put, build good relationships, and build a history with others that leads to trust.

Drifting from one local church to another destroys our ability to minister effectively. We become diffuse and lack sufficient understanding of others that would enable us to obey the "one-another" passages. Instead of becoming a blessing to others, diffuse Christians who are too restless to stay put begin seeking blessing for self. Like wine tasters, they constantly sample different groups, but never growing deeply enough to become effective givers.

Building the temple correctly

God arranges the stones as he builds his temple, but we are also involved in this process, as God works through human agency in reaching and incorporating new people into his building. In 1 Corinthians 3, Paul considers the project of building God's temple from the human side. This passage is a completely different discussion, and instead of the building materials standing for people, here the materials stand for our work for God. People working in the body have two alternatives: works that are flammable (wood, hay, or straw, v. 12), or non-flammable (gold, silver, jewels, v. 12).

The non-flammable works of ministry stand for building God's temple correctly—with sound doctrine, correctly motivated, and in a cooperative, God-dependent attitude. God will reward such works (v. 14). The flammable materials are inappropriate for a temple and God will burn them away, signifying that they will not be rewarded (v. 14-15). Fortunately, the one who did inferior work is not condemned (v. 15). Worse are those who would corrupt the temple; them God will either "destroy" or "corrupt" (v. 17).[29]
The main lesson is in verse 10: "Whoever is building on this foundation must be very careful." Already in the earliest times, false leaders were infiltrating the church for self-serving reasons. These wrongdoers are probably the same ones that come up in 2 Corinthians, where Paul says, "These people are false apostles. They are deceitful workers who disguise themselves as apostles of Christ" (2 Corinthians 11:13).

Self-serving false leaders were the scourge of the early church, as they still are today. Every effort to prevent evil workers from becoming leaders in the church has failed, from rule making to

---

[29]The word here doesn't necessarily mean "destroy." The semantic range of the word could include the idea of spoiling or corrupting. The lexicon says, "phtheirō vb.; destroy (1Co 3:17; 2Pe 2:12; Jude 10+); 2. LN 20.23 harm (2Co 7:2+), 3. deprave, corrupt, perversion (1Co 15:33; 2Co 11:3; Eph 4:22; Rev 19:2+)." James Swanson, *Dictionary of Biblical Languages With Semantic Domains: Greek* (New Testament), electronic ed., GGK5780 (Oak Harbor: Logos Research Systems, Inc., 1997).

requiring official credentials, to regional or worldwide "accountability" organizations or Magisteriums. Satan is simply too smart to be blocked by any such external means. Only the discerning, well-taught body of Christ can either prevent such people from coming into leadership, or remove them if they do. Once evil workers take over leadership of a church, all hope of positive change is in vain. Only removal of such leaders can save the group.

The Dividing Wall

Paul also reveals that in the new temple, no longer has a dividing wall like that in the original temple. The dividing wall was a wall separating the court of the gentiles (where non-Jews could enter) from the holy place. In Ephesians 2:14-16 he says,

> For Christ himself has brought peace to us. He united Jews and Gentiles into one people when, in his own body on the cross, he broke down the wall of hostility that separated us. He did this by ending the system of law with its commandments and regulations. He made peace between Jews and Gentiles by creating in himself one new people from the two groups (NLT).

Here again he stresses the unity of the body of Christ, superseding the old rules of the law, and based on the mystical union of all believers. Racism and other forms of prejudice have no place in the temple of God. In fact, the mystical union removes every kind of prejudice—race, socio-economic, and gender: "There is no longer Jew or Gentile, slave or free, male and female. For you are all one in Christ Jesus" (Galatians 3:28).

The point of the temple

We have seen how the picture of the church as the temple of God works with all its symbolism. But a final question remains: What was the main point of the temple, and what does that say about the church?

When he dedicated the temple, Solomon talked about two main purposes for the temple.

In the first place, the temple symbolized a place of access to

God. In 1 Kings 8:30, Solomon prayed, "May you hear the humble and earnest requests from me and your people Israel when we pray toward this place. Yes, hear us from heaven where you live, and when you hear, forgive" (NLT). You can again see from his words that he knew God lived in heaven, not in the temple. But the temple stood as a symbolic statement that God was accessible. Of course their access was indirect and through the mediation of priests—not like our direct access in the mystical union. The veil separating God from the people was torn from top to bottom when Jesus died on the cross, clearly signifying that he achieved a new level of intimate access never known under the old temple system (Hebrews 10:19-20).

But the temple stood for more than this. In 1 Kings 8:41-43 Solomon went on to pray, "In the future, foreigners who do not belong to your people Israel will hear of you... all the people of the earth will come to know and respect you, just as your own people Israel do. They, too, will know that this Temple honors your name" (NLT). And in verse 60 he adds, "Then people all over the earth will know that the Lord alone is God and there is no other" (NLT). God intended the temple to be a testimony, demonstrating his true nature to the whole world. All the awesome symbolic rituals in the temple were really foreshadowing the work of Jesus, as the book of Hebrews explains. Central in this demonstration was the grace of God made possible through substitutionary sacrifice.

God's temple is still supposed to make a strong statement to the world about God. Now the people of God, personally indwelt by the Holy Spirit and united spiritually to each other and to God, are the supreme statement that God loves people.

The big picture

The picture of the temple shapes key aspects of healthy group ethos. From the temple we get a statement of belonging, of diversity, of interdependency, and of how our corporate solidarity makes a powerful statement about God to the watching world. At the same time, this picture rebukes the individualism, formalism, and disengagement in faulty modern conceptions of the church. By urging our people to view themselves as God's temple, we correct human tendencies toward selfishness and autonomy. We can well challenge modern church members on whether they are willing to let God build them into the wall. Or are they reserving the right to hop around like Mexican jumping beans?

Under modern conditions of perpetual motion (mostly for the sake of earning more money through promotions and new jobs) the New Testament picture of the church as God's temple crumbles into nonsense. One famous leader of a megachurch told me that their studies showed that thirty percent of their people leave each year. Can you imagine what this realization would do to your philosophy of ministry? What would be the point of equipping people or discipling them if they are going to be gone in an average of three years? Leaders will discard all long-term approaches in churches where they see their members as short-term guests.

Instead, we should call on our people to hold still and let God work. Although some leaders doubt it, modern people will decline opportunities to move around for the sake of money because they want spiritual stability and fruitfulness. The problem is that few leaders ever call on them to do so. I asked the mega church leader mentioned earlier if they ever called on people to consider forsaking promotions involving moving in order to develop better, more stable ministries. He thought about it for a minute and admitted they had never made that call. But we should make the call. The American habit of moving every few years is devastating to children and shatters community, as even secular authorities warn. The church has to call its people to put first things first and allow God to build them into a solid, lasting temple of the Lord.

Some people may ignore that call, but our experience shows that many will listen. They listen mainly because they have become convinced that their spiritual health as well as their children's depends on building spiritual and relational stability in their lives instead of more wealth and worldly prestige. Also, people who have built significant ministry don't want to move away from those they have loved for years. As shocking as it may seem to secular Americans, some things matter more than career advancement, and God's people stand at the top of the list.

Chapter Eight

Pictures: God's Family

Sometimes, Jesus and the apostles refer to the church as the family of God. Like all these pictures, some aspects of the metaphor don't fit. For instance, we don't choose which earthly family we come into, whereas John says that as Christians, we "were born, not of blood" but through faith (John 1:13). Likewise, children in earthly families are minors without decision-making responsibility, but we are responsible adults. So, just as with all these pictures, we have to determine which aspects of family life are relevant and which are not.

Here are some typical passages that represent the body of Christ as God's family.

> Don't let anyone call you 'Rabbi,' for you have only one teacher, and all of you are equal as brothers and sisters. And don't address anyone here on earth as 'Father,' for only God in heaven is your spiritual Father. And don't let anyone call you 'Teacher,' for you have only one teacher, the Messiah (Matthew 23:8-10, NLT).
>
> There was a crowd sitting around Jesus, and someone said, "Your mother and your brothers are outside asking for you." Jesus replied, "Who is my mother? Who are my brothers?" Then he looked at those

around him and said, "Look, these are my mother
and brothers. Anyone who does God's will is my
brother and sister and mother" (Mark 3:32-35).
Then Peter began to speak up. "We've given up
everything to follow you," he said.
"Yes," Jesus replied, "and I assure you that everyone
who has given up house or brothers or sisters or
mother or father or children or property, for my sake
and for the Good News, will receive now in return a
hundred times as many houses, brothers, sisters,
mothers, children, and property—along with
persecution. And in the world to come that person
will have eternal life. (Mark 10:28-30).
Therefore, as we have opportunity, let us do good to
all people, especially to those who belong to the
family of believers (Galatians 6:10; See also
1 Timothy 3:15; 5:1-2 and 1 Peter 4:17).

In addition to these, over 210 verses from Acts to Revelation
refer to fellow Christians as "brethren," "brothers," or "sisters." So
the early church clearly drew heavily on this picture to define their
identity. Of course, addressing God as our heavenly father is also
very common.

Elements of the picture

Modern people have problems getting all they should from the
picture of the church as the family of God. So many of us have grown
up in families too dysfunctional to call forth pleasant mental images.
A family is supposed to summon images of love, closeness, and
loyalty. Members of healthy families sacrifice for each other and will
do anything for the good of the family.

People showing real affection for others outside the context of
sexual attraction is becoming increasingly uncommon in our western
world. Visitors from developing countries quickly notice that
Americans in particular stand farther apart when talking, feel
awkward with physical touch, and generally express less affection

for friends and even family members than do people in their own countries. Western culture is relatively cold.

Early Christians greeted each other with a "holy kiss," and Paul often reminds them to keep doing so. He seems zealous to see Christian groups openly expressing closeness and affection to each other. Most groups feel kissing each other might be too jarring in our culture, but we need to find analogous ways to express affection. One key to developing groups that seem affectionate is to build real relationships where people actually *feel affectionate* toward each other. Too often, churches try to put on a show of affection by encouraging group hugs, or smiling introductions to those sitting nearby at a church service. But is this closeness and affection? Often, the people involved in these activities don't even know each other!

The picture of the family of God powerfully contradicts the modern church in its disengagement. We cannot stretch the concept of being like the family of God to fit definitions that involve merely attending a worship service while lacking closeness to the others there. Alienated Americans need to make friends in fellowship, and then invest in those friends until they begin to feel affection for them. Groups where people have engaged in relational investment for years become places where anyone can sense true warmth.

Belonging

The image of the church as God's family ministers to our need to belong. As members of God's family, we all should gain a strong sense of belonging—one of our basic needs as humans. When the people of God believe this picture, we finally gain the potential to overcome the galling sense of loneliness so many of us feel in the West. Instead of feeling adrift in a mobile culture where people pass each other like pieces of debris floating down a river, we find the life God created us for: the life of love. But merely joining ourselves to the body of Christ is not enough. The closeness God intends requires consistent, long-term investment.

Belonging to a loving family means our lives become each other's business. Unlike the rest of the world, we now have a basis for speaking the truth into each other's lives, including reproof.

Christians in the body of Christ feel able to address each other in ways they would never address outsiders. Only our common commitment to each other and to the will of God provide a basis for speaking the truth in love, even when it hurts. We will consider the nature of loving discipline in a separate chapter.

Exception Passages

In a handful of passages, Paul changes the picture to reflect himself as the father, or even the mother! In 1 Thessalonians 2:7-12 he says,

> But we were gentle among you, like a mother caring for her little children. We loved you so much that we were delighted to share with you not only the gospel of God but our lives as well, because you had become so dear to us... For you know that we dealt with each of you as a father deals with his own children, encouraging, comforting and urging you to live lives worthy of God.

Here Paul compares his care, affection, and admonition to the actions of a mother and a father. He is not saying he *is* their parent, but that his actions were like those of parents. God is the father. Christian leaders are brothers and sisters just like all Christians. Leadership is a ministry just like other ministries, and those who take on such ministries are not responsible for the needs of their adult following in the same way parents are responsible to meet all the needs of their helpless children. Instead, leaders are responsible to equip their members to meet each other's needs.

Paul also saw himself like a spiritual father to Timothy (1 Timothy 5:1; Philippians 2:22), and the Corinthians (1 Corinthians 4:15). These references are apparently based on his role in leading them to Christ. It's an affectionate and authoritative title, but not related to the larger teaching of the body of Christ as God's family, with God as the father.

The big picture

As members in God's family, we should never feel the loneliness and disconnectedness that are inevitable apart from God. But none of this is easy or automatic. Believers who show up expecting their church to make them feel like they're part of the family are guilty of sin. We are not deposited into the body of Christ to passively demand service from others. Instead, we all have to learn how to build the Christ-centered relationships with other believers that make a group actually seem like a family.

The picture of the family of God is not pointing to a strange cozy feeling that mystically comes over a group. This picture is calling us to live out the new relational capabilities God has given us in sacrificial love of others. As a group takes that charge seriously over time, the picture of God's family seems less and less far-fetched and unreal. No phony outward acts of pseudo-closeness are necessary. People know they are close and those wandering in from the world can see the closeness with their own eyes.

Chapter Nine

Pictures: God's Field

Agriculture was a big part of life in the ancient world, so it's no surprise to find images of the church from farming. In one passage, Paul calls the church "God's field."

> I planted, Apollos watered, but God was causing the growth. So then neither the one who plants nor the one who waters is anything, but God who causes the growth. Now he who plants and he who waters are one; but each will receive his own reward according to his own labor. For we are God's fellow workers; *you are God's field* (1 Corinthians 3:6-9 the "you" here is plural).

Paul uses this picture to teach on Christian ministry. He discusses the cooperative attitude he and Apollos had, compared to the competitive and fleshly perspective then dominating the Corinthian church. By pointing to a cultivated field, Paul calls our attention to several points.

Results

First, he mentions the limitations of human workers. Neither he nor Apollos was able to cause growth. They were only able to do a ministry (planting or watering) and let God's power bring about spiritual results. He goes on later in the chapter to say each worker will be rewarded based on his own works—that is, not on the results, but on the work he did and his motives for working.[30]

This is not to say results don't matter at all. Results are important, and the harvest is the ultimate goal of both Paul's and Apollos' work. However, our results may not be immediate, and they are not "ours" either. Perhaps another will harvest the seed I planted, and I should be fine with that. Further, results must be kept in a strictly subordinate position. We get our theology of ministry and the church from scripture, not from our calculation of what will yield the best results.

We should seek to maximize our results within the limits of God's will, and indeed, this is exactly why Paul had come to Corinth in the first place. He said, "I have become all things to all men, so that I may by all means save some," and that he ran the race "in such a way, as not without aim; I box in such a way, as not beating the air" (1 Corinthians 9:22, 26). Paul cared about results and pursued objective goals in his ministry. However, he also believed that God is finally the one who provides results in our ministry.

This is where pragmatic arguments about the church break down. Pragmatism is a view that judges all things by results. Under pragmatism, the question is not "is it true?" or "is it right?" but "does it work?" Entire books on the church come out today that hardly mention scripture. Their argument is based entirely on common sense strategies for getting results. If we argue the case this way, we shouldn't be surprised when our people use a pragmatic test for truth. The result will be fleshly, worldly, and unspiritual. To get the best results, people will run the church like a business and use manipulation instead of biblical persuasion. The focus will shift to the external where results are measured, and internal realities will be ignored or discounted. God may have to discipline such a church.

---

[30]The nature of "wood, hay, and straw" or "gold, silver, and precious stones" clearly relate to the "quality" of each man's work (vs. 13), not the quantity of results. This is the context of the argument from the beginning of the chapter, where he rebukes fleshly ministry involving jealousy and strife (vs. 3). He goes on in the next chapter to say, ""Therefore do not go on passing judgment before the time, but wait until the Lord comes who will both bring to light the things hidden in the darkness and disclose the motives of men's hearts; and then each man's praise will come to him from God" (1 Corinthians 4:5). So here again, motivation, not just results are the basis for judgment.

The realization that we don't have control over the time or amount of harvest should comfort us. Nothing is worse than feeling responsible for something we can't control. Fortunately, God expects faithfulness, not immediate results (1 Corinthians 4:2). If we are faithful, no doubt we, or someone, will see results eventually, as God promised in Galatians 6:9, "Let us not lose heart in doing good, for in due time we will reap if we do not grow weary."

Boundaries

Paul says that "neither the one who plants nor the one who waters is anything, but God who causes the growth." This statement uses *hyperbole* (deliberate exaggeration) to make its point. Actually, the workers are *something*, but compared to God, they are like nothing. After all, he also calls himself "God's fellow worker" later in the same passage (v. 9). But Paul is not drawing attention to our importance in this passage. He is calling attention to our limitations, and the corresponding outlook—that only God's power can win people.

Only the servant who has deeply embraced the truth that God causes the growth can possess the full humility Paul demonstrates here. This passage provides a basis for "boundaries" in ministry. In this context, having boundaries means we don't feel responsible for everything, only for our own part. We do our part, whether planting or watering, and we don't feel responsible for others' reactions and decisions. We can entrust God with the outcomes in ministry; then we become free from the distracting burden of anxiety over how our ministry results reflect on our egos. This passage also rejects "co-dependent" models of ministry where we feel we have to make people do and think the right thing.

Accepting your limitations in ministry, along with the reality of God's faithfulness prevents what some call "burnout" in ministry. People commonly burn out when they take too much upon themselves. Just be sure you are diligently planting or watering, and leave the rest to God.

Cooperation

Paul's view of farming also leads him to say, "Now he who plants and he who waters are one" (v. 8). Although the Corinthians were competing based on which leader they preferred (v. 4), the leaders themselves were not competing at all. Such lack of competition will only come to those who have understood their own limitations, and have fully accepted the need for the function of the other workers in the field.

As a young Christian worker, I used to drive myself to the limit of endurance and beyond. Every year I would do great until I suffered my annual physical and emotional breakdown. Then, half the work for that year would crumble apart while I withdrew and tried to recuperate. Older, wiser voices eventually called my attention to this passage and another one later in the book "The body is not one member but many" (1 Corinthians 12:14). Both of these argue against a messiah complex, where we think we have to do everything. My teachers convinced me that viewing myself as the only one who could help people was arrogant and unfaithful. You can tell you have this problem if you are unable to say "no" when asked to help anyone or do anything. After serious dealings with God on this issue, I became able to trust his working through other members more, and no longer have exhaustion breakdowns.

Ancient farming was usually a team project carried out by an extended family, and it didn't matter who planted, who watered, or who reaped. The important thing then, as now, is the harvest. Unity and cooperation are the hallmark of mature Christian workers who understand the larger picture, including God's part in ministry. Paul explicitly says that jealousy and strife, which result from workers focusing only on their own part of the whole task, are telltale signs of a fleshly outlook (v. 3). Fleshly workers may even undermine other competitors or rejoice when they fail.

Hard work

In another passage Paul says, "The hard-working farmer ought to be the first to receive his share of the crops (2 Timothy 2:6

NASB)." In context, the hard-working farmer refers to a dedicated Christian worker.

Any one who has farmed knows that hard work is essential. No lazy farmer can expect to see a successful harvest. Proverbs rebukes lazy farmers: "The sluggard does not plow after the autumn, so he begs during the harvest and has nothing" (Prov. 20:4). Fall is the only time for plowing in their system, and in the same way, Christian workers who "miss the moment" end up with nothing. The so-called "sluggard" farmer gets rough handling in both Old and New Testaments. The sluggard is one who is more intent on cultivating personal comfort and avoiding exertion than on accomplishing anything. The author of Proverbs says,

> I passed by the field of the sluggard, and by the vineyard of the man lacking sense; And behold, it was completely overgrown with thistles, its surface was covered with nettles, and its stone wall was broken down. When I saw, I reflected upon it; I looked, and received instruction (24:30-32).

What he learns should be obvious: "That could be my vineyard if I'm as lazy and self-indulgent as this guy." Farming is hard work, and we should assume that doing Christian work will be difficult and taxing, even if we do have boundaries as mentioned above. Some Christians are so super-spiritual they reject hard work and accountability. They feel something has gone terribly wrong if they feel fatigued when serving God. But anything as difficult as farming will tire us at times, and we should expect that.

Consistency

We can draw lessons from additional features of successful farming, because in the next verse Paul says, "Consider what I say, for the Lord will give you understanding in everything" (v. 7). It seems like Paul expects us to ponder these pictures for more meaning.

Consistency is essential to successful farming. Farmers work in rain and shine, heat and cold. Plants cannot understand the farmer's personal problems that might cause him to fail to weed or water his crops. They wither without care, whether the farmer's excuses for failing to do so are good or bad. Even during winter (or for them, the dry season) when they expect no harvest, farmers continue to work, sharpening their tools, repairing equipment and buildings, and doing a host of other work in order to be ready for the next growing season.

So too, when working with people. We've all seen that highly gifted person who disappears so often that people never build confidence in his reliability. Less gifted people often end up counting for more in the body of Christ for the simple reason that they are there when they are needed and make their contribution consistently.

Patience

Patience is indispensable for good farmers. No amount of fretting and worry will hurry the day of harvest. Crops require a full growing season, and the wise farmer knows he must patiently wait until harvest time to reap. But in today's churches we see impatience sometimes so severe that it undermines God's whole intent for the church. Church leaders in the west have demonstrated a fixation on quick results, even if those results are of such inferior quality that they lead to disaster in the long run.

Many western Christians are enamored with spiritual shortcuts. For instance, we want shortcuts to spiritual health and deliverance from sin through a variety of pathways involving miracles or esoteric insights. Plodding, steady, spiritual growth seems too un-miraculous for quick fix Christians. But God's real miracles usually come through the slow, steady path of growth.

Likewise, when it comes to evangelism and church growth, Americans tend toward fascination with approaches that provide quick, even astonishing, numeric growth. Christian magazines and books resound with stories about churches that went from nothing to thousands in a few years or even a few months. Even though studies show that such rapid growth churches are usually full of transfer Christians, the reading public will spend millions on books explaining how they can get the same results. I read these books and stories as well. It's so intriguing to read stories of powerful spiritual awakenings.

When pondering rapid growth stories, we should remember that God does work rapidly at times when he sparks supernatural revival, and he has worked that way at our church during certain periods. But is explosive growth in a short time really the norm for healthy Christian ministries? Is this something we should seek or desire?

In our experience, rapid growth can cause huge problems, including chaos, compromise, poorly trained leaders, and loss of community—especially if the growth is mostly by conversion. Think about it: If hundreds or even thousands of people swarm into your local church in a short time, how could you establish every-member ministry? How could your people possibly practice the one-another passages? How could the church raise up credible spiritual leadership in proportion to the growth? The biggest thing explosive growth usually gets us is a big ego-trip (and I've been there). It too easily establishes an ethos centered on numbers that ignores depth. These results are not because leaders have darkened hearts. Rather, such results are virtually inevitable under extreme rapid growth conditions. There is simply no way to develop spiritual depth and quality body life when growth exceeds a certain level.[31]

To develop a good farm, we need to convince people that building quality and depth in a self-replicating discipling ministry is more important than rapid numeric growth. We need to convince members that winning converts is more important than winning large numbers of transfers.[32]

Like a patient farmer, if church workers build quality they will

---

[31] Peters suggests that limit is at or less than 25 percent growth per year. George W. Peters, *A Theology of Church Growth*, (Grand Rapids: Zondervan Publishing House, 1981). I believe the limit is significantly less than that. If we accept the estimate of one million Christians by the year 100 AD, the early church experienced roughly 11 percent growth per year—more than enough to reach the entire world within the next century, That seems plenty rapid to me.

[32] Thumma and Bird found in their 2008 survey of mega churches that "nearly everyone, including visitors, described himself or herself as a "committed follower of Jesus Christ... barely 2% (roughly 500 people among the entire 24,900 survey respondents) said they were *not* a committed follower of Christ." Scott Thumma and Warren Bird, *Not Who You Think They Are: The Real Story of People Who Attend America's Megachurches* (Hartford CT: Hartford Institute for Religious Research, 2009) 5. Although some had been out of church before coming to the mega church, hardly any were non-Christians.

eventually reach large numbers of people, and those people will be more mature and better equipped than people won through approaches targeted to rapid growth. Merely warehousing or entertaining large numbers of people is not our mission. But leaders and members have to take the long view if they are to successfully pursue a discipling, multiplying, every-member strategy. Here is a good example where values need to interact with theology, and the image of God's field guides us toward patience.

Some self-replicating approaches are very impatient as well. Many small group models call for doubling each group and planting new ones every six months. This model is so aggressive it could begin with one six-person small group, and win every adult on earth in 13 years! That's impatient, and the model isn't working. Maybe we should consider a more patient approach that allows time for adequate training and spiritual growth before members are thrust into leadership roles.

Even if such approaches occasionally result in large numbers, we have more to consider from a biblical perspective than pragmatic, short-term results. The Bible teaches that people have to grow out of their moral and relational problems through a gradual transformation process including community, struggle, learning, counseling, prayer and practice. Projects like letting "the word of Christ richly dwell within you" so you can teach and counsel each other "with all wisdom" (Colossians 3:16) take more than six months! It usually takes six months just to build enough trust to begin discovering a new believer's major moral and relational problems. Impatient leaders are unwilling to undertake the long haul implied in a disciple making approach.

Learning also suffers in impatient churches. Paul's call to "be diligent to present yourself approved to God as a workman who does not need to be ashamed, accurately handling the word of truth" (2 Timothy 2:15) makes no sense under impatient approaches. Impatient churches usually shortcut to formulaic, script-like teaching that holds no one's interest, or they dismiss all efforts to teach and simply argue for unguided singing and sharing sessions that are even less interesting and not transformative at all. Impatience and over-simplifying theories lead to weak, confused, and non-transformative groups. Claims to the contrary by some groups in the west appear to be largely fictional.[33]

Jesus on farming

Jesus also used farming as a picture of the church in the kingdom parables found in Matthew 13. In the parable of the soils, a planter sows seed (the word of the kingdom) on different kinds of soil (v. 3-9, 18-23). The four types of soil (rocky, pathway, weedy, or good) stand for different types of individual hearers. As in the 1 Corinthians passage, the sower should realize that results will be different based on factors beyond his control, including the activity of Satan and individuals' willingness. According to this pattern, most efforts to spread the gospel fail for one reason or another. Only seed landing on good soil has a good outcome. This low frequency of success in evangelism again points to the need for patience and consistency.

Within the church, "the worry and cares of the world, and the deceitfulness of riches" pose the biggest threat (Matthew 13:22). Christians (living plants) distracted with the world-system (the

---

[33] Leaders in Xenos have been intrigued to hear claims from organic or "simple church" enthusiasts that their people have planted hundreds of house churches in the U. S. rapidly and spontaneously with little or no leadership training and no oversight. These claims flatly contradict our own experience, which shows that, while people may plant such groups, the groups tend to stagnate or fizzle out. In our multiple trips around the country to observe these explosively growing "networks," we have found them to be mostly imaginary! In some cases, "networks" supposedly containing half a dozen house churches actually contained none. What one writer called a network of "six or seven" house churches turned out to be nothing more than three Christians meeting in a coffee shop discussing plans for planting their first house church. Other "networks" contained nothing more than a single small group made up of long-time Christians who said they had yet to win their first convert. Even worse, we found proof that some authors who claim to have planted hundreds of house churches are claiming to have planted house churches that were actually planted by other, established churches. The people in these groups denied any involvement with the "network" that supposedly planted them. Not one of the groups we visited were reaching significant numbers of non-Christians to faith. Perhaps there are significant house church planting events going on somewhere in America—they are definitely going on in other countries. But we have never found one, and we have wasted so much time trying that we are no longer actively looking. The best home group planting we have found comes from local churches that train, deploy, and oversee their groups. In overseas (real) church planting movements I have visited and studied, they have training, organization, accountability, and discipline at a fairly high level. Two of the world's leading experts in church planting movements have told me (agreeing with my observations) that there are no actual church planting movements in America at present. Yet, according to a recent Pew poll, "Homes are the most popular alternative venue to churches and other houses of worship. About 7% of Americans [over 20 million people!] say they attend religious services in someone's home. Attending services in homes is somewhat more common among Protestants (9%) than among Catholics (4%)." "Eastern, New Age Beliefs Widespread: Many Americans Mix Multiple Faiths," (Pew Forum on Religion & Public Life December 2009) 6.

weeds) invariably become unfruitful. Churches where the ethos includes accommodation with Satan's world system are doomed to an unspiritual future (James 4:4).

We also notice that even responsive people bear fruit at different levels depending on their makeup and the field where they are assigned to work (Matthew 13:23). God doesn't expect all Christians or all groups to be alike or to bear equal fruit. Each group should focus on what God has called them to do, not on how well others are doing.

In the parable of the wheat and the tares (v. 24-30), the results are again mixed through no fault of the sower. The evil one makes certain we will have mixed results as he attempts to frustrate the God's purposes—in this case through infiltration. Both parables teach that God has decided to let things happen in this mixed way until the "time of the harvest" (v. 30) when God sets everything right. Jesus was warning that the history of the church will include the good and the evil, the real and the false.

The big picture

The picture of the church as God's field uses an activity people already knew to explain key aspects of the church. God expects workers in the body of Christ to tend his field with hard work, patience, consistency, good sense, and cooperation. We have to trust God to bring the ultimate results. We must struggle to embed these elements into the values system our churches if we want health. People who pursue ministry with steady, hard-working consistency become more stable and really happier than those impatiently tapping their feet as they wait for explosive growth events. If our people adopt this kind of ethos, God will provide growth and the harvest when the time is right.

Chapter Ten

Pictures: Jesus' Bride

Marriage, sibling, and parent-child relationships are the closest we, as humans, know. God uses all three to picture his relationship with us. But marriage is uniquely used in connection with the church.

The Old Testament

In the Old Testament, God often calls Israel his betrothed, his beloved or his bride. Unfortunately, he often connects these pictures with his people's unfaithfulness—especially in the prophets, such as Ezekiel, Jeremiah, Hosea, and Isaiah. A poignant example of this imagery is found in Lamentations 1:2, 8, 9:

> She [Jerusalem] weeps bitterly in the night,
> And her tears are on her cheeks;
> She has none to comfort her
> Among all her lovers.
> All her friends have dealt treacherously with her;
> They have become her enemies...
> Jerusalem sinned greatly,
> Therefore she has become an unclean thing.
> All who honored her despise her
> Because they have seen her nakedness;
> Even she herself groans and turns away.
> Her uncleanness was in her skirts;

She did not consider her future;
Therefore she has fallen astonishingly;
She has no comforter ...

The statement, "Her filthiness was in her skirts" (KJV) and the allusion to "all her lovers" both refer to the well-taught concept of "spiritual adultery." God declares that when his bride serves other gods, it is similar to human adultery in its moral loathsomeness, and in the pain and damage it causes. In some passages, he uses quite lurid language for shock effect (e.g. Ezek. 23). He is slamming home the lesson that committing adultery against God is a devastating sin.

The New Testament

In the New Testament, the church is the future Bride of Christ, which means we are currently betrothed, or promised to him. The wedding itself is the wedding feast of the Lamb and the New Jerusalem, pictured in Revelation 19:7-8.

Betrothal in the ancient world was a more serious commitment than engagement in our day. Getting out of betrothal required a divorce, and they considered fornication during betrothal to be adultery; essentially, betrothal stands between modern marriage and engagement. Violating our betrothal commitment to Jesus is a serious fault, and the result can only be similar to that experienced by Jerusalem when Jeremiah wrote Lamentations: our lovers will abandon us and even feed on our flesh when we least expect it.

Paul

In 2 Corinthians 11:2-4, Paul says,

I am jealous for you with a godly jealousy; for I betrothed you to one husband, that to Christ I might present you as a pure virgin. But I am afraid, lest as the serpent deceived Eve by his craftiness, your minds should be led astray from the simplicity and purity of devotion to Christ. For if one comes and preaches another Jesus whom we have not preached, or you receive a different spirit which you have not received, or a different gospel which you have not accepted, you bear this beautifully.

In this passage, adultery (seduction and loss of virginity) refers to their defection to false teachers. In the case of the Corinthians, these were probably Greek influenced teachers using popular Greek views to lure people away from the true gospel. In our own day, we have every reason to think false teachers will use the wisdom of our own culture to tempt us. Contemporary false teachers will cater to our sin nature by telling us Jesus came to help us gratify ourselves with money, or they may reassure postmodern young people that their relativism and refusal to stand for truth are okay with God.

Paul calls faithfulness "the simplicity and purity of devotion to Christ" (v. 3). The picture of the Bride of Christ calls forth ideas of faithfulness, devotion and the subjective enjoyment of our relationship with Jesus. Some Christians are tempted to become bored by the same old truths, and in place of our simple relationship with Christ, turn to a more sophisticated and trendy ideology.

Paul speaks again using the language of marriage in Ephesians 5:25. There we read,

> Christ also loved the church and gave Himself up for her; that He might sanctify her, having cleansed her by the washing of water with the word, that He might present to Himself the church in all her glory, having no spot or wrinkle or any such thing; but that she should be holy and blameless.

The emphasis in this passage is on Jesus' unconditional and sacrificial love for his bride, the church. The passage is not arguing that the church needs to *become* spotless and without wrinkle. Rather, in God's view she *already is* spotless because of Jesus' finished work. The imperative in this passage is for husbands to love their wives as Christ loved the church—not tapping their toes, waiting for their wives to become perfect, but loving unconditionally and sacrificially as they do "their own bodies," nourishing and cherishing them, "just as Christ also does the church."

By implication, Jesus is also calling his bride to respond to her new status appropriately, which includes heart-felt faithfulness and devotion to the one who has so served her. As the bride of Christ, we should tolerate no higher loyalty than him.

James

James charges his readers with spiritual adultery because they have fallen in love with the world-system.

> You adulteresses, do you not know that friendship with the world is hostility toward God? Therefore whoever wishes to be a friend of the world makes himself an enemy of God. Or do you think that the Scripture speaks to no purpose: "He jealously desires the Spirit which He has made to dwell in us?" (James 4:4-5).

Here, their love of money, pride, and prestige call forth the rebuke for adultery. Just as Jesus warned that we cannot serve both God and money, James warns his readers that they have to chose either life and vitality with God or mediocrity and spiritual death with the world-system.

Arguably, this passage applies to the contemporary western church in a way so painful it could bring tears to our eyes. Instead of leading people in our culture out of slavery to the world-system, many churches have embraced that system and its values.

Accommodation to western time priorities

In my opinion, the biggest single reason churches in the modern west are unable to live out God's vision for *koinonia* is accommodation. Accommodation means modifying the word of God to meet the expectations of your audience. Church history reveals that this has always been a big problem for the church. The church has consistently tended to follow the thinking of her culture, rather than the teaching of the word of God.

Today, we have accommodated the Christian gospel to western culture, so that materialism, career, personal comfort, and private living have crowded out any possibility of living according to the New Testament pattern. We leaders in the modern church have failed to win our own people away from the values system of our culture, and instead have bought into that system ourselves, promoting it as the way of God.

Western Christians, including pastors, are torn. They know the "one another" passages are in the Bible, and should be obeyed in a community setting. But as so many pastors and home group leaders have said to me, "Our people are really busy!" That's supposed to explain why we, as modern people, can't be expected to do what Bible teaches.

It's true—there's no way we can live a typical American lifestyle with our kids' multiple sports leagues, our large SUV payments, daycare bills, time for entertainment, extra hours at work and the gym, and still obey the "one another" passages. Something has to give. Especially with the increase in committed hours for the average American during the past two decades, the whole New Testament picture of the church (such as the one-another passages) has to be consigned to the trash heap of history or radically reinterpreted in the most superficial terms.[34] Unfortunately, either option involves willful disobedience to God in a central area.

So, what's the answer?

---

[34] "Children are being driven in recent years more than ever before, according to Hofferth and Sandberg of the University of Michigan in a 2001 study of kids 3-12 from 1981 to 1997." In these charts we see how time allocation has changed during those years for typical kids.

Cited in Alissa Quart, *Hothouse Kids: The Dilemma of the Gifted Child*, (NY: The Penguin Press, 2006) 69, 70. This shift in kids' priorities is a mirror of what adults, including Christians are doing with their own time. This graph from the Economic Policy Institute shows parents have followed the same pattern. This is a sociological shift in American culture, measured repeatedly with high reliability. See Suniya S. Luthar "The Culture of Affluence: Psychological Costs of Material Wealth" *Child Development*, 2003; Vol. 74 (6): 1581–1593. M. Csikszentmihalyi "If we are so rich, why aren't we happy?" *American Psychologist* 1999;54:821–827. B. Kantrowitz "Busy around the clock." *Newsweek* 2000 July 17;136:49–50.

Clearly, if we want to honor God, if we believe his will is best for our lives, if we believe the Bible is inspired and binding on all people, we will have to break ranks with American culture's values system. We simply cannot follow God in areas like radical fellowship when our time commitments fill our lives with higher priorities. Surely, we must realize that we can't take teaching like the one another passages seriously and still expect to match our neighbors in the world-system who have nothing to do but gather money and serve themselves.

A young man recently told me after a church meeting, "I just attend here when I have time... I'm working on a degree right now." This statement, which in different forms is very common today, really amounts to idol worship. Instead of fitting his degree into whatever is left over after he has "loved God with all his heart, soul, mind, and strength," and "fervently loved one another from the heart," it's just the opposite. He might spend some time with the people of God if all the more important things are already covered. This is spiritual adultery. This is love of the world-system.

Those who believe in New Testament-style church life don't *find* time for fellowship, we *make* time! We do the same thing people in the world do—we list out our priorities in life and begin cutting from the bottom. But unlike people in the world, our commitment to Christ *and his body* should be at the very top of that list.

Today millions of American evangelical Christians live in daily disillusionment, feeling that God or the church has let them down. Yet, many of those same believers have never made the connection between their own insistence on living according to a western cultural values system, and the spiritual poverty they sense in their churches and their own lives. The biblical call to "be holy, for I am holy," (1 Pet. 1:16) means Christians are to be *different* than their culture; that's what the word "holy" means. And to be different than our culture doesn't mean we should be meaner or more harsh. It means we put God ahead of other things in life.

Intimidated leaders

Pastors understand better than others how body life is supposed to work, including how Jesus' betrothed should be faithful to him. But they feel powerless to resist a consensus so strong it seems insane to question it. What pastor wants to see his church collapse as people storm out, covering their ears? Consider the following examples of suggestions that would probably result in a complete loss of credibility for any Christian leader who made them:

- That our people should strongly consider taking jobs that pay less and require fewer hours, so they will have more time to invest in relationships and ministry.
- That couples should consider living on only one income for the sake of their children, even if it means moving to a smaller house and driving well-used cars.
- That Americans stop saying they're "barely making it" when in fact they live at the highest level of income in the world, both today and throughout history.
- That walking Christians should not stress success in the world system for their kids (such as scholarships, sports ascendancy, or attending top universities), but instead urge their kids to succeed in spiritual growth, learning how to build quality relationships, and how to build a fruitful ministry.
- That Americans are not short on time, but in fact have the same number of hours in their week that everyone else in the world has, including those in the New Testament church.
- That playing video games or watching TV for thirty hours per week is not as important as building up the people of God.

Some pastors shudder in dread when they imagine themselves arguing these kinds of points in front of their church. The result could be a lynch mob, or at least a thundering stampede to get out of that church. Leaders have an important choice to make at this point: whether to play to the expectations and demands of their people, or to trust God with their future.

In a word, I believe there is a direct connection between simple living and the spirituality of the church. When Christians get caught up in the world-system—what Jesus called, "the worries and cares of the world and the deceitfulness of riches" (Mt. 13:22), all fruitfulness is choked out. If the church is afraid to call its people to a life of simplicity, they will not have time to do what the New Testament teaches. Once that happens, all our fussing over other issues becomes pointless.

Worldly Christians see the church as a compartment in their lives—maybe even an important one. But before devoting time to anything spiritual, comes that which "I have to do," (meaning the things of the world). So, if I get done with these things I have to do, there will hopefully be some time left over for the things of God. Instead of seeing our lives as being "in Christ" (and consequently in the body of Christ), we see ourselves as first under obligation to the world.

How could a community ever do what we're reading about in the "one another" passages based on a few hours per week, no matter how spiritually eager people are? It isn't going to happen. So, unless we are ready to challenge the values system of our materialistic culture with a different way of life, we can kiss the whole New Testament picture goodbye.

The challenge we throw down has to be positive. Simple living isn't merely something we're forced into because materialism is too devastating to accept (although we can certainly make that argument). The even more important point is that simple living is fun, it's healthy, it makes you and your kids happy, and it makes possible the awesome vision of the New Testament church.

Repentance
James also shares encouragement and solutions in the following verses:

> But He gives a greater grace. Therefore it says, "God is opposed to the proud, but gives grace to the humble." Submit therefore to God. Resist the devil and he will flee from you. Draw near to God and He will draw near to you. Cleanse your hands, you sinners; and purify your hearts, you double-minded. Be miserable and mourn and weep; let your laughter

be turned into mourning, and your joy to gloom. Humble yourselves in the presence of the Lord, and He will exalt you (v. 4:6-10).

Christians who fall in love with the world-system are committing spiritual adultery with God's sworn enemy, Satan, whether they realize it or not. He is the "God" or "ruler" of this world-system (1 John 5:19; 2 Corinthians 4:4; John 12:31).[35] Satan used idols and the occult to lure people away from God in Old Testament times, and still does so today in many lands. But in the west, he has cultivated materialism and uses the attractiveness of prestige in the world-system to accomplish the same goal.

Those caught in adultery can only humble themselves, draw near to God, and throw themselves on his mercy. Thank God, his mercy endures forever! The call to cleanse our hands and hearts, to be miserable, mourn, and weep are all pleading for repentance from the heart, including our faulty motives.

Preparation

Engagement is a time when couples prepare for marriage. During the last months before the big day, they plan the wedding and collect the things they will need for life together, including a place to live. Although still living apart, their current living situation becomes increasingly irrelevant in anticipation of their new life. The focus shifts from single living to married life.

All this fits the picture of the church as Jesus' bride-to-be. He has gone ahead of us to arrange a place to live (John 14:2). That leaves the church with the task of getting herself ready. As a bride approaches her wedding she wants to be at her best. Engaged women have been known to go on diets and begin working out to look their best. They carefully select the dress, flowers, and other adornments for a beautiful wedding. Brides dream of dazzling the audience when they make their appearance. As they plan the ceremony, they compile lists of friends to invite. All these adornments and gathering

---

[35] I have written on this in much more detail in Dennis McCallum, *Satan and his Kingdom: What the Bible Says, and How It Matters to You*, (Minneapolis: Bethany House Publishers, 2008).

of friends could be a picture of the church building both the character of her members and gathering others into herself.

Engagement is also a time for couples to cultivate and deepen their relationship with each other. They should enjoy a growing mutual understanding. Especially in the ancient world, where dating was unknown, betrothal was the only time when a new couple spent significant time with each other (usually in the presence of their parents). In the same way, the members of the bride of Christ should cultivate their knowledge and appreciation of Jesus. Building the body of Christ includes deepening our own and others' relationship with him. Our focus should be on the new home he is preparing, not our old residence in the world. Getting ourselves and others ready for our wedding day should keep us quite busy until he gets here.

The big picture

Although westerners' view of marriage is becoming as distorted and diminished as their view of family in general, people in successful marriages know that the union forged in a family is without parallel in the awesome joy it provides. Likewise, groups who insist that loyalty and fidelity to Jesus are totally reasonable and attainable, experience the joy only known to the faithful people of God. What an extraordinary picture this makes when Jesus calls the church his bride! Remember, the bride is the church, not the individual. This is yet another reason why all of our lives become each other's business.

Healthy churches recognize spiritual adultery when they see it, and continue to argue unashamedly that complete faithfulness to Jesus is the only reasonable standard. They refuse to play games with God by looking the other way when people agree together to accommodate their lives to the world-system. People in churches like this gravitate toward simple living because they realize the power of the world to captivate their affections and mislead their children. They know better than to flirt with anything that powerful and destructive.

Chapter Eleven

Pictures: God's Flock

The health of the local church depends absolutely on its leadership. The New Testament has a lot to say about leadership in the church, and it often uses the picture of a shepherd (or pastor) to make its points. Like all the other pictures, this one only matches in certain areas, not in others. For instance, if it weren't for other analogies such as the army or the body, one could easily use this picture to teach a sedentary version of Christianity where the leaders take care of everything. Humans share some characteristics with sheep, but unlike sheep, we are also responsible, free-choosing moral agents.

Jesus, the good shepherd

Jesus is our model for leadership. He is the owner and leader of the church, a position he executes through the Holy Spirit. But he also delegates leadership to human leaders from first to last in the Bible. Anti-leadership models of the church promoted by some today are simply not biblical.

Jesus describes his leadership model in John 10 where he calls himself the good shepherd.

> I tell you the truth, anyone who sneaks over the wall of a sheepfold, rather than going through the gate, must surely be a thief and a robber! But the one who enters through the gate is the shepherd of the sheep.

The gatekeeper opens the gate for him, and the sheep recognize his voice and come to him. He calls his own sheep by name and leads them out. After he has gathered his own flock, he walks ahead of them, and they follow him because they know his voice. They won't follow a stranger; they will run from him because they don't know his voice (v. 1-5).

Protection

Here Jesus calls attention to the difference between true and false shepherds. The robber in this account is Satan. Jesus later contrasts the robber, who comes "only to rob and kill and destroy," with himself, who came to give abundant life (v. 10). The whole account stands in the context of intense struggle and conflict. Both robbers and wolves threaten the sheep, and this calls our attention to one key feature God has in mind for leaders—protection.

God appoints leaders to help protect people in the body of Christ from menacing dangers. Here we see the difference between humans and sheep. Sheep are almost completely helpless, but humans need to learn to protect themselves. So we should not expect leaders to protect us from *all* dangers, any more than God does. But this does explain why early leaders like Paul and John removed false teachers and dangerous leaders from the church (1 Timothy 1:20; 3 John 9,10). It also accounts for other forms of discipline we will discuss in Chapter 20.

Personalized guidance

Unlike the sneaky robber, Jesus pictures himself coming legitimately. These are his sheep, and they know his voice. They won't follow a stranger's voice. His words aptly describe ancient patterns of village shepherding. In Palestine, the wet season produces grasses widely, but during the dry season, only high pastures in the mountains still have fodder. Therefore, during the wet season villagers would stay at home in their village, and share a common sheepfold. They could all release their flocks into the same stone corral without worrying about getting them mixed up. The reason was that shepherds actually knew their sheep, and the sheep knew their shepherds.

Unlike today, where sheep are processed in large flocks and only live for a short time, ancient shepherds kept their sheep as long as possible. Only when animals were old would they make it into the stew pot. With small flocks and long tenure, shepherds treated their sheep more like pets than farmers do today. They gave their sheep names and had different whistles for each one. In the morning, shepherds could come to the shared corral and call their sheep. Without hesitation, the sheep would come and follow their shepherds as they had been trained to do.[36] The fact that he knew their names and their call was a mark of legitimacy, but it also shows that he had a relationship with each one. When Jesus calls each one of us by name, he shows his individual knowledge and concern.

Of course, human leaders are not Jesus, so they can't necessarily have a direct relationship with each person in the church. But this model does suggest that the flock should know its shepherd. I think this argues in favor of indigenous leaders for local churches instead of the modern system, which more closely mirrors a corporate model.

Today, most churches select their pastors from a database instead of recognizing those in their midst who function as leaders.[37] When the church raises up indigenous leaders (leaders from within their own group) like they did in New Testament times, the people know their leaders from long experience with them. They know the life, service, and character of such leaders by direct experience in the local church.

Loyalty and sacrifice

Jesus also taught the importance of good shepherds being loyal to their flocks, and not leaving them just because a wolf appears. He says, "The good shepherd lays down his life for the sheep" (v. 11). He

---

[36] For these, and many other interesting insights on ancient shepherding practices, see W. Phillip Keller, *A Shepherd Looks at Psalm 23*, (Grand Rapids: Zondervan, 2008).

[37] Or churches can retain a search company that "can earn $40,000 or more for a successful hunt," according to Bobby Ross Jr., "The Workers Are Few: Gap exists between what large churches need and what seminaries produce," *Christianity Today*, posted 7/14/2009

was referring to his death on the cross, but he also expected human leaders to live sacrificially for the sake of their sheep:

> You know that the rulers in this world lord it over their people, and officials flaunt their authority over those under them. But among you it will be different. Whoever wants to be a leader among you must be your servant, and whoever wants to be first among you must be the slave of everyone else. For even the Son of Man came not to be served but to serve others and to give his life as a ransom for many (Mark 10:42-45).

Serving, sacrificial leadership is our model, based on Jesus' own life.

The "hireling"

Jesus calls disloyal shepherds "hired hands" (John 10:12). He explains that such a one, "runs away because he is a hired hand and cares nothing for the sheep" (v. 13). What a horrific picture! The "hireling" (KJV) is one of the most repugnant images in the New Testament. To be entrusted by God with the awesome responsibility of caring for his flock and then to abandon them for the sake of personal profit is reprehensible in the extreme.

The church has largely ignored Jesus' teaching in these passages during most of its history. Probably the worst example was the medieval church when nobles could buy a diocese and become a bishop. It was a good investment because they obtained rights to the tithes (collected as a tax, not voluntarily) from that district. Often, such men knew nothing about spiritual leadership and sometimes didn't even live in the area they supposedly pastored.

Today, the church is often wracked by scandals, but one of the biggest scandals never makes the news. Pastors in the modern western church move from church to church, hoping to move into progressively higher positions each time they abandon one flock for another. Like the hireling in Jesus' story, the concern is often not for the flock, but for personal profit. Successful senior pastors may even be hired away from their flourishing churches to pastor a megachurch. The smaller church simply can't match the pay and perks in the larger church.[38]

Of course, some pastors leave to start new churches, which could be a valid and even admirable reason for leaving. It would be especially admirable if they first raised up new leaders to replace themselves and don't leave their group in a lurch. Others are transferred by their denomination, sometimes against their will. Still others leave because their church fired them or pressured them out.

In the early church, the leadership came up from within the local church with few exceptions. Leaders chosen in this way were well known to their groups, who "knew their voice." Bringing a stranger in from out of town was not unprecedented, especially if a local church had more explosive growth than they could handle, like when both Barnabas and Paul were sent to Antioch (Acts 11:22, 25, 26). Some quality preachers and evangelists would also travel to other cities as guest speakers. Thus the church at Corinth had heard teaching from Paul, Apollos, and Peter (1 Corinthians 1:12). But in 99% of local churches, importing leaders from elsewhere is something nobody would have considered. New Testament leaders might even be paid for their work if the church decided they needed more from them than their secular jobs allowed (1 Timothy 5:17). But local churches expected to raise up their own leaders, not take them from some other group.

Still less justifiable would be leaders leaving one church to get a higher paying job at another. Yes, some were trying to do just that even in New Testament times, but Paul denounced them bitterly, as in 2 Corinthians 1:17: "You see, we are not like the many hucksters who preach for personal profit. We preach the word of God with

---

[38]The top reason pastors leave their church is that they "wanted a different community," according to a study by Ellison Research based on a sample of 872 Protestant church ministers nationwide. But the second and third highest reasons were "promotion" and "wanted a larger church." In one of the strangest findings, they learned that "87% of Southern Baptists pastors feel pastors in their denomination don't tend to stay at one church for enough years." Yet those same preachers were most likely to change churches. James Draper argues, "Wanting a different community, a promotion and better pay are all legitimate reasons for job changes if you are in a corporate environment, but it is a dangerous trend for the pastoral ministry." About half of all transfers admitted it was for "better pay," "a bigger church," or "promotion." *Facts & Trends* September/October, 4, 5, 6. I can only assume that the real number is higher yet.

sincerity and with Christ's authority, knowing that God is watching us." The Bible mentions these cases to teach us what *not* to do.

Ask yourself: What moral justification could a large church feel for hiring a pastor away from his smaller flock? I don't know the answer, and I'm surprised at the silence in church literature in critique of this practice. It happens all the time, and few seem to feel it's a problem. Congregations are often heart-broken when they lose a pastor they trusted, and it can set them back for years. In America, the average senior pastor has pastored nearly three different churches, and that doesn't count the churches where they served as youth or associate pastors, so the real total is probably four or five.

At best, this reflects an unhealthy wanderlust, or a "grass is greener on the other side" attitude on the part of pastors. It does not reflect loyalty to their flocks. Many of these transfers come as the easy way out of conflict or other problems in the church, for all the world just like the hireling in Jesus' teaching. Meanwhile, research shows that churches' success is strongly associated with the longevity of their top leadership.[40]

Moving around is commonplace in the corporate world, where people pursue personal advancement by transferring. But how can this be reconciled with the idea of community? Even though only perhaps 50% of pastor transfers are based on ambition, the pastors they replace create another batch of transfers. The significant percentage who are dismissed by their churches can't be blamed, but how can we blame the church when they have been taught that churches should pick leaders based on this system?

Results of the modern system

I am convinced that the effects of frequent transfers by church leaders (when no local replacements have been trained and deployed) are debilitating to local churches. The weaknesses caused by this system are all around us.

1. People in churches abandoned by their pastors often

---

[40] Thom Ranier, *Breakout Churches*, (Nashville: B&H Publishing Group, 2005) 56, 57

become cynical. Many leave the church, adding to the flood of the disillusioned and transfers to other churches. Those that remain keep up their guard, making certain that they don't make the mistake of trusting a pastor in the future.

2. Committees and boards come to have more power, and they distrust future pastors. One new pastor reported his board welcoming him with the comment, "We just want you to remember one thing; this is our church. We were here before you came, and we'll be here after you leave." How is that for some chemistry in your group? This situation was headed straight down to disaster. Most churches wouldn't be this crass, but the underlying thought is there.

3. Strange pastors coming into a new church, for whatever reason, have a huge job ahead. They don't know the people, they don't know which of them are the most spiritual, they don't usually know their staff either. Building relationships at a level where people's strengths and weaknesses become apparent can take years. Many important relationships that should exist with key non-staff opinion leaders will probably never be built, as they would have been with indigenous leadership.

4. Gaining trust at a deep level from a congregation usually takes years. And having people's trust is very important in one's ability to motivate others. Just as American leaders finally gain real trust with the group, it's time to move again!

5. The New Testament concept of modeling becomes impractical under this system. People aren't close enough to their ever-changing leaders to model their own lives after them, and they often see such leaders as hirelings unworthy of being modeled.

6. Having upwardly mobile preachers means the focus shifts from long-term ministry approaches to quick

results. This whole system pressures leaders to show what they can do in the period of a few years, not for decades or for life. It would be hard to exaggerate the effect this has on leaders' thinking. People wonder why the church persists in trusting programs and gimmicks for its growth, but this system virtually guarantees such a result.

7. Personal discipleship and strong equipping of the saints could theoretically go forward in churches with short-tenured pastors, but it's unlikely. Discipleship and equipping are long-term strategies that take years to develop results. But in the mobile preacher scenario, quick results are all that matter. The well-trained force of workers would only begin to become effective when it's time for their pastor to go. Long-term approaches lead to slow growth in the short term. But a church that grows from 400 to 800 looks a lot better on the resume than one that grew by 50 but did quality equipping that opens the door for multiplying groups in the future.

8. The modern system explains in part why church leaders in the west thirst for transfer growth. When making out one's resume, numbers matter, and nobody asks whether they are transfers from area churches or converts.

9. It's probably hard for short term pastors to lead their church into actions that could offend significant numbers of their skeptical members (like practicing church discipline or preaching unpopular messages).

10. I have personally talked to scores of ex-church goers who report becoming disillusioned with the church when a trusted pastor (including a youth pastor) left for no apparent reason other than advancement. Others still attend, but will no longer lead or take responsibility because of their cynicism. Extrapolated nationwide, this could account for millions of dropouts and quitters.

This list could go on. Nobody knows the full price the church in the west pays for ignoring Jesus' picture of the loyal, sacrificial shepherd. People may complain that I'm comparing today's pastor selection system to hirelings, but how does Jesus identify a hireling? Hirelings probably look just like other shepherds until the telltale moment when he, "leaves the sheep" (John 10:12).

This discussion has been negative, and it should be, but there are legitimate ways leaders can leave their churches. When leaders raise up other leaders who can take their place so they can go to the mission field or to another location to begin a new church, or even to help a struggling church, this is healthy. But such leaders have just as much concern for the group they're leaving as for their new mission.

The failings of the modern system should also suggest the weakness of basing a large church on one person. In the early church, they always selected several elders in each city (as we'll see later), and elders were actually church leaders, not just committee bureaucrats. Such churches could give up a key leader without much damage, because several other quality leaders were right behind him.

The benefits of loyalty

As a pastor who has led in one group for forty years, I see the difficulties as well as the benefits of longevity in one leadership role. I'm sure some people in our group would just as soon see me move on, but most share with me the appreciation of longstanding relationship. People who stay with their groups for decades gain a knowledge of people that surpasses anything a new pastor could reasonably attain. I've watched people develop through all phases of life, and I've even reached the point where I work with the adult children of my friends from the old days. When I see how people's trust in my judgment and character is strained at times, even after so long together, I marvel at what pastors must experience when moving around every few years.

While I realize some leaders are gifted for starting new groups and feel an entrepreneurial restlessness, this is completely different than merely taking over leadership of someone else's group. I can't help feeling that the modern system works against community, trust, and more personal approaches to ministry, and in favor of gimmicks and programs as the answer.

When older leaders retire, this becomes another reason churches might need a new leader. But one would think that leaders in ministry long enough to retire would have raised up new leaders from their church who could take over. The fact is, the American church has little interest in raising up indigenous leadership beyond lower, volunteer roles. I believe this is a foundational mistake that leads to cascading problems in many areas, including the loss of motivation in members and the loss of an organic ethos in the church.

Paul

Paul's best discussion of the church as a flock comes in Acts 20:28-31, when he addresses the elders from Ephesus:

> So guard yourselves and God's people. Feed and shepherd God's flock—his church, purchased with his own blood —over which the Holy Spirit has appointed you as elders. I know that false teachers, like vicious wolves, will come in among you after I leave, not sparing the flock. Even some men from your own group will rise up and distort the truth in order to draw a following. Watch out! (NLT).

Paul is mainly concerned in Acts 20 with protection. He reveals the disturbing fact that the wolves will often come from within the existing leadership. That often happens, and the church has to be strong enough to protect itself through church discipline (which we'll discuss later). Too often, the sheep and fellow leaders are too loyal to leaders who go bad. Jesus put it on all Christians to gain discernment when he warned, "Beware of the false prophets, who come to you in sheep's clothing, but inwardly are ravenous wolves" (Matthew 7:15). He went on to give instructions for discerning the good from the evil: "You will know them by their fruits. Grapes are not gathered from thorn bushes nor figs from thistles, are they?" (Matthew 7:16-17).

But leaders should also play a key role in protecting the flock, just like all shepherds. That's why Paul insists in another passage that leaders must "be able to exhort in sound doctrine and to refute those who contradict" (Titus 1:9). It's not enough to exhort in sound doctrine. When contradictory voices rise, leaders have to be strong enough to expose error, especially since people often fail to recognize subtle false positions. Leaders are too often reluctant to discipline one of their colleagues for a variety of reasons, and as a result, apostate false teachers have been able to completely take over entire denominations in our day.

Peter

Peter's best discussion of the church as God's flock comes in 1 Peter 5:1-5:

> Therefore, I exhort the elders among you, as your fellow elder... shepherd the flock of God among you, exercising oversight not under compulsion, but voluntarily, according to the will of God; and not for sordid gain, but with eagerness; nor yet as lording it over those allotted to your charge, but proving to be examples to the flock. And when the Chief Shepherd appears, you will receive the unfading crown of glory. You younger men, likewise, be subject to your elders; and all of you, clothe yourselves with humility toward one another, for God is opposed to the proud, but gives grace to the humble.

Peter stresses the humble, serving attitude good leaders should have. He points out that being a good model is just as important as what leaders teach. He also agrees in this passage that leadership should be a team affair, not a single celebrity. When he says to "shepherd the flock of God among you" he is referring to the universal New Testament practice of appointing groups of elders (or bishops) in each town. This plurality doesn't come out in some translations because the word "you" can be either singular or plural in English. But in Greek, it's clear that he refers to a singular flock and plural shepherds.

Peter probably had a special feeling about the importance of the stewardship shepherds of God's flock enjoy. Jesus challenged Peter himself on this in John 21:15-17. That was when Jesus repeatedly asked Peter, "Do you love me?" Each time Peter said "Yes," Jesus gave him a similar charge: "Tend My lambs," "Shepherd My sheep," and "Tend My sheep." The message seems pretty clear: if we love Jesus, we should be concerned for his sheep. This isn't just a message for professional leaders. This message is addressed to anyone who loves Jesus. When we develop a Christ-centered heart, he will direct us very quickly to love those he loves. After he has done everything for us, this is one thing he leaves us to do for him: "Tend my lambs" (John 21:15).

The big picture

For true church health, we need to teach and model biblical versions of leadership. Healthy churches favor indigenous leadership at all levels. Their members know their leaders are not hirelings, but sacrificial lovers of the flock. Members in these churches have seen their leaders lay their lives down in a hundred ways over the years. People feel inspired to become leaders themselves. The idea that leaders like this would run off in search of higher pay is laughable.

Churches with institutional definitions of leadership become pathological. There, leadership becomes a privilege or a celebrity position. Weak churches live in fear that their hireling leaders will leave just like previous leaders. Members view leadership as something for outsider professionals, not for themselves. Transient pastors compete with neighboring churches for numbers so their resume will look good. Unless modern western churches turn their view around on these central issues, we can anticipate nothing but more decline.

Section 3

Lessons From Stories and Letters

The New Testament pictures of the Church form a beautiful mosaic
of metaphors. Each one touches on our experience in a way that
evokes our feelings even as it yields profound insight. But we also
have additional material on how to develop healthy communities in
the form of stories, especially the book of Acts, and letters intended
to teach crucial lessons about the church. We now turn to these
stories and letters.

Chapter Twelve

Of Wine and Wineskins

Church structure gets a lot of attention in studies on the church. People focus on things like whether to have home groups and what type. They argue about what style of worship is best, how many meetings to have, what kind of meetings, and so forth. Some of this is warranted, because some structures are more suited to promote New Testament style body life than others. But structures are not the secret to church health. I have visited healthy churches with vastly different structural arrangements. At the same time, churches often try to imitate the structure of successful churches but find none of the results they expected.

Jesus made the priorities clear in his comments on wineskins.

> No one tears a piece of cloth from a new garment and puts it on an old garment; otherwise he will both tear the new, and the piece from the new will not match the old. And no one puts new wine into old wineskins; otherwise the new wine will burst the skins and it will be spilled out, and the skins will be ruined. But new wine must be put into fresh wineskins. And no one, after drinking old wine wishes for new; for he says, 'The old is good enough' (Luke 5:36-39).

The context for this parable was Jesus' refusal to comply with expectations based on Jewish tradition but not based on the Bible. He taught that what matters is the wine (what God is doing), not the wineskins (structures humans construct to embody what God is doing). He also reveals the need to change wineskins whenever God begins to do something new (new wine), rather than clinging to old wineskins that will crack and spill the wine. Notice "wineskins" in this context means man-made structures (like rabbinic hand-washing), not God-ordained features of the church, which should never change.

But Jesus is not teaching that wineskins are of no importance; indeed they *are* important, becuse bad ones could crack and spill the wine, which in this context stands for people failing to hear, believe, or live the gospel. Wineskins are important enough that we need new ones from time to time.

When we apply this principle to the church, we see that all churches create structures, or wineskins, through which they practice church life. Some work better than others. Our way of meeting, our system for equipping, our favorite way to celebrate the Lord's Supper, the times at which we meet, the way we talk, and many other structures make up our chosen wineskins. Jesus suggests a pragmatic test to determine when we need new wineskins: the question is always, "Do our wineskins hold the wine?"

This point alone suggests why imitating other groups' wineskins is a bad idea: they are in a different situation and have different people, different history, etc. There is no "true" or "correct" wineskin. Jesus' point is to avoid being hung up on one set of wineskins and thus end up out of step with changes that new wine requires. If we don't want to end up with old, stiff wineskins, we should reevaluate our skins frequently to see whether they are still suitable and be willing to change. Like an organism, we should be adaptable and flexible to new conditions.

Applying New Testament structures

What are we to think about the way the New Testament church operated? Are these patterns mandatory or optional? We need a way to assess New Testament practice in the area of structures. We can break the material down into three categories for this process:

1. Precepts

The New Testament writers sometimes give direct instructions that are not optional. We could call these "precepts." Precepts would include the one-another passages we studied earlier, as well as preaching the word and staying faithful to true doctrine. These have to be carried out, or we have forsaken biblical Christianity altogether. Some structural features are included as precepts. For instance, the church must assemble (Hebrews 10:25), we should pray together (Matthew 18:19, 20), we should take the Lord's supper, we should practice church discipline, etc.

2. Principles

Other structural features aren't specifically commanded, but do appear to rest on the basis of underlying principles. Examples here could include plurality of eldership, which, as I will argue, is based on biblical theology concerning human nature: that humans are fallen and need accountability. Also, any local church has to provide smaller meetings where people can build relationships and practice ministry with each other, as we saw earlier. Exactly what kind of meetings we create is up to us as the Holy Spirit leads, but we need something. Any time a structure is required in order to be faithful to theological principle, we should implement that structure if we are to have a healthy church.

3. Examples

Other early church practices are not clearly based on either principle or precept. For instance, some early church groups met on the first day of the week. Paul taught daily in the schoolroom of Tyrannus. The Jerusalem group fed widows. Early groups of Christians greeted each other with a "holy kiss."

We don't have to follow all the examples of the early church, because some are based on cultural features no longer present, and others (like holding lectures in the schoolroom of Tyrannus) weren't even followed in all New Testament churches.

But before discounting these examples consider this: Since the early church was so successful, do we have good reason to think our ideas are better than theirs? Also, why would God include so much narrative about what they did unless he wanted us to learn something from it? In my opinion, any time we want to diverge from the example of the early church, the burden should be on us to show why we think breaking away from their pattern is warranted.

Judgment calls

Clearly, people might disagree on which New Testament feature falls into which category. For instance, some believe meeting on Sunday belongs in the precept category (because John calls it "the Lord's day" in Revelation 1:10), while others see it as only an example (because Paul says all days are alike in Colossians 2:16 and Romans 14:5-6). Some think women wearing head coverings is a precept, while others argue that because the cultural setting no longer attaches the same meaning to head coverings, it would be meaningless.

We are not going to try to settle all these issues here. The leaders of each local group need to decide what they think is binding, or at least wise, and what is not.

New Testament examples become more compelling when we see them practiced in different locales rather than just one. They also carry more weight when they are not clearly linked to a particular cultural norm (like women wearing head-coverings, or holy kisses).

Take the example of house churches. Early church meetings usually happened in homes. Paul says, "Greet Priscilla and Aquila, my fellow workers in Christ Jesus. Greet also the church that meets at their house" (Romans 16:3; see also 1 Corinthians 16:19; Colossians 4:15; Philemon 1-2). This example is widespread, rather than being limited to one or two locations.

Some have argued that house churches were only the result of persecution—that they had no other option if they were to stay secret. But even when large venues were available, as in Ephesus or Jerusalem (suggesting persecution was negligible) they continued to meet in homes (Acts 2:46; 5:42; 20:20). Also, house churches weren't linked to cultural expectations. Both Jewish and Greco-Roman people practiced religion in special temples or buildings, not in homes. Therefore, the early church was going *against* cultural expectations when holding church meetings in homes, and that shows strong intentionality.

Are we sure we want to dismiss this example? Scripture never commands us to have our meetings in homes, but we can marshal some good, common sense arguments suggesting it might be a good idea. Aside from the fact that the early church did it, homes feel personal, and they limit the size of the group, keeping it small enough to be intimate and interactive (1 Cor. 14:26). Many people own or rent homes, so most groups have plenty of places to meet. The cost for meetings is negligible. Also, some of the most striking movements in the church today (like that in China) are based mainly on house churches. If we think we have a better idea than house churches, I believe the burden of evidence is on us to show why we would not follow such a successful example.

Watch how your structures might affect group ethos. I know of churches that hold their main worship services at their church buildings, and afterward hold "house church," "mini-church," or "small group" meetings in the Sunday school rooms there in the same building immediately after the worship meeting. I think that's a questionable adaptation. These people are getting their involvement with the people of God out of the way in one day, instead of having it spread through the week. They aren't moving their meetings into neighborhoods where different groups can be easily invited. Having large and small group meetings back to back makes it unlikely that people will spend much time with their small group. Further, Sunday school rooms are ill suited to sitting and having lengthy personal conversations. Modern substitutions for early church examples often work against intimacy and depth in body life.

Extra-biblical structures

Adding structures unknown in the New Testament may be permissible, but it can also cause problems. For many churches, the problem is not that they lack biblical structures, but that they have added too many other structures not called for in scripture, and this can choke out vitality or lead to confusion. New ideas come into every church, and trying these usually shows innovation and freedom. However, as years go by, these ideas tend to build up more and more activities and features, even after people have forgotten why they are there.

Some structures may have lost their effectiveness long ago, but people in the church view them as their pet projects, and canceling them would hurt their feelings. Such favorite structures become like the sacred cows in India: nobody will kill them, even though they visibly suffer and gradually die from hunger. Likewise, leadership teams tend to add on more activities and structures without deleting a similar number of older, ineffective ones.

Considering the problem today of people's perceived time shortages, we are under more pressure than ever not to multiply unnecessary church functions. When people feel busy, they begin cutting activities, and too often, they will cut the important things instead of the unimportant. Leaders in the church today must have the strength to kill the sacred cows. They should simply delete activities from the public schedule unless they are clearly advancing the kingdom. At times, we may need to cancel even worthwhile things in order to do even better things. We can still allow people to do what they want, but we should point out that airtime in announcements is limited and must be focused on central efforts.

Aside from adding too many extra-biblical structures, there is the greater danger of adding structures that do positive harm. These are activities and rules that may not be morally wrong, but have nothing to do with our mission or vision as God's people. They may, in fact, give an implied message that could harm the church.

Area churches have called on us over the years to join in on numerous such activities, and it's never easy to say no to friendly churches in town. Christians take interest in Jesus marches, revivals, festivals, citywide prayer meetings, political agitation, demonstrations, and a host of other things that could potentially sap the strength of a church to pursue its central mission. Even when such activities are not wrong, they may cause a diffusion of effort and attention that leaves people feeling too busy to invest where they should. For instance, I believe the American church's over-involvement in political action has hurt our ability to reach large portions of our population.

We can allow people freedom to pursue outside activities as they choose. But to make these matters into church issues waters down our ability to win people's devotion to more worthwhile pursuits. Many of the problems with today's churches come not from ignoring biblical structures, but from adding pointless things to them.

In the following chapters, we will focus mainly on structures and practices in the precept or principle category. Your judgment may differ from mine at points, but be consistent with your understanding of the New Testament, and don't compromise just because our culture prefers other ways.

Non-organic structures

Leaders should also consider how introducing some structures might imply a non-organic understanding of the church. For example, some churches organize their home groups geographically. New people entering small groups or home churches register with the office which sends them to a group in their part of town. This sort of system makes sense if people are regularly walking into your church with no personal connection there. But be sure you're flexible: attendance at a home group in one's area should be optional in order to allow for more important organic, or relational considerations.

For instance, suppose a member sacrificially befriended and witnessed to a coworker for a year and finally won the person into the church. It's natural that she would want her friend to join her own small group, even though it meets in a different "zone." Which is more important: that people get to continue building friendships and disciple those they have won to Christ, or that they attend a home group in their area? Arguably, relationships are more important than geography, and that makes home groups more organic.

We could cite similar examples in a number of areas—how churches define membership, how liturgical they are, how formally they dress and speak, etc. In many of these areas, the lack of clear biblical instructions means that we have freedom to do what we think best. These are judgment calls, so again, I'm not arguing that churches who see it differently are rejecting scripture. However, I do think it's important that whenever introducing new rules or structures, leaders consider whether these will inhibit or facilitate an organic vision of the church. I also believe the spirituality of a group is more important than its structures.

The big picture

Church structures and church quality are not the same thing. But structures can affect the quality of a group when they carry implicit messages or take up people's time. Always think through how your approach to structures might be affecting the ethos of the church, and reassess at least annually. Make sure you are practicing the parts that are required, and evaluate the other parts for possible change.

Chapter Thirteen

The New Testament Pattern of Ministry

We have already studied how all the members in the body of Christ are supposed to play their roles, ministering to other believers and reaching out to those who don't know Christ. This picture is crystal clear in the New Testament; in other words, it's a precept, not just an example. Groups usually develop an *ethos* or a view of ministry that tends to determine their definition of success and well-being. This philosophy of ministry may or may not match that we see in the New Testament.

Tragic changes

As the early church moved into the second century, the menace of false teaching brought about a tragic change that lingers to this day. Gnostic and other heretical leaders were so influential that many thousands were abandoning the apostolic gospel. In this setting, leaders increasingly felt the need for ecclesiastical authority that could be easily identified as legitimate. They thought the church needed strong official leadership that could be regulated. That way, they could protect the people of God by denouncing and excluding false teachers.

While false teaching increased, the earlier stabilizing authority wielded by the apostles disappeared as the apostles died off. This missing piece from the previous picture in Acts and the epistles suggested to early leaders that they needed a supra-local authority similar to the apostles. Earlier, Timothy could rebuke misbehaving elders in public (1 Timothy 5:20), and Paul could turn false teachers out of the church (1 Timothy 1:20). Jesus had also authorized the apostles to declare true Christian doctrine in their power to bind and loose (Matthew 10:40; Luke 10:16; John 14:26; 15:26-27; 16:13). Who would have the power to do such things now that the apostles were gone? Bishops increasingly claimed that power for themselves.[40]

In all likelihood, there were other motives as well. We can't rule out the possibility that some of the men calling for more exclusive control were motivated by power-thirst. After all, they were fallen men, just like everyone else. Then too, people knew that the body of Christ was a worldwide entity, so it seemed like churches in different localities should have some supra-local cooperation similar to that seen in Acts 15 with the Jerusalem Council.[41]

By early in the second century, the office of bishop became "monarchical," meaning that each city or district would have only one bishop. Now bishops didn't have to deal with plurality, but lacked any local accountability. In addition, bishops increasingly insisted that nobody's teaching was valid but their own. They began to argue that the original apostles had imparted their authority to subsequent bishops in an "apostolic succession."[42] Teaching biblical

---

[40] This remarkably early (about 110 AD?) development can be seen in Ignatius of Antioch (unless, as some scholars think, these passages are forgeries from two centuries later). He argues, "Let no man do anything connected with the Church without the bishop," and, "He who does anything without the knowledge of the bishop does [in reality] serve the devil." That the pressure of heresy was the driving force behind this restrictive new teaching is evident in this passage and in the letter to the Philadelphians: "Keep yourselves from those evil plants which Jesus Christ does not tend [heretics].... For as many as are of God and of Jesus Christ are also with the bishop." Ignatius of Antioch, "Letter to the Smyrnaeans," "Letter to the Trallians," and "Letter to the Philadelphians," in Alexander Roberts and James Donaldson, eds., *The Ante-Nicene Fathers, Vol. 1*, (Grand Rapids, Mich.: Eerdmans, 1985), 66, 80, 89, 90.

[41] The need to form regional or worldwide linkage between churches has resulted in Episcopal, Reformed (Presbyterian), and Congregational approaches. Each have their arguments. In the Episcopal system (used by Catholics, Orthodox, Episcopalians, Anglicans, Methodists, and others) the apostolic, or extra-local authority resides in bishops who rule regions. In the Presbyterian system, churches elect representatives to a "Synod" that has extra-local authority. Congregational churches do away with apostolic authority other than the Bible. Each local church can decide for itself what to do. While congregational churches may form national or international associations (like Baptists and others have done) these have no authority over the local church.

[42] According to the Catholic Encyclopedia, the idea of an apostolic succession is backed up by 2 Timothy 2:2: "[W]hat you have heard from me before many witnesses entrust to faithful men who will be able to teach others also." Clearly, he was telling Timothy to pass down what he had heard from Paul—his teaching—not the authority of an apostolic

doctrine and other functions increasingly came to be reserved for bishops or their delegates. By the end of the second century, the Old Testament term "priests" reappeared, now applied to church leaders.[43]

Most damaging in this shift was the formation of a universally accepted separation between leaders and members in the church— the so-called clergy-laity distinction. This difference between the clergy (from the Greek *kleros*, meaning "lot" or "heritage," i.e. they inherited the leadership role from the apostles) and the laity (from the Greek word *laos*, meaning "people") was far more than a mere recognition of leadership offices. The clergy-laity distinction explicitly denied lay people their right to minister the word. It moved teaching, preaching, counseling, and leading groups into the exclusive province of the clergy.

The clergy also came to hold the exclusive right to minister the "sacraments"— eventually seven sacred rituals that confer the grace of God according to Catholic and Orthodox churches. The ability to minister the sacraments with true, supernatural power came to clergymen through the sacrament of ordination. In this ritual, priests were given the power to change bread into flesh and wine into blood. The worst part of the rise of the clergy was their claim that they, alone, had right to interpret scripture. This had the effect of taking the Bible out of the hands of average Christians.

The clergy-laity distinction had a devastating impact on the spirituality of the church. People came to view their involvement in church as a chance to receive ministry. They no longer viewed it as a chance to minister to others. The clergy left only financial giving and relatively low skill roles to normal Christians. Under constant

---

office. The New Testament taught that the apostles had authority in doctrinal and practical matters, but it never taught that they would pass this down to others. Another passage used to back up the succession is Acts 1:15-26, where they chose Matthias to replace Judas, thus suggesting the apostles felt the need to keep up their number. But this will hardly support a succession, since the main requirement for the new man was that he had "accompanied us all the time that the Lord Jesus went in and out among us—beginning with the baptism of John until the day that He was taken up from us—one of these must become a witness with us of His resurrection" (Acts 1:21-22). This passage in fact shows that men from later generations would not qualify to have apostolic authority (see also John 15:27, which makes the same point).

[43] "Priest" in *Oxford Dictionary of the Christian Church*: (Oxford University Press 2005)

clergy-laity teaching, Christians came to accept their own spiritual incompetence. Their focus became securing their own salvation and seeking personal blessing.

Even the Reformation, which made numerous positive changes in the theology of church leadership, continued to accept the clergy-laity distinction as valid.[44] To this day, many Protestant congregations believe that only clergy are qualified for sophisticated ministry, including ministering the word of God. Anabaptist and later pietistic and Pentecostal groups called this belief into question.

Contemporary correction

Today, growing numbers of theologians are rejecting the idea that the clergy have special ministry prerogatives. They recognize that this is a concept found only in the Old Testament and later church history. In the Old Testament, the Levitical priests were a distinct class, and the ministry they did was not open to other Israelites. But in the New Testament, we are all priests (1 Peter 2:9). Leadership is just one ministry in the church, and it functions like other ministries.

Even leaders with offices such as elder and deacon are no more authoritative in their views on scripture than others in the church, and leadership should be open to anyone, as long as they meet the biblical requirements. Leaders serve through providing protection and direction, and by equipping other believers to develop their own ministries. They are facilitators and equippers (Ephesians 4:11-12), but they stand under the authority of scripture just like other members. Their only unique authority regards the operation of the ministry, including the right to make decisions on how the local

---

[44] As William Pauck explains the Reformers' perspective, "All Christian believers, therefore, are ministers, servants, priests, by virtue of their faith in the Word of God, but not every one of them can or should assume the function of preaching, teaching, and counseling. For the sake of order, certain ones must be set apart from the group of believers to undertake the office of the preacher... 'We are all priests,' wrote Luther, 'insofar as we are Christians, but those whom we call priests are ministers [*Diener*] selected from our midst to act in our name, and their priesthood is our ministry.'" Wilhelm Pauck, "The Ministry in the Time of the Continental Reformation," in *The Ministry in Historical Perspectives*, H. Richard Niebuhr and Daniel D. Williams, Ed. (New York: Harper & Rowe, Publishers, Inc. 1956, 1983) 112. Calvin says, "Neither the light and heat of the sun, nor any meat or drink, are so necessary to the nourishment and sustenance of the present life, as the apostolic and pastoral office is to the preservation of the Church in the world." Ibid. 115.

church carries on its work—and they should be respected in those decisions (Hebrews 13:17).

The shift to the clergy-laity distinction was a mistaken turning back to the Old Testament economy. Instead of regulating ministry and access to the Bible, the post-apostolic fathers should have protected the church by teaching their people to read and to interpret the Bible correctly—something they could have done at any time. Around the world, Christians have historically been leading proponents of universal education, usually so people can read the Bible. Instead, church leaders were more interested in control than empowerment.

Unfortunately, the clergy-laity concept also fits in well with Americans' determination to spend most of their time pursuing personal peace and affluence. By leaving the ministry to the professionals, American churchgoers can justify doing little more than coming to watch the show.

Over-reaction

Unfortunately, some modern critics of the clergy-laity distinction are reacting by denying the validity of offices or positions in the church, such as elders and deacons. Some teach that elders have no authority from God other than their ability to persuade others—in other words, no more authority than anyone else in the church. This will not stand up to biblical scrutiny.[45]

My own group began with this understanding. During the Jesus Movement, many groups saw no reason for authority and wanted nothing to do with the sort of hierarchical approach they had seen in the traditional church. The result in our group was theoretical anarchy, although there were *de facto* leaders at different times based

---

[45] The "Simple Church" movement is the most outspoken group arguing against any formal church offices. Frank Viola explains this vision of New Testament-style body life: The group must be "gathering under the Headship of Jesus Christ without a clergy, where the members know one another deeply and are experiencing a depth in Christ, where decisions are made by the community, and where every-member functions in the meetings (services) without any man controlling, directing, facilitating, or dominating... (1 Corinthians 9:2; 2 Corinthians 3:1-4)." Frank Viola, "Rethinking the Five-Fold Ministry," (http://tallskinnykiwi.typepad.com/tallskinnykiwi/images/FIVEFOLD.doc) 4. I agreed with Viola's assessment of the fivefold ministry concept. But notice that to be "New Testament" a meeting and associated group has to be completely lacking in human leadership of any kind. Actually, New Testament believers are expected to respect and obey their leaders as we will detail in the chapter on leadership.

on people's respect for those people. But respect was not universal; sometimes they respected one person, sometimes another. Division of opinion became common. Nobody had the right to say what was going to happen next.

In this environment, different interest groups tended to form around different opinion leaders. It was usually easier to let everyone do what they wanted and try to talk some people into joining into what I thought we should do. Sometimes other opinion leaders would tear into my reputation, trying to convince people not to go the way I was suggesting. I probably did the same thing in return, although that's harder to remember for some reason. Many in the group seemed to feel it was their personal responsibility to make sure nobody got any more influence than anyone else.

The only rule we could agree on was that if someone went off to one side and started a new group from scratch, he or she would be in leadership of that group. That became a strong incentive for starting new groups; in fact, it was the only way to get anything done! Our main meeting increasingly suffered from gridlock and squabbling. In the vacuum of authority, we sometimes referred our decisions to Christians from other groups, just in order to get things moving. Another reaction was simply to disengage from the leaderless group. People preferred the newer groups that had leaders and took less interest in what was happening at the central group. Several times, groups of angry dissidents who didn't get their way left the church, never to return.

We knew on a pragmatic level that we had problems, but studying the Bible finally changed our minds for good. We saw that in one passage after another the Bible plainly calls on Christians to respect and obey their leaders (Hebrews 13:17; 1 Corinthians 16:15-18; Philippians 1:1; 1 Thessalonians 5:12-13; Titus 2:15; 1 Peter 5:5).[46] One of our problems was that none of us felt comfortable being called an "elder" at nineteen or twenty years of age. But we had also

---

[46] Of course, we should remember that spiritual authority is given to leaders for the direction of the ministry—not for other things, like what people do in their households.

harbored a super-spiritual theology that discounted the need for human leadership. We finally established an eldership five years after our group began, and things have gone better since then.

We won't defeat the clergy-laity idea today by dismissing all spiritual authority and leadership. That only creates chaos, disunity, and lack of fruitfulness. Instead, we have to convince all Christians in our churches that God has placed them there to minister, not to be ministered to. Quality leaders push for this, and without strong proactive leadership, we have little chance of seeing a properly mobilized church.

Full mobilization

The ideal standard for ministry in the local church is this: everyone ministering to his or her full potential, and everyone receiving ministry as needed. This is the picture we saw earlier in the image of the church as a body. Of course, it's an ideal. We'll never fully reach that standard in this life, but we can get much closer than most churches in the west have so far, and we should strive in that direction.

To come anywhere near this picture we will have to work hard to build in a number of key convictions and features that make up good ministry philosophy:

- First, we will have to argue the case that God's will and his provision for every Christian includes ministry. Ministry is not optional in the Christian life. It is a means of growth, just like prayer, scripture, and fellowship. Given the beliefs of most modern western Christians, we will need to argue this case often and with power. Members must become convinced that they will never know true spirituality without developing a significant ministry (John 4:32-35; 13:12-17, 34, 35; Acts 20:35; Romans 12:10-13; Philippians 2:1-4; Colossians 2:19; 1 Thessalonians 5:14-15: Hebrews 10:24, 25).
- God created humans to be significant and to accomplish things, according to Genesis one and two. He gave the original humans rulership and significant creative work

to do, and this was before the fall. People today still long for significance, and as Christians we should recover our intended sense of significance based on the important roles God gives us to play in the most important project going on today—the development of his kingdom. Unless church leaders show members how to do these significant things in the spiritual realm, they automatically turn to the world for their significance. Leaders have to convince their people that serving God is significant and important—more important than getting ahead in the ways of the world.

- We have to achieve success at some level in evangelism. Unless new Christians are coming into the body of Christ, the concept of every-member ministry eventually breaks down. People lose motivation because they can see that the other older Christians around them are in no particular need of nurture, training, or counsel (for more on this point see the chapter on outreach).

- Leaders need to teach on key modalities of ministry that lie close to the vision for their church (as explained in Chapter 14 on equipping). For instance, in our church we teach most often on evangelism, personal discipleship, how to lead small group ministries, and how to serve the poor. At other times, we offer specialty classes on grief counseling, divorce care, youth ministry, children's ministry, disability ministry, church planting, preaching, prayer, parenting, prison ministry, substance abuse counseling, Bible teaching, etc. We should also encourage members to initiate many other ministries in the church. The leaders are not the only ones who can show initiative in getting new ministries going.

- We will need to establish structures, such as ministry teams or groups where different kinds of ministries can go forward. Some of these will require ongoing oversight and even funding. Those ministries that bear abundant fruit deserve "airtime" before the church. Announcements and short "ministry highlights" help people understand ministry opportunities.

- We have to convince our opinion leaders that people have not been discipled unless they have developed a defined, significant ministry. Personal holiness without serving is a nonsense concept (Galatians 5:6, 13-14).

- The opinion leaders in the church have to decide how to view those in the group who are "do-nothings." Is it okay to do nothing? What should we say or do to those who take in, but never give out? Your answers to those questions indicate how hard-line or soft your church ethos is. Judging from the parable of the talents and other passages,[47] doing nothing with our stewardship from God is a very serious sin. It's a sin of omission, so it may not call for extreme church discipline, but omitters should be challenged, pleaded with, warned, and powerfully admonished, both during teachings and in person. They have to be persuaded that they are missing out on what God has for them. We may also need to challenge their right to take up space in crowded smaller groups of various kinds.

- Any modern, western church that takes a stand that doing nothing is a serious sin must prepare to lose people. Hundreds of other churches in any metropolitan city will welcome omitters, patting them on the back and thanking them for showing up. Once people realize this you can expect them to transfer, and you shouldn't worry about such losses. You cannot build healthy ethos by tacitly endorsing sins of omission. On the other hand, a church that has a strong ethos of action and involvement won't

---

[47] After showing the man who buried his talent being cast into outer darkness, Jesus went on to tell another parable where those who failed to do good for others were judged with the words, "Truly I say to you, to the extent that you did not do it to one of the least of these, you did not do it to Me" (Matthew 25:45). In fact all the parables about being ready for the coming of the Son of Man in Matthew 25 are about sins of omission. So is the parable of the good Samaritan (Luke 10:30-37).

lose many members to a competing vision of lazy self-gratification. The members of active groups enjoy being used by God and aren't interested in doing nothing.

The big picture

A church where most people have gained a vision for developing their own ministry is an awesome church! Groups like this are so energized, so participatory, and so eagerly engaged that the difference is night and day. No matter how difficult it is to sell the whole church on a vision for becoming equipped, effective ministers for God, we dare not let down or back off in any way on this crucial point. This is a message we *must* sell our people on if we want to see a healthy church.

Groups that abandon the New Testament insistence on every-member ministry are engaging in sinful accommodation that will demolish good ethos and ultimately incapacitate the church and all of its members. Likewise, watch out for diluted and self-serving definitions of ministry. If people become convinced that they only need to put some money in the plate or that, "my family is my ministry," they end up ignoring the whole body of New Testament teaching in this crucial area.

Chapter Fourteen

Equipping God's People

We already saw that Paul teaches,

Now these are the gifts Christ gave to the church: the apostles, the prophets, the evangelists, and the pastors and teachers. Their responsibility is to equip God's people to do his work and build up the church, the body of Christ (Ephesians 4:11-12 NLT).

God gives leadership gifts for one key purpose: equipping God's people for ministry. If the church today is to be animated by a New Testament caliber ethos, we must be an equipping community.

Based on several recent studies, we can safely say the church in the west is not adequately doing this job. People are being entertained, preached to, and taught to sing. But according to authorities, most American Christians do not know the Bible, do not know how to lead others to Christ, cannot counsel others, don't know how to give generously, aren't ready to teach God's word, and cannot discern false teaching when they hear it.[48]

---

[48]It's hard to know where to start when documenting biblical ignorance in American Christianity. Barna finds that of "born-again Christians," 10% believe that people are reincarnated after death, 29% claim it is possible to communicate with the dead, and 50% contend that a person can earn salvation based upon good works. "Americans Describe Their Views About Life After Death" October 21, 2003. In another study, he found that most "Christians" in America don't even name the Bible as their source of moral knowledge: "six out of ten evangelicals (60%) rely on the principles contained in the Bible as their main source of moral counsel. In contrast, only two out of every ten non-evangelical born again adults (20%) do the same." One of his most telling tests is that referred to as the "biblical worldview" survey. To pass the test, respondents have to agree with six statements like "Jesus lived a sinless life

Goals

When is a Christian equipped? What should a local church shoot for when equipping people? To answer these questions, ask yourself what kind of person you would trust to, for instance, lead a group in your church with maturity and life-giving power. Let me suggest a number of things I would like to see in people I would trust in that role:

- In the first place, they would have to know their Bibles. Ministry is all about God's word, and Paul implies that workers who cannot handle the word of God accurately should be ashamed (2 Timothy 2:15). To know and handle the word accurately several things are needed.
- They need to be familiar with the flow of the biblical story from beginning to end. The parts of the story only make sense in context of the whole.
- They need to know principles of sound interpretation. Unless they can interpret passages in context and in harmony with the language used, and without contradicting other parts, they are dependent on others and not ready to lead. We have not equipped our people if they have to continually come to older leaders and ask what things mean.
- They need to have an integrated understanding of the key themes in scripture. By "integrated", I mean they have to have thought through the claims about issues like God, humans, the world, angels, the church, how to grow spiritually, heaven, hell, etc. in a way that doesn't result in contradiction and inconsistency. Merely knowing

---

on earth" or "God is the all-knowing, all-powerful maker of the universe who still rules that creation today," so this is hardly a rigorous definition. He found in 2005 that only 5% of American adults have a biblical worldview, and that "8% of Protestants possess that view, compared to less than one-half of one percent of Catholics." "Most Adults Feel Accepted by God, But Lack a Biblical Worldview," The Barna Group: August 9, 2005. Os Guinness says, "The truth is, for those who think, the present state of American evangelicalism is appalling. As a spiritually and theologically defined community of faith evangelicalism is weak or next to nonexistent; as a subculture, it is stronger but often embarrassing and downright offensive." Os Guinness, *Fit Bodies Fat Minds* 15. J.P. Moreland argues that we live in the most anti-intellectual period in the history of Christianity. *Love God With All Your Mind: The Role of Reason in the Life of the Soul*, (Navpress, 1997) Chapter 1.

many details about the Bible doesn't mean one has a useable, balanced theology.

- They need to be able to apply the word to daily situations and human need in a liberating way. They will need this when counseling or teaching younger believers. Field experience as well as library work are required to get to this point.
- They need to have practiced what scripture teaches in a way that transforms their own characters. They need to be able to model Christian living, so equipping must include formation of Christian character and a biblical values system.
- They need practical ministry skills in a number of areas, demonstrated by examples of success. For instance, to lead others into a lifestyle of prayer, evangelism, discipleship, and building others up, they need to have succeeded in these pursuits themselves. Otherwise, they are guessing when giving ministry advice and coaching.
- They need to know how to love others, including their own families, deeply, and in a way recognized and appreciated by others. Only in this way can they become models people will admire and imitate.
- The Bible calls on normal Christians to counsel each other with "all wisdom" that comes from having God's word richly dwell within us (Colossians 3:16). It also calls all believers to develop discernment based on field experience working with people (Hebrews 5:12-14).
- They should at least have a basic knowledge of false perspectives in theology and ministry. Unless they are familiar with faulty approaches, they will have poor discernment and will be unable to refute challenges Satan launches against their ministries.

Remember, this level of equipping isn't for a few key people, but for all Christians in the church. Isn't this a minimal list of what we would like to see from role models in the church? According to many church leaders, the answer is apparently "No." In one church after another today, the qualifications for leading a home group amount to nothing more than the ability to raise your hand to volunteer—that, and maybe a half-day training session combined with a set of detailed lesson plans that remove almost all need to think for oneself. Instead of sophisticated, competent leaders, people in such groups find themselves confronted with someone no further ahead spiritually than themselves. The task of leading through scripted ministry approaches is so over-simplified that nobody feels challenged when doing it or sitting under it.

Raising the bar

Which of the goals above could be safely removed or reduced? I agree with critics that if any of these things are unnecessary, we should remove needless goals in order to avoid over-qualifying people. Time is precious, and we don't want to discourage would-be learners. At the same time, if we care about the quality of ministry in the church, we will not put ill-equipped people in charge of it. But even to acquire basic proficiency in all these areas is probably a multi-year, hard-working project for new Christians.

Priority

Ask yourself why people's schools, companies, and professions are so prepared to demand excellence and years of training at the highest level and nobody thinks that's strange. Doesn't the kingdom of God deserve something similar? Why are the institutions of the world the only entities that can call on people for long-term sacrifice and brain-wracking memory and creativity? We're not surprised to see people devoting long hours of study toward earning their degrees, so why shouldn't we expect something similar for the far more important task of serving God?

When a church is growing by conversion growth and using organic principles, the need for well-equipped workers becomes intense. We may feel strong temptation to take shortcuts because of the shortage of qualified ministers in the church—shortcuts like sending out untrained and ill-equipped leaders. Rapid growth churches may send people into battle armed with rubber bands. (Over-heated growth leading to compromise is one of the perils of winning large numbers of transfers from other believing churches.) But if we throw unequipped people into positions where they fail, or merely go through the motions, we set ourselves and them up for disappointment that could be dangerous. We could find people unwilling to lead in the future if we send them into situations they are not equipped to handle.

If we accept the need to release normal Christians into ministry, but also that they should be fully equipped to succeed, then the ministry of equipping acquires a new urgency. We will have to go all-out to advance the equipping task as quickly as possible. We will need money and time from our best and brightest in substantial quantities for such a challenging task.

Classes

According to Acts 19:9 and 20:31, Paul probably held classes when he settled down for a prolonged period of ministry, as at Ephesus. Classes are good for equipping, because they can convey a large amount of content in a comparatively short time.

Most churches have some classes for equipping, but they are often too light. How churches can equip people based on a few weeks of classes is a complete mystery to me. We teach a concentrated series of classes, each lasting three hours per week for ten weeks. Leaders in our church take a minimum of seven of these classes in series. Each has homework every week, quizzes, and graded finals. Over twenty percent of all students fail each class, so they're not soft. Adults pay around sixty dollars to get into each one, or twenty-five for college students. The tuition is not mainly for offsetting the expense of the classes. Rather, putting some money down helps people value the classes more and work harder, to avoid wasting money.[49]

---

[49]Curriculum, including class handouts and lecturer's notes for most of these classes are available free of charge to interested churches on our website: www.xenos.org.

Many church leaders today think a program like this is too extreme. That's when the negative observations flow, with downcast eyes, "Well, our people are really busy...." But the biggest problem is not with our people being too busy; it's with their leaders. The fact is, people love taking these classes, including busy, family people. We even see people go back and repeat one or more, just to freshen up. I've had countless adults and students come up to me glowing with the thrill of discovery as they describe how they are learning things they never realized before. As students gain a sense of mastery with their Bibles and their skills in working with people, they become excited and motivated to share those skills. A few years ago when we made a "light" version of some of our classes for over-worked people with families, hardly anyone registered for them. They continued registering for the 'heavy' versions. So it's clear: leaders often under-estimate members' willingness to study, learn, and sacrifice.

People will only love taking classes when churches put their best people on the task of teaching. Good teachers need to carefully design and re-work classes year after year. The classes need to be challenging, interesting, and stimulating (not childish, like some classes offered in churches today). Senior pastors and other top leaders should devote regular time to teaching.

An equipping church needs a sizeable budget for equipping, and the willingness to prioritize equipping by releasing top staffers from other duties. Offering top quality classes every year is not easy or cheap. I often study church budgets, and in most churches, I can't find anything devoted to equipping the saints. That's not to say they aren't spending anything, but it's probably such a small number that it doesn't deserve its own line in the budget.

You can have volunteers teach some classes and these can be quite good as well. But don't leave your whole equipping program to volunteer work. To get the quality needed, you have to enable key people to devote more time and effort than is reasonable for volunteers.

The power of ethos

Any thought that people can't be equipped today because they're too busy is false. The problem is usually with leaders who don't believe in their people's capabilities. People in strong equipping churches love to take classes, study, and use their training because everyone assumes it's natural. The group's ethos is that people would be foolish to not get equipped and build ministries. They see nothing strange about sacrificing time and effort on the things of God.

Low expectations yield low results. Modern assumptions that the New Testament picture of the church is no longer feasible indicate a lack of vision, and in my opinion, unfaithfulness to our call. If we view our people as incapable of becoming quality leaders who can "accurately handle the word of God" (2 Timothy 2:15), they will probably meet our expectations every time.

You quickly see a group's values system in what they prioritize. Failure to prioritize equipping says the church doesn't believe every-member ministry counts for much.

Personal Discipleship

If we have any hope of recovering the New Testament picture of the church, we will need to recover personal mentoring from the ash heap of history. Some signs look good, especially in non-western churches. In the west, we just have too many important things to do. We can't find time for meeting with younger Christians to build love relationships and to train them in the word, character development, and how to build a personal ministry.[50]

We know Jesus did it. We know Paul was let down over the wall in Damascus by "his disciples" (Acts 9:25). We know he told Timothy, "The things which you have heard from me in the presence of many witnesses, entrust these to faithful men who will be able to teach others also" (2 Timothy 2:2). We know most churches in New Testament times probably didn't have classes, and that classes are

---

[50] Barna gives convincing evidence that intentional discipleship is in eclipse in modern Ameica. George Barna, *Growing True Disciples*, (Ventura, CA: Issachar Resources, 2000), Chapter 3, "The State of Discipleship."

inadequate for forming character and ministry skills in young believers. We know there were no theological schools like seminaries in the first century, and therefore the New Testament church must have raised up virtually all leaders through personal discipleship. So the biblical case for personal mentoring is strong.

Widespread personal disciple making was lost during the rise of the clergy in the second and third centuries for the most part and has only occasionally been practiced since, usually with excellent results. But just when interest in making disciples was rising in America during the Jesus movement, the "shepherding movement" left a sour taste in everyone's mouth and set discipleship back dramatically.[51] Today, interest is again rising.

Personal mentoring brings qualities to the equipping process that no class can bring. I meet with a number of young men every week, and these are the best times of my week. These times are when I feel God working through me intensely as I come to grips with real issues in people's lives. Most of our meetings are two hours or so. We have time to share what's happening in our lives, study together, and pray. If I had to cut things from my schedule, these "hang-outs" would be the very last thing to go. Even more importantly, each of these young men meets with other young men to do the same thing. I believe the most important thing I can do for our church is to deliver high quality leaders for their future.

When a church gets the vision for making real disciples, the future looks good. By gradually spreading the practice across the church, such groups can anticipate a future with scores and eventually hundreds or even thousands of trained, competent Christian workers. All of them will be looking for opportunities to serve. Multiplication becomes possible.

Multiplication happens when, instead of just adding people to the church, each member seeks out people she can win and disciple.

---

[51]The Shepherding movement grew out of a group centered in Pensacola Florida, and spread nationwide during the 1970s. They taught that you need a discipler, or "shepherd" whom you obey in all areas of life. They theorized that by learning to obey a human shepherd, you would learn to obey God. Their mistaken understanding led to authoritarianism and spiritual abuse. The movement was stamped out of existence by the rest of the church in America during the '80s.

As individuals duplicate themselves, groups tend to multiply. The church grows, and not just in numbers; qualitative growth matches quantitative growth. This concept is as good today as it ever was and has tremendous potential to raise up large numbers of quality Christian workers.

I know Christians who don't share this vision for personal disciple making, and I feel sorry for them. They're going to miss the lifelong joy that comes from cultivating such friendships with young Christians and the eternal rewards that come with it.

The process

For detailed information on how to make disciples I recommend people read our book on the subject, *Organic Disciplemaking*.[52] The basics of making disciples include: building a quality friendship; gaining and imparting vision; teaching what the Bible says and how to interpret it; and teaching and modeling prayer, fellowship, and how to build a personal ministry. Helping disciples gain victory over personal sin problems and build godly character is the most difficult part—especially when we include sins of omission, attitude problems, self-absorption, and relational problems. We may need to confront issues at times in loving discipline.

If your disciple matures and wins a ministry, especially winning another disciple, coaching begins. Here you monitor your person's thinking and actions when he's working with others, helping him to ask the right questions, read situations, and measure his words. In churches where home groups duplicate themselves, you will likely see your disciples begin leading their own groups. By guiding new leaders through the first year or so of leading a group, you can significantly shorten the learning curve.

To begin with a self-centered, carnally-minded believer and end with a self-feeding, stable, relationally healthy minister for God is a

[52]Dennis McCallum and Jessica Lowery, *Organic Disciplemaking: Mentoring others into maturity and spiritual leadership*, (Houston: Touch Publications, 2006). You should also read Rober Coleman, *Master Plan of Evangelism*. (Revell, 2006). Coleman is unexcelled for vision and theory. Our book starts where his leaves off with practical ideas.

several year project—if things go well. A significant percentage of people we try to disciple will never make it. But God put us here to give our lives away in real Christian love. If we adopt a ministry philosophy in harmony with that, he will bless us with eventual success. Of course, if you have some authentically mature believers to work with, the time could be shortened considerably.

The harvest of discipleship

In a church where people buy into personal disciple making, you can anticipate several good changes:

First, people realize that disciple making is a meaningful ministry where God might use any serious Christian. Instead of feeling clueless about how they could affect the kingdom of God in a lasting and powerful way, people dare to consider the possibility that even they could be used by God for something important. Delivering even one replicating disciple is equivalent to a lifetime of work. Instead of one servant of God, there are now two.

When disciple making succeeds, people experience changes that are deep and lasting. Most discipling relationships lasting several years are close enough to reveal people's real underlying needs in a way no other ministry could. When two believers dare to build a close relationship before God and his word, things come out. The life-changing power of love and truth come into operation. When Paul taught that we can "speak the truth in love" to one another, resulting in spiritual growth and maturity, this is the kind of thing he had in mind. Disciple making can release the church from the deadening task of baby-sitting to move on to real service.

As the number of people being discipled and making disciples increases, the disciple making church will see an end to people's sense of disconnection. People engaged in relationships at this level feel love in the church—something many in modern western churches do not now experience.

Under a proper model of disciple making, people stop seeing spiritual growth as primarily an inward thing benefiting themselves. They realize that God gives us life change so we can give ourselves out to others. Healthy disciples begin seeking opportunities to minister. Can you imagine what a church full of people like this would be like? A community where most people were looking for an opportunity to love and serve others? Anyone entering a group like that would soon realize this is no ordinary group of people. The whole church would seem warm, welcoming, and eager to relate.

Discipling churches have no shortage of volunteers, good giving, and consistent efforts at personal evangelism.

As discipleship networks spontaneously form and expand, people enjoy being with each other, following up on how things have developed. This is different from churches where people feel relatively distant from others in the group.

A discipling church is a wonderful church. But none of this is easy. Only years of patient teaching, modeling, prayer, and pleading will have any chance of establishing a disciple-making ethos in a group, whether the group is large or small. To be fair, discipling groups also have conflict and friction at times because of the closeness in relationships. But that's all part of the picture God would have us pursue.

If this is not a part of your church, start with yourself. Find a person or two to befriend and mentor. As you and your friends share the benefits, you may find a few others who will work with you on the project, including finding their own people to mentor. It has to spread gradually through the church; you can't impose this church-wide and expect people to understand. Authors Bill Hull and Greg Ogden have written excellent books on working disciple making into existing, more traditional churches.[53] Why not read those books and make a plan for introducing disciple making into your church?

Leadership support

Even well-equipped leaders tend to lose their way unless we provide ongoing help, encouragement, and further equipping. Businesses and professions have realized this and require ongoing training for their people. The church should do likewise.

---

[53]Bill Hull, *The Disciple Making Pastor*, (Grand Rapids: Baker Book House Co., 1988), and *The Disciple-Making Church*, (Revell: 1998). Greg Ogden, *Transforming Discipleship: Making Disciples a Few at a Time*, (Downers Grove: InterVarsity Press, 2003).

We see Paul doing this on numerous occasions. At one follow up session in Troas, he began teaching one evening and continued until a guy named Eutychus fell out of the window around midnight (Acts 20:7-12). Paul raised him from apparent death and went inside to continue lecturing until daybreak! That must have been an intense seminar.

Churches that provide ongoing equipping for their established leaders might offer classes for leaders, peer challenge groups that focus on Bible study and support between leaders of different groups, open houses, where top leaders host other leaders for sharing and edification, and monthly or quarterly leadership meetings for teaching and motivation. Leadership retreats are also great for instilling morale and good ethos in the church.

Equipping and church planning

Leaders plan a way forward when planting a new church or when looking to improve an existing group. With so many possibilities, these sessions can be quite confusing. May I suggest that in your next planning session, equipping might be the best place to start? For many churches, their best move would be to upgrade their level of equipping. This could include blocking out time for top leaders to plan classes and even take more coursework themselves. Their job descriptions will have to be altered, clearing away less important tasks so they have time to lead the charge toward a well-equipped membership.

Don't lead your church based on the lowest common denominator. If some in the group aren't willing to invest the time for equipping, start with those who are willing. The others will catch on later.

The big picture

A well-equipped church puts an ill-equipped one to shame. Imagine yourself walking into a meeting as a new person in a well-equipped church: People there would be looking for new people to talk to. They would have answers to questions and experience dealing with people. If you decided to get involved, you would get help at every step. Making friends wouldn't be hard; established believers would be taking the initiative. Any smaller group you attended wouldn't be a boring discussion where people pooled their ignorance. Instead, you would hear stimulating conversations from people who have thought long and hard about the issues at hand. Being around growing believers with good attitudes is always fun, and the work of the kingdom gets done.

The key to victory in equipping is that strong leaders establish a belief in equipping as part of the group's ethos. In our church, probably like many churches, some groups live like this and enjoy the fruit of spiritual living at a high level. Others have lost the right perspective and are suffering as a result. To revive the right outlook, leaders in those groups have to convince most people in their group that only a fool would miss the opportunity to be equipped and to build a ministry; it's fun, it's fruitful, it's fulfilling, and it's God's will.

Chapter Fifteen

The New Testament
Pattern of Worship

Many theologians rank the proper worship of God as the first priority for the church. Properly understood, I agree. But too often this argument is taken to mean that the corporate worship service on Sunday morning is the most important activity in the life of the church. The problem here is that this defines worship as a "worship service," often with a liturgy, characterized by a set order of ritual, song, etc. But most of this definition comes from Old Testament practice and flies directly in the face of New Testament teaching.

Further, many Christians simply take worship to be identical to music. As David Ruis says in *Ministry Today*, "For most of us worship equals music... worship and music are simply one and the same."[54] None of these definitions is remotely close to that given in the New Testament.

To understand what the Bible teaches on worship, we need to trace the concept all the way through te Bible, understanding the vocabulary of worship as it's used during different periods. No one has done a better job at this than David Peterson in his excellent book, *Engaging with God: A biblical theology of worship*.[55] One of Peterson's main points is that the Old Testament understanding of

---

[54]David Ruis, "Canned Worship," *Ministry Today*, Aug. 2009 37.

[55]David Peterson, *Engaging With God, A biblical theology of worship*, (Downers Grove Ill: InterVarsity Press, 2002)

worship was explicitly reinterpreted in the New Testament, and that failure to recognize this leads to a diminished view of worship.

A Change in Sacrifices

We saw earlier how Peter teaches that all Christians are priests in 1 Peter 2:5 and 9. Whereas in the Old Testament only select Levites had this privilege, today every Christian is a priest, and Jesus is our high priest (Hebrews 7:17-19).

What do priests do? In the Old Testament period, their main function was to carry out the worship of God through offering two main kinds of sacrifices: sin offerings, for moral offenses, and various thank offerings to express gratitude for God's goodness and blessing.

In the New Testament all types of sin offerings are cancelled because Jesus fulfilled those through his death (Hebrews 9:11-14; 10:1-14). Presenting sin offerings now would be like "nailing him to the cross once again" (Hebrews 6:6 NLT). But we still can offer thank offerings to God in gratitude for what Jesus has done. This is what Peter is referring to in 1 Peter 2:5 when he says that we "offer up spiritual sacrifices to God." Peter doesn't specify here what these sacrifices are, except to say that they are spiritual, not physical. However, by studying other passages in the New Testament we discover several different "sacrifices" through which we can worship God. Repeatedly, the language of Old Testament worship through thank offerings signals that these have been re-interpreted in our day.

Different Ways to Worship

Self-sacrifice

In Romans 12:1, Paul says, "Therefore I urge you, brethren, by the mercies of God, to present your bodies a living and holy sacrifice, acceptable to God, which is your spiritual service of worship." Offering ourselves completely to God is our main form of worship. Notice that this plea is for Christians. He addresses it to "brethren" and bases it on the previous discussion about God's grace for Christians.

In Old Testament times, Israelites offered various kinds of thank offerings to show God their gratitude. God called these pleasing sacrifices a "soothing aroma" (see Lev. 3:5,16). Considering what God has done for us, how can we say "Thank you!" to God? Not by offering an animal, but by presenting to God something much more precious—our very selves. We can "sign over the title deed" of our lives and say, "God, I want the rest of my life and every part of my being to be one long expression of my gratitude for the gift you have given me." When we do that, God says it is "holy" and "well-pleasing" to him.

Paul calls this our "service of worship"—a term in Greek (*leiturgeo*) from which we get the English word "liturgy." The elaborate worship service enacted by the Old Testament priests no longer has a place in Christian worship; God has replaced the old ritualistic way with this very personal sacrifice.

Giving

Hebrews 13:16 says, "And don't forget to do good and to share with those in need. These are the sacrifices that please God." To "share" means we give generously to the poor and to God's work. Every financial gift is like a thank offering to God, and therefore should be viewed as worship.

Paul agrees: "I am generously supplied with the gifts you sent me with Epaphroditus. They are a sweet-smelling sacrifice that is acceptable and pleasing to God" (Philippians 4:18). Although many Christians don't think of giving as worship, this is the same language the New Testament uses for all types of worship.

God thinks offering your money is an act of worship like praising him. Whether you support your local church, other Christian workers and ministries, or help the needy, giving for the sake of the Lord counts as worship in the New Testament. Giving your money is a way to give of yourself. Money costs us our time, effort, and creativity. Giving is also an expression of our trust in God's faithfulness to meet our own material needs, which Paul says God will fully supply (Philippians 4:19).

Praise

Hebrews 13:5 uses the language of worship and thank offerings: "Through Christ then, let us continually offer up a sacrifice of praise to God, that is, the fruit of the lips that give thanks to his name." Praising and thanking God for all that he is and all that he does for us is like a pleasing thank offering. The New Testament repeatedly stresses the importance of thanking and praising God (see 1 Thessalonians 5:16-18; Colossians 3:15-17).

Why is this? God doesn't need to hear thanksgiving from us; he is self-existent and needs nothing. Our gratitude pleases God because he approves of the attitude behind thanksgiving. Appreciation signals spiritual health in his people, but ingratitude signals selfishness. Christians who feel sorry for themselves are ignoring astonishing blessing from God and focusing only on what they want in addition but haven't yet received.

Thanksgiving also signals trust. Especially when under trial, a crucial question for Christians is, "Have you given thanks to God?" Inability to thank God during trials means we don't fully believe his promises concerning how trials bring us maturity and changed character. Thanking God when we are suffering is a major act of faith—an act of worship—and we feel the effect immediately. You feel your spirit lifting as you reflect on the great things of God and his constant love.

The author of Hebrews emphasizes that we should worship God with praise "continually," not just during a worship service. Individual Christians can praise God throughout every day, but when the body assembles, it is natural to praise him together. Corporate praise and worship were probably a regular feature of New Testament meetings, but no gathering is ever called a "worship service."[56] Early Christians praised God both in song and in prayer. Many believers

---

[56]D. A. Carson notes how "'cultic' [ritual] language is used in the New Testament to refer to all of Christian life" and the "lack of any mention of worship when the New Testament writers provide purpose clauses as to why the people of God meet together." Based on this, he cites a number of scholars who "conclude that we should stop thinking of 'worship services' and meeting together 'to worship' and the like." These include Howard Marshall, Aboyd Luter Jr., John P. Richardson, and Alastair Campbell (but not Carson himself). D. A. Carson, "Worship Under the Word" in D. A. Carson, Ed. *Worship by the Book*, (Grand Rapids: Zondervan, 2002), 25.

find singing praise to God particularly edifying. For these people, music uniquely opens channels to the heart. Music is also a good way to allow all to participate in praising God at the same time. But we also have multiple New Testament examples where individuals and groups turn to God in prayer and praise him that way.

How did the early church practice corporate worship? We have information on two large meeting formats in the New Testament at Jerusalem and at Ephesus. Both are described as teaching meetings (Acts 2:46, 19:9, 20:29). Communion, which is a way to express thanksgiving, was practiced in house churches (Acts 2:46), where it was a part of the "love feast" (1 Corinthians 11:19-20). Paul describes interactive house church meetings in 1 Corinthians 14, where we find our only specific mention of singing hymns in a meeting (v. 26).

Based on this information, we can conclude that the early church saw home churches as the best venue for corporate worship in praise. It makes sense that a more intimate, participatory meeting might be the best place to worship God together. That doesn't mean anything is wrong with the modern practice of worshiping in large gatherings, but it does call into question whether it is a specifically biblical practice.

Ministry

Paul speaks of his own apostolic ministry in this way: "The grace was given to me from God, to be a minister of Christ Jesus to the Gentiles, ministering as a priest the gospel of God, that my offering of the Gentiles might become acceptable, sanctified by the Holy Spirit" (Romans 15:15-16). Here is the language of temple worship again, this time referring to Paul's evangelistic work.

Earlier, in Romans 1:9, he says, "For God, whom I serve [*latreuo*] in my spirit in the preaching of the gospel of His Son, is my witness as to how unceasingly I make mention of you." *Latreuo* is one of the main words for temple service, or worship, here applied to Paul's preaching of the gospel. Peter explains it in similar words: "You are royal priests, A holy nation, God's very own possession.

As a result, you can show others the goodness of God" (1 Peter 2:9).

Leading others to Christ is worship, provided we do this work with the right attitude—to please God, not people. Hebrews 13:16 says other types of ministry should also be viewed as worship when it refers to "doing good." By implication, Paul teaches that loving and serving others is worship in Ephesians 5:2, saying, "Walk in love, just as Christ loved you, and gave himself up for us, an offering and a sacrifice as a fragrant aroma." Loving and serving (ministering to) others is worship for us, just as it was for Jesus. Every day, God gives us dozens of creative opportunities to say "Thank you!" to him by bringing his love to others.

Lifestyle or meeting type?

Worship scholar David Peterson says,

> Contemporary Christians obscure the breadth and depth of the Bible's teaching on this subject when they persist in using the word 'worship' in the usual, limited fashion, applying it mainly to what goes on in Sunday services... When Christians become preoccupied with the notion of offering God acceptable worship in a congregational context and thus with the minutiae of church services, they need to be reminded that Paul's focus was on the service of everyday life.

He also worries about "a dangerous tendency towards introversion in many churches. Indeed, congregational worship in some contexts can be like 'a narcotic trip into another world to escape the ethical responsibilities of living a Christian life in this world.'"[57]

I agree. We simply don't see the centrality of a serving life in today's talk about worship, even though many teachers tip their hats to the idea in a cursory way. In one book after another, the authors point out that worship is one's whole life lived for Jesus, but then go right on to spend the rest of the book discussing how to do worship services.

---

[57]David Peterson, *Engaging with God*, 18, 187, 188.

When you look at all the different things the New Testament calls worship, you realize that early Christians viewed worship as a way of life. We worship God when we give ourselves to him and to others in various ways. Worship is the God-centered life. This is different from how many understand worship today. For many western Christians, worship is something you do at a particular kind of meeting—a worship service—understood in the usual way.

Confusion

Viewing worship as a worship service narrows the definition in a way that ignores or marginalizes the other modalities of worship, and is really just a tiny chip out of the whole picture. Although most pastors and theologians agree that worshiping God involves your whole life and is not limited to the worship service, their people often miss this point.

Then there are other problems. Historically, the church has drawn its definition of worship services from the Old Testament in a way not found in the early church. The medieval church consciously emulated the Old Testament with the re-introduction of formal priests, altars, incense, and the view that Sunday was a holy day similar to the Sabbath. These are formalistic features that were superseded in the New Testament because Jesus fulfilled them, and are therefore inappropriate in our new, more intimate level of relationship with God. The medieval church also re-introduced the legalism found in the Old Testament.

The Reformers made serious improvements by eliminating much of the formality and priestcraft of medieval Christianity, but they also kept a number of features relatively unchanged. One of these was concept of the worship service itself. Although they centered it more on the word of God and got rid of some specifically Old Testament features, churches kept the holy day, the altar, the fixed order of worship (liturgy) and some lesser features. Most of these are unimportant, but defining worship in terms of a meeting type is serious. I think it deforms the biblical picture and introduces something not found in the New Testament.[58]

The church should worship God, and understood correctly, I agree that worship is at the center of what the church does. But if worship is winning others to Christ, ministering to people, praise, giving, and total commitment to God, this is a very different picture than attending a worship service.[59]

Worship service fixation

When people combine the importance of worship with the meeting, or adopt an "experience" definition of worship, the result is a fixation on worship services that threatens the overall New Testament picture of the church.[60] Pastors commonly see the worship service as their most important role in their churches and the most important thing going on in their churches. So do their people.

I went to one pastors' workshop where we broke up into groups of six and wrote down the top three areas of strength in our own churches. When we compared notes, all five of the other pastors had listed "worship" as their top strength, and they were not using the word as the New Testament defines it. Each went on to explain how awesome their music program, dance, and so on were, all referring to their worship services. When we went to the second most important strength, three of them put "innovation in worship" "diversity in worship" and something else about worship. Worship, understood as a meeting type or as music, dominated the thinking of these pastors, and they were not unusual.

---

[58]Of the five words used to refer to worship in the Septuagint (the Greek translation of the Hebrew Old Testament), only once is one used in the New Testament to refer to the activity at a Christian meeting ("While they were *ministering [leitourgeo]* to the Lord" Acts 13:2). Even this was not a regular meeting of the local church, but a prayer meeting for leaders. Instead of worship, the New Testament emphasizes edification as the main reason for meeting. Even in the Old Testament, Peterson points out that while worship "found expression in cultic [i.e. temple or tabernacle ritual] activity, the reference was normally to the honoring of God by total lifestyle. When Christians imply that reverence is essentially a matter of one's demeanour in church services, they show little understanding of the Bible's teaching on this subject!" David Peterson, *Engaging with God*, 73.

[59]Carson thinks, "The notion of a 'worship leader' who leads the 'worship' part of the service before the sermon (which, then, is no part of worship!) is so bizarre, from a New Testament perspective, as to be embarrassing." D. A. Carson, *Worship by the Book*.

[60]Harper and Metzger plainly state, "Worship is about God's people experiencing his presence." I think that definition is alien to the New Testament. Brad Harper and Paul Louis Metzger, *Exploring Ecclesiology*, 93.

In the dozens of large churches we have studied, the majority of people attending worship services do not even belong to a home group; fifty percent participation in home groups is well above average in America. Very few exceed half. But is this good? If half of a church of hundreds or thousands does nothing but attend the worship service, is that a legitimate version of the church as pictured in the New Testament? Are these people carrying out the vision for Christian living pictured in the "one-another" passages? Are they even worshipping under the New Testament definition?

Most pastors I've talked to are unhappy that the majority of their people remain relationally disengaged and are not in home groups. But most of them have not made the connection between their own understanding of the centrality of the worship service and their people's lack of interest in small group fellowship.

Today, a growing number of Christian leaders see small group or home church involvement as the heart of church life, instead of just another add-on. But I'm afraid most of their people have not bought into the vision, and the fixation on the worship services is probably largely to blame. Most church leaders aren't willing to risk losing attendance at their worship services for the sake of higher involvement in small groups. Of course, this is not the only reason home groups fail to flourish, but I suspect it is a big reason.[61]

Formalism

When people think worshiping God requires a fixed, recognizable service, they assume that a certain form is necessary. This is formalism—a focus on outward forms more than on inner, heart realities. When God cries out against formalism, he says he is angry "because this people draw near with their words and honor me with their lip service, but they remove their hearts far from me, and their reverence for me consists of tradition learned by rote" (Is. 29:13). Jesus also criticized formalism when he refused to follow traditional washings and quoted the verse above from Isaiah. Then

---

[61]So do other authors such as Wolfgang Simpson, *The House Church Book* (Ventura: Barna Books, 2009) xix. and M. Scott Boren, *The Relational Way*, (Houston: Touch Publications, 2008).

he added, "Neglecting the commandment of God, you hold to the tradition of men" (Mark 7:8).

Both of these were extreme cases of formalism, but even at lesser levels, formalism is harmful. The focus on forms and external rites reflects an impersonal understanding of how to relate to God. We don't relate to each other in formalistic ways, because we understand that it would be odd and impersonal to recite the same thing to each other each time we meet. Personal communication is spontaneous and responsive to the situation; it never involves reciting formulas.

To the extent that people understand worship as requiring a certain form, they are viewing their relationships with God as distant and not fully personal.

Positive fruit

When people understand worship as a lifestyle centered on God, they realize that worship is something they do every day and every hour. Such people no longer live the dual life of going to worship but then being hardly different from other people the rest of the week. Instead, people with the New Testament view are actively looking for ways to worship throughout the week.

People who are constantly looking for opportunities to worship through service and giving are active, fruitful members. Praising and thanking God should go forward all day long. People come to view their efforts to share their faith as a love offering to God rather than a duty. They begin to view every gathering from small groups to one-on-one meetings as potential acts of worship. Awareness of constant, relational interaction with God should replace a "Sunday-go-to-meeting" mentality. These attitudes can form a crucial basis for powerful New Testament-style ethos.

Chapter Sixteen

The Ministry of the Word

The New Testament church was a community of truth. Paul says the church is the "pillar and support of the truth" (1 Timothy 3:15). God has given something to the church so valuable that Paul could refer to it as "the treasure which has been entrusted to you" (2 Timothy 1:14). When we realize how valuable the truth from God is, we also realize we can anticipate constant attacks from the father of lies, all calculated to distort, undermine, or de-emphasize the truth. If we in the church don't fight for, preserve, and dispense the truth of God, certainly nobody else will, and this awesome treasure God entrusted to us will be cast to the ground and trampled underfoot. We will have only ourselves to blame for the resulting impotence and spiritual death in the church.

The best way to guard the truth, according to the New Testament, is to disseminate it so widely that too many understand it for the enemy to silence. We saw earlier that the early church in Jerusalem "devoted themselves continually" to the apostles' teaching. That never changed. Wherever we follow the early church, the word of God is central.

The public preaching of the word

The early church gathered in home groups where they could form and deepen relationships and where people could minister to each other. But they also gathered in larger groups to hear the public preaching of the word. The home meeting with a few close friends is one perspective, and it's a needed one. But when the sizeable congregation assembles, bringing together people from many other home groups, we see a different perspective—what God is doing in the whole city—and this is needed also. Deep and powerful preachers of the word are not very common, so it makes sense that house churches gathered to share access to highly gifted teachers. If home groups are unable to duplicate until they each have someone who can preach like Paul or Peter, duplication may never happen.

Preaching is a spiritual gift God gives to certain leaders so they can minister the word in power to sizeable groups of people. Without the preaching of the word, smaller groups tend to drift off and fizzle. They need to see themselves as a part of something larger. When leaders stand before the church and declare the word with passion and spiritual conviction, the whole church tends to unify around the great truths of God. They see their way. They are called to account. They gain vision.

New Testament calls to preach the word are among the most virulent imperatives we have. Think of Paul's parting instruction to Timothy. He sounds like he's swinging his arm around three times before throwing this punch:

> I solemnly charge you in the presence of God and of
> Christ Jesus, who is to judge the living and the dead,
> and by His appearing and His kingdom: preach the
> word! (2 Timothy 4:1-2a)

More emphatic language would be hard to imagine. He had earlier instructed him, "Until I come, give attention to the public reading of Scripture, to exhortation and teaching" (1 Timothy 4:13). You can tell Paul considered public Bible teaching and preaching central in the life of the church. Without it, he warns, people "will not endure sound doctrine; but wanting to have their ears tickled, they will accumulate for themselves teachers in accordance to their own desires, and will turn away their ears from the truth and will turn aside to myths" (2 Timothy 4:3,4). The darkness of human selfishness and love of bizarre mythology is always lurking just beneath the surface. To lead the church into this fate, leaders need only fail to preach the scriptures.

Just as some people gravitate to mass meetings, and feel aversive toward small group fellowship and transparency, others gravitate only toward intimate meetings, and see no value in larger gatherings to sit under substantive Bible teaching. In a church like ours, where many house churches share large meetings, we have noticed over the years how some home groups see great value in coming together while others see little need and tend to have little participation in such meetings. I've come to view low participation in our so-called "central meetings" as a predictor of illness in those groups. These are the groups that tend to lose their way. They become provincial—focusing only on their own little band, and eventually their inwardness tends to implode.

The ministry of the word in smaller groups

While public preaching is biblical and effective, we have every reason to believe that home groups in the New Testament also centered their time on the word of God. They probably didn't focus on preaching as much. But Paul makes it clear that along with hymns, prophecies, and tongues, they would bring a "teaching" (1 Corinthians 14:26). In our church, where people see their home churches as their main venue for fellowship (more people attend home churches than our large meetings), we encourage a guided discussion format. Guided discussion allows everyone to share insight, while providing some set up for the passage, and needed background and explanation.[62] Groups pass discussion-leading responsibilities from person to person among more knowledgeable believers in the group.

Our earliest description of a secret Christian meeting comes from second century author Justin Martyr in his *First Apology*:

> And on the day called Sunday all who live in cities or
> in the country gather together to one place, and the
> memoirs of the apostles [the New Testament] or the

---

[62]See our free training material for guided discussion at http://www.xenos.org/classes/discussion/index.htm

writings of the prophets [the Old Testament] are read, as long as time permits; then, when the reader has ceased, the president [the one leading the meeting] verbally instructs, and exhorts to the imitation of these good things.[63]

After this, they stood, prayed together, took communion, and gave money to a common pot for the poor. So even at this late date, Christian meetings still centered on the reading and teaching of the word. Group reading was ideal for the significant proportion of people who were illiterate. Only much later did churches move to a ritualized meeting format.

Some modern small group and simple house church advocates argue that home meetings should be unplanned and spontaneous. There should be no leader and no regular reading and teaching of the word of God, just singing, prayer, and prophetic words.[64] This simply doesn't square with the New Testament picture. If only apostolic figures taught the word, why would James need to say, "Let not many become teachers?" (3:1). Why would teaching and preaching be listed right along with other spiritual gifts?

Even prophecy, which Paul strongly encourages, probably involved the word. The idea that prophecy consists strictly of subjective messages from God, unrelated to scripture, ignores the role of prophecy throughout the Bible. Prophets often preach correct application of scripture and admonish or rebuke those who ignore

---

[63]Justin Martyr, *First Apology*, (Roberts-Donaldson English Translation) "Chapter LXVII – Weekly worship of the Christians."

[64]In *Pagan Christianity?* Viola and Barna argue against preaching and teaching from house to house as a regular part of church life. They think only apostles preached during special times. They claim that, "The earliest recorded Christian source for regular sermonizing is found during the second century," and "the contemporary sermon delivered for Christian consumption is foreign to both Old and New Testaments," 89, 88. But Paul characterized his times with the Ephesians as "teaching you publicly and from house to house" (Acts 20:20)—a practice he pursued "daily" according to Luke (Acts 19:9). The Christians in Jerusalem "were continually devoting themselves to the apostles' teaching" (Acts 2:42). Paul's call to Timothy to "preach the word" (2 Tim. 4:1,2), to "give attention to the public reading of scripture" (1 Timothy 4:13), his inclusion "if anyone has a teaching," (1 Cor. 14:26), and his reference to elders who "work hard at preaching and teaching" (1 Timothy 5:17), all point to the fact that early church meetings centered substantially on the word of God and preaching/teaching. Nor was their teaching and exhortation impromptu and unprepared. Paul calls on Timothy to be diligent so he can "handle accurately the word of truth" (2 Timothy 2:15). That implies studying. Paul's "teaching daily at the schoolroom of Tyrannus" (Acts 19:9) would hardly have been impromptu either.

God's word. In that role, prophecy can be an aspect of preaching. Paul also calls the others in a meeting to "pass judgment" on what prophets say, which also would involve a scriptural assessment (1 Corinthians 14:29).

When we consider how insistent both New and Old Testaments are that spiritual growth and maturity come through the word of God, why would anyone suggest that smaller meetings focus merely on subjective sharing and words of prophecy? In house churches I have visited around the country, they rarely mentioned scripture, or never discussed it at all. When they did mention the Bible, it was usually just a short devotional reading of a few verses without interpretation or context. No wonder many find such meetings boring! Repeatedly, people complain that home group meetings aren't interesting enough to justify the time investment.

By contrast, the New Testament church believed the word of God should "richly dwell within them," and that "teaching and exhorting one another" should be based on scripture (Colossians 3:16). They thought mature Christians should be teachers of the word, and that only spiritual babies were "unaccustomed to the word" (Hebrews 5:12-13). When Paul left groups, he commended them to the word "which is able to build you up and to give you the inheritance among all those who are sanctified" (Acts 20:32). He reminds the Colossians that "the word of truth... is constantly bearing fruit and increasing, even as it has been doing in you also since the day you heard of it and understood the grace of God in truth" (Colossians 1:5-6). The list goes on.[65]

When churches teach their people how to handle the Bible and convince them to spend time communing with God through his word, they can't wait to share and discuss the insights God gives them. Home group members look forward to feeding on the word together and learning from each other. Bible discussions are especially intriguing to non-Christian guests when groups know how to keep

---

[65]John 8:31,32; John 17:17; 2 Timothy 2:15; 3:16, 17; Romans 10:17; Hebrews 5:11-14; Romans 15:4; 1 Peter 2:2

things real and in plain language. Part of every discussion is how the truth under discussion has worked out in people's lives. Avoiding technical language and learning how to articulate truth in a way everyone can understand is good training for future ministry.

A weakened ministry of the word

The ministry of the word should be a priority in both large and small meetings, because God works through his word. When churches downplay the importance of learning the word, their members remain spiritually immature. According to Paul, those who partake only of the milk of the word are, by definition, spiritual babies (1 Corinthians 3:1-2).

One of the perils of popular preaching today is the emphasis on topical preaching. These topical series can have catchy titles and are often popular with members and their guests. But the negative is that people aren't learning the Bible like they would under expository preaching. I'm not saying it's wrong to teach topics, but I firmly believe that expository teaching—where you explain entire books of the Bible, one passage at a time—results in superior retention. The earlier chapter on equipping covered other ideas for strengthening members' depth in the word.

Under a weak ministry of the word, fleshliness begins to permeate the church. People aren't being convicted of their sin by the word, and instead, feel their carnal attitudes are legitimate. In the absence of a well-rounded understanding of scripture, people begin simply assuming their thoughts and feelings are the voice of God. Such subjectivity poses a real threat to the health of any local body. Experience can easily become the standard instead of truth. Members have no way to prioritize things and end up clamoring for ministries that don't contribute to the church's mission. Studies show that non-Bible teaching churches are also weak in evangelism.

Our choice in the church is simple: we either base things on the word of God or on the word of man. That should be an easy choice for Bible-believing Christians.

The big picture

People don't naturally assume that God's word is what they need. They must be taught and convinced that the word is important. When a church adopts a high view of scripture, revelation becomes the gateway to all other things God wants for the church. Unless people in the church totally respect the word and have a good knowledge of it, we simply have no chance of convincing them to exert effort toward any of the goals we have discussed so far.

Chapter Seventeen

Other Lessons on Leadership

Recognizing and developing quality leadership is one of the most important tasks for any local church. Churches with weak leadership are usually doomed to boring meetings, low motivation levels, and confusion. The idea that quality groups might spring up without the stimulus of strong leaders is na ve. That's simply not how it works. God uses leaders. Yet, as we saw earlier, real quality leaders are not just concerned with leading. They immediately set out to train up other leaders. Godly leaders are not eager to hoard leadership to themselves. They want to see others sharing in the leadership task.

Ego-driven and high-control leaders have little interest in training up other leaders. They are happiest when everyone is focusing on them. They love being the center of attention and won't accept changes that interfere with that goal. High-control leaders don't trust others to lead. Training makes little or no difference in their view; they simply cannot trust the judgment of others in the church.

Churches that want the blessing of godly leaders have to take serious stock of what the Bible says about leaders, and act accordingly. Scripture gives several boundaries to leadership in the church.

Indigenous

New Testament communities nearly always drew leaders from

within their own local churches. A system like that used today would have been unthinkable. As we saw earlier, seminary students usually don't have time to develop a ministry while doing graduate level study, so they come out inexperienced and are placed in a group they do not know.

New Testament churches raised up leaders from within their own ranks. They didn't look to institutional criteria like degrees for who should lead. They didn't believe they were *creating* leaders or hiring leaders in from outside. Instead, they were *recognizing* those whom God had made leaders in their midst.

Chosen by God

The New Testament teaches that God selects leaders, especially upper level ones. Jesus chose the apostles (John 15:16). The Holy Spirit gave prophetic words to indicate his choice of Paul and Barnabas (Acts 13:2) and Timothy (2 Timothy 1:6; 1 Timothy 4:14) after having selected Paul on the road to Damascus (Acts 9). Just as in the Old Testament, where God called great leaders like Moses and David, he assigns this task to chosen people in the church. Paul states that " [i]t was he [God] who gave some to be [various types of leaders]" (Ephesians 4:11-12) and that God "has arranged the parts in the body, every one of them, just as he wanted them to be" (1 Corinthians 12:18).

On a different level, all Christians lead at times, and in that sense all of us are to influence others for God. All of us should plan to lead our children. In this lesser sense, none of us needs anything more from God than his will as already expressed in his word; all Christians are to be servants and models of Christian living. But at higher levels of leadership, it becomes far more important that we see clear signs of divine choosing.[66]

When looking for signs of divine election of leaders, nothing is more convincing than a lengthy record of God changing the person's

---

[66]Although they should be linked, there is a difference between God's choice and one receiving a calling. People say God called them, but whether this is really God or their own desires may be hard to discern at times. In any case, "calling" is not what Paul directs Timothy and Titus to when looking for good leaders. Instead, he is looking for external indications of maturity and divine election based on their way of life.

life and using that person in the local church where he leads. This is the kind of credential Paul refers to in 2 Corinthians 3:1-2: "Are we beginning to commend ourselves again? Or do we need, as some, letters of commendation to you or from you? You are our letter, written in our hearts known and read by all men." Instead of letters of recommendation, Paul pointed to the way God had used him to establish the church in Corinth—the surest mark of true, God-ordained leadership.

In the apostolic period, the leader's record of sacrificial service and godly character counted for more than any degree ever could (if schools like today had existed). They chose who should lead in an organic way. This is the best explanation for why Paul left Timothy at Ephesus and Titus on Crete. He charged both of them to select leaders, but to do so gradually (not "hastily" 1 Timothy 5:22), based on eye-witness evidence of character and proven service. Paul could have selected leaders himself, but he apparently felt the need to have these workers watch for the hand of God over a longer period. Here we see a key benefit of indigenous leaders: The church can bear witness to their choosing.

There were traveling church planters and teachers in the early church, and occasionally a group like the one at Antioch would bring in outside help, like Barnabas and Paul (Acts 11:22-26). This would have been to help with the group's overwhelming growth (v. 21—note the "great number that believed"). When revival strikes, groups may not be able to raise up leaders fast enough to keep up with growth. But these unusual cases shouldn't obscure the fact that in almost all cases, leaders were recognized from within the group itself. Even in Antioch, Paul and Barnabas came in alongside the existing leaders there, *not to replace them*. We see in Acts 13:1 that the main leadership of the group included at least five men, so this is not a case of bringing in all new leadership like churches do today. Rather, they were reinforcing existing leadership.

Practical implications

If we accept the argument for indigenous, God-ordained leadership in the church we will be driven to other conclusions as well.

First, we should exercise caution when giving or providing ministry to a young Christian. We should provide *opportunities* to build ministry, but should remain reluctant to install a young worker into a well-developed ministry built up by someone else. Otherwise, we might simulate from the human side what God should provide from his side. The result could be that a person appears to be chosen by God, when in fact we installed the person in the position artificially. Installing a person into a developed ministry could result in the "turtle on a fence post" syndrome.

Suppose you were walking through a pasture and noticed a turtle sitting on top of a fence post. What would you think? One thing is clear: someone put the turtle there! Turtles aren't capable of putting themselves on fence posts, and they really don't belong there. No turtle in this situation would be very happy about it. Leaders who don't belong in their roles are like these turtles. Someone has placed them where they don't belong, and nothing good is going to come from it. God would not have placed them there. We may harm both the church and the individual when we interfere with God's selection in this way.

Instead of installing young, unproven workers into leadership of well-developed ministries, it makes more sense to offer them opportunities to follow up with new people and form discipleship friendships. From these, a larger ministry may develop, and we could see the marks that God is using the person in others' lives—one of the best signs that someone is a leader.

Favoring indigenous leaders and following organic principles for leadership selection is just a matter of respecting God's ordering of the church. Under the organic paradigm, God leads the church, and we are just watching for his leading and trying to move in concert with him. This is the key to power in all ministry—not us deciding what needs to happen and making it come to pass; but rather discovering what God is doing and getting in line with that.

Problems with the modern system

The modern system results in strangers leading groups they do not know. This is a significant move away from organic principles.

Churches expect their hired leaders to lead even though they come in having no idea who the people in the church are, and no history with them. No wonder such leaders turn to programs.

Secondly, when churches tell their own members they should lead, but every time a top position opens they hire someone from outside, what does this say? Why would we hire leaders from who-knows-where based on professional criteria? Christians in the local church would never see their own people rise to upper levels of leadership. This approach suggests that members are only good enough to lead at lower levels, because whenever we need leaders in an important role, we go outside the church to a pool of professionals. This tells our people that it's pointless to excel at ministry and perpetuates the clergy-laity distinction.

The modern system isn't easy on those playing the role of professionals either.[67] Seminary students are uprooted from their churches and any ministry they may have developed when they go away to school. The experience of leaving active ministry to go live with Christians for several years has a distorting effect on the students' outlook. In my opinion, young Christian workers should study the books while keeping it real by serving people and struggling for their faith in the midst of the unbelieving world. Real-life ministry has a way of clarifying what is far-out and useless in our scholarship and what directly contributes to meeting people's needs.

Other seminary students have never developed a ministry of any kind and go to seminary without any practical experience. These

---

[67]Many books have been written about the ill health in the lives of American pastors. Think about these findings reported by Dr. Richard J. Krejcir, based on studies completed at Fuller Seminary and several related studies:
Fifteen hundred pastors leave the ministry each month due to moral failure, spiritual burnout, or contention in their churches.
Fifty percent of pastors' marriages will end in divorce.
Eighty percent of pastors feel unqualified and discouraged in their role as pastor.
Fifty percent of pastors are so discouraged that they would leave the ministry if they could, but have no other way of making a living.
Eighty percent of seminary and Bible school graduates who enter the ministry will leave the ministry within the first five years.
Seventy percent of pastors constantly fight depression.
Almost forty percent polled said they have had an extra-marital affair since beginning their ministry.
Seventy percent said the only time they spend studying the Word is when they are preparing their sermons. Dr. Richard J. Krejcir, *Statistics on Pastors: What's Going on with the Pastors in America?* http://www.lifechristiancounseling.com/pastors/Statistics%20on%20Pastors.pdf p. 2.

students are particularly vulnerable to reaching unwarranted conclusions about ministry. They study ministry from books, trying to imagine what it's really like. The result is something like going to a bike-riding school for several years before learning to ride. What is wrong with this picture? Sadly, a large number of younger Christians come out of seminary with weakened faith and bad habits, often questioning the reliability of scripture.[68]

Advantages of indigenous leaders

Churches that focus on raising up indigenous, divinely elected leaders gain terrific benefits.

- The leaders are well known to the church and already trusted.
- Everyone in the church knows that leadership is open to anybody gifted and called to lead.
- Motivation to excel in ministry increases.
- Because they are real leaders, not turtles on fence posts, indigenous leaders do better work.
- No other churches have to have their leaders lured away by a more powerful local church.

Offices

The New Testament recognizes two offices involved in leadership in the church. These offices are for recognized leaders, or ministers, but ministry is not limited to them. Everyone in the church should minister, as we have seen. But some serving believers should be recognized as particularly accomplished and mature, and these are formally designated as either elders or deacons.

These offices are different than the later concept of the "clergy." As we saw earlier, the clergy/laity distinction was a disenfranchising

---

[68]Having seminaries makes a certain amount of sense. In fact, we host a branch campus for Trinity Evangelical Divinity School at our church. I attended seminary and benefited from it, as did most of our elders. Top scholars are a rarity, requiring a special calling and years of preparation. Pooling such scholars together where many churches can share in their expertise and the expense saves immense costs for local churches.

The problem is not mainly with seminaries, but with the church's system for choosing leadership. In my opinion, churches would do better if they sent young, upcoming leaders to seminary after they have demonstrated strong gifting in preaching, teaching, and leadership. These are the ones who would benefit most from seminary. Other leaders should be trained in the local church.

of most Christians from their birthright as practicing ministers. Offices imply none of that. These offices are nothing more than the church agreeing on who is reliable and mature. Someone has to lead, and these are the ones whose lives demonstrate they are best suited to that role. Having people hold formal offices avoids the problems expressed in the phrase "everybody's job is nobody's job." We need to know who is responsible for direction in the church, but recognizing some as elders and deacons doesn't remove anyone else's ability to minister.

Elders or Bishops

The first office is "elder" or "bishop" (correctly translated "overseer"). The office of elder is identical to the office of bishop. You can see this in Acts 20, where Paul meets with "the elders of the church at Ephesus" (v. 17) and reminds them that God "has appointed you as overseers" (v. 28). Again in Titus 1 he instructs Titus to be careful who he recognizes as "elders" (v. 5), because "an overseer must lead a blameless life" (v. 7). So the words are interchangeable.

"Elder" comes from the word *presbeuteros*, which means an older man, and therefore describes a person who is relatively spiritually mature. "Bishop" comes from the word *episkopos*, which literally means an *overseer*. The word "bishop" therefore, describes what the person does (i.e. oversees the local church), while "elder" expresses what they he is (a mature, reliable Christian). So, these words refer to the character and function of top leaders in the church.

Character qualities

When discussing who should be an elder, Paul emphasizes spiritual maturity and character over gifting. The qualities needed for elders in 1 Timothy 3 and Titus 1 are mostly character traits. People may be very gifted and knowledgeable, yet spiritually immature. Immature people can get into leadership, where they harm the church (see Diotrophes 3 John 9). For those interested, Appendix 1 contains a chart detailing the character qualifications for elders. These character qualifications are important, because Paul is trying to tell Timothy what to look for when searching for mature Christians. In that sense, these criteria apply to all of us as pictures of what we should aspire to.

Invalid criteria

Ignoring or hedging too much on these character qualities poses a mortal danger to the local church. Good groups can be ruined when unspiritual leaders get control, and history is full of examples. Insisting on these biblical traits is our best protection against ending up with leaders subject to Satan's manipulation. Unfortunately, some churches pay scant attention to the biblical qualifications for elders.

Some churches seem to choose elders for their prominence in the community, their wealth, and their business acumen. One elder in a large area church told me that the net worth of his board of elders must be astronomic, but he doubted that half the men could describe what it says in John 3:16. We could speculate about the motives churches may have for putting "successful" people into eldership, but the key point is that God forbids partiality to the rich in James 2.

Other churches go by a seniority system, where the old guard keeps control of the church, even though spiritual younger people are available. This also spells eventual doom for the vitality of the church.

"Nepotism" is when people place relatives or friends into places of leadership in the church for no reason other than favoritism. This lacks integrity and undermines God's intended choice of leaders. It can also lead to resentment and cynicism in the church.

So in several ways, churches may go astray from the path Paul prescribes for choosing leaders.

Functional capabilities

Paul stresses character most, but he also mentions some capabilities indicating ministry competence. Specifically, he seeks those who lead well and suggests looking at how they lead in their families as a clue (Titus 1:6 and 1 Timothy 3:4). He says that if someone doesn't lead his family well, Timothy has no reason to think he will lead the church well (v. 5).[69] This idea of watching to see if a potential elder leads well accords with Jesus' statement that his sheep know his voice and follow him willingly. Discerning good leadership should not be a mystery—just look behind the leader and see if anyone is following.

Paul also wants elders to be knowledgeable in the scriptures and good at teaching. In Titus 1 he says an elder must be "holding fast the faithful word which is in accordance with the teaching, so that he will be able both to exhort in sound doctrine and to refute those who contradict" (v. 9). Deacons are also expected to know and practice scriptural teaching (1 Timothy 3:8), but this extra requirement (that elders be able to refute those who contradict), implies a higher level of knowledge. Refuting false doctrine requires studying what opponents teach, and why, in addition to what the Bible teaches.

In 1 Timothy 3 Paul says elders should be "able to teach" (v. 2) which may be a weak translation for the word *didastikos*, which means "skilled at teaching." Elders may not have the spiritual gift of teaching, but they should be practiced enough to do a good job when needed. Being skilled at teaching implies that the elder's teaching results in people learning—and learning in this context means people learn to *do* what he teaches, not just hear what he said. In other words, both teaching and leadership are probably in view.

These functional criteria are important because in middle-aged church culture, most of the people in the church might be considered qualified as elders in the sense that they avoid gross sins like drunkenness and generally stay out of trouble. But at the same time, they may not actively and powerfully serve the church, and they are therefore not suitable as elders.

---

[69] I disagree with translating the word *prohistemi* here as "to manage." This is a word meaning "to stand before" and originally came from a commander standing before his troops, or going before them into battle (leading). It can also mean to go before someone to protect them, and as such includes the idea of "caring for" someone. But the primary meaning is leadership, and the word is translated that way in other New Testament passages (Romans 12:8; 1 Thessalonians 5:12). The context in 1 Timothy 3 is finding good leaders, not managers.

Relative, not absolute

Each elder we recognize should have all of the character and functional qualities given. But these qualities are not absolute. Nobody is "above reproach" in the sense that no one could reproach him for anything. Instead, we have to understand these qualities as being relative to the rest of the church. Compromises are unavoidable, but a church is better off with imperfect leaders than with no leaders.

Plurality

In each and every group in the New Testament for which we have information, leadership is based on a group of leaders, rather than a single "pastor" or "priest." In the early chapters of Acts, the apostles led the church in Jerusalem together. In Acts 14:23 we read that "Paul and Barnabas also appointed elders in every church...." These were mostly new churches in small villages. The groups must have been relatively small, yet each group got "elders" in the plural, which points to an intentional policy. Later, Paul left Titus to "appoint elders [plural] in every city [singular]" on Crete (Titus 1:5). Peter agreed with the practice when he called on elders to "shepherd the flock [singular] of God among you [plural]" (1 Peter 5:2). Timothy was busy appointing multiple elders in the city of Ephesus. Clearly this was the universal practice in the New Testament church.

Having plural elders working as a team protects the church from the caprice that one leader might bring. Elders are accountable to each other in a plural eldership, which can prevent one of them from being taken out through temptation, false teaching, or other failing. Satan finds it harder to deceive a local church if he has to mislead a whole group of elders. The need to win the agreement of the other elders softens extremism.

Plurality doesn't always work perfectly; but it is clearly better than having only one leader. By the second century the early church abandoned plurality in favor of the "monarchical bishop." The change happened gradually, as one city and then another would lose elders and fail to replace them. Increasingly, church leaders began to deliberately avoid having accountability, preferring to be the centerpiece of the church. They also feared false teaching and felt they could control it better with single leaders.

Plurality of elders is not necessarily equality of elders. Within a group of elders, one or more of them might have more experience, knowledge, or gifting that result in respect or persuasiveness beyond that of newer elders. This probably always happens to some extent as leadership groups evolve. Peter was the leader of the elders in Jerusalem, and later his place was taken by James, Jesus' half brother. Having a lead elder in an eldership group can help set an agenda and get things moving, avoiding gridlock. Such elders might have more influence than others during discussions, but they all should have one vote on decisions.

In the early days of our church, we accepted an argument that elders should be co-equal and all decisions must be unanimous. This turned out to be a straight jacket that took nearly two decades to change. Because we believed that no decision could be taken unless every elder agreed, decisions would linger on for weeks or even months of endless debate. In the end, we realized nothing in the Bible says decisions have to be unanimous. We realized that the practice really takes power away from the majority and gives it to the single elder who dissents from a decision. It imposes an unreasonable bottleneck on every decision. Today, we still prefer agreement, but if we can't all agree, we go by majority vote, which makes a lot more sense.

Deacons

We also see Timothy qualifying another office called "deacons" in 1 Timothy 3. "Deacon" means a servant or a minister. We don't know exactly what deacons did in New Testament times. Many assume that the seven men chosen to oversee a social ministry in Acts 6 were deacons, and therefore conclude that deacons should minister in practical areas like feeding widows, while elders lead the ministry of the word. In many churches today, deacons handle physical issues like taking care of the church's buildings and benevolence gifts. They may also seat people and handle collections.

But careful study of Acts 6 doesn't support this conclusion, and I think it's a damaging conclusion that diminishes the role of deacons.

The evidence

First, the men selected for this ministry were never called deacons. When a dispute broke out involving the ministry of feeding widows, the apostles said, "It is not desirable for us to neglect the word of God in order to serve (*diakonein*) tables" (v. 2). Some think this implies that these men were deacons, even though the word is being used in its normal sense of "service," rather than as an office. At the same time, the apostles refer to their own ministry as "the ministry (*diakonia*) of the word" (v. 4). So both the apostles and these seven were serving, and they referred to both ministries (of service and the word) using a derivative of "deacon." This could have been an *ad hoc* administrative need they filled with suitable men apart from any notion of the office of deacon.

On the other hand, even if these men were considered deacons, we see no indication that their ministry was mainly tied to physical service ministry. Stephen, one of the seven, was a miracle worker and a premium debater and preacher who was mighty in the word (6:8, 10 and chapter 7). His knowledge of scripture and ability to argue his case so infuriated the men at the synagogue of the freedmen (a group that apparently included the still-unconverted Paul) that they killed him.

Another one of the seven, Philip, was a greatly used evangelist. He sparked a revival in Samaria that led most of the city to faith. He also won the first gentile to Christ when the Spirit led him to the Ethiopian eunuch (Acts 8). Based on the example of these two, we can see that the seven men in Acts 6 ministered the word as well as service, and were among the best.

Finally, the requirements for deacons are strict, and that also suggests the office of deacon is a high office, probably involving leadership. We see no clear case for limiting deacons' roles to serving tables.[70]

In all likelihood, deacons were ministers serving in a variety of roles, including preaching and leadership, under the oversight of the elders. Second and third century developments, including the rise of the monarchical bishops and priests, led theologians to relegate deacons to service ministry only and to view it as a lay office, not as clergy.[71]

Why two offices?

Some New Testament churches, like those at Jerusalem, Ephesus, and Antioch, had hundreds, if not thousands of people.[72] If groups this large viewed leaders of individual home churches as elders, it would result in a huge number of elders. Such a large body would find it practically impossible to work together in one council.

Churches simply don't need more than a handful of elders to do the coordinated decision-making implied in our descriptions of plural elderships. Yet, such large groups must have included scores or even hundreds of house churches.[73] These conditions probably

---

[70]So also argue Mark Driscoll and Gerry Breshears, *Vintage Church: Timeless Truths and Timely Methods*, (Wheaton: Crossway Books, 2008) 74-77.

[71]For Catholics, deacons are usually a stage on the way to ordination as a priest. In Orthodox churches, they are sort of helpers for priests. Anglicans and Lutherans view deacons as "assisting pastors in human care ministry and other roles with the goals of caring for those in need and freeing pastors to focus on word and sacrament ministry." Among Baptists, definitions vary more, but usually refer to work of service, and helping run services by passing out communion, taking collection, or seating people. See a good article in "Deacons" in *Wikipedia* http://en.wikipedia.org/wiki/Deacon. Nearly all traditions see the passage in Acts 6 as pivotal.

[72]Recent authors like Rodney Stark "*The Rise of Christianity*, (Princeton: the Princeton University Press, 1996)" have tended to discount the large size of some New Testament churches, but without good reason. We know the church in Jerusalem was huge—at least 5000 according to Acts 4:4 (unless we are to understand that these were only the males in the group, which is the best translation!). Even though this group was scattered later by persecution, James is still able to describe the group as "many thousands" thirty years later (Acts 21:20). The church in Antioch was described as a "large number" early in its history—an expression that could hardly be less than hundreds (Acts 11:21). The church at Ephesus was huge. The pile of books they burned was valued at 50,000 days' wages (Acts 19:19). During the few years Paul ministered there, "all who lived in Asia heard the word of the Lord, both Jews and Greeks" (Acts 19:10). Demetrius was able to argue persuasively that the Christians were so numerous in Ephesus that the idol crafters and the cult of Artemis were in danger of being abandoned (Acts 19:24)—this in spite of the fact that the temple of Artemis was one of the ancient wonders of the world. Any estimate based on a serious consideration of these statements couldn't be lower than thousands of members. So we see that some churches numbered in the thousands, requiring more that one level of leadership.

[73]House foundations excavated in Jerusalem and other Greco-Roman cities show that living rooms were much smaller than today's rooms. Most of these rooms were only twelve by twelve feet or smaller, so the house churches in them couldn't have been very large—probably ten to fifteen people at most. A few may have met in the homes of the rich, perhaps reaching a size of thirty. In churches of hundreds or thousands (see previous footnote), we can infer that there must have been scores or hundreds of house churches.

led to the need for a second office in the church. Home church leaders couldn't all be elders, because there were too many. Instead, they probably designated most as deacons, and only the most experienced as elders.[74]

Deacons then, should be leaders who work under the oversight of the elders in a local church. They could lead the smaller groups, like home churches or small groups, or other ministries like the service ministry in Jerusalem.

Qualifications

Like elders, deacons had to demonstrate character, knowledge, and functional qualities before being recognized (1 Timothy 3:8-13). The character qualities are similar to those of elders and you can study them in Appendix 2. Functionally, they must know and practice the word according to verse 9, which says they must be "holding to the mystery of the faith with a clear conscience." But they are missing the requirement that they be able to teach.

Paul also insists, "These must also first be tested; then let them serve as deacons if they are beyond reproach" (v. 10). Deacons should have a publicly known record of godly service in ministry. Here again, the signs of divine election on their ministry point to who should be deacons. Only those who have demonstrated the ability and commitment needed in real-life ministry should be recognized as deacons.

Gender

Deacons were definitely both male and female. 1 Timothy 3:11 says, "Women must likewise be dignified, not malicious gossips, but temperate, faithful in all things." Here the NASB and most translations imply that these were the wives of deacons, although NASB adds the possible translation "deaconesses" in the margin.

I think deaconesses should be in the text as the preferred reading. Otherwise, we are left wondering why Paul would stipulate

---

[74]Interestingly, Titus is given no instructions for deacons, possibly because the towns in Crete were smaller and the groups small enough that they didn't need two levels of leadership.

requirements for deacons' wives, but not for elders' wives. That makes no sense. Besides, in Romans 16:1 Paul recommends "our sister Phoebe, who is a deacon in the church in Cenchrea."

Elders were normally—and maybe always—men in the early church, unless Titus 2:3 is referring to female elders (*presbutis* – here translated as "older women"). But many churches today see this as a *description*, not a *prescription*. In other words, even though they had all male elderships, that could have been for strategic reasons rather than theological reasons. Women were not easily accepted as leaders in ancient cultures. The main theological backing for male-only eldership is 1 Timothy 2:12, where Paul says, "I do not let women teach men or have authority over them. Let them listen quietly (NLT)." But various interpretations of this verse and context have been advanced, including some that see this as a temporary and local restriction, or not a restriction on their leadership at all.[75] Whatever the local church decides on this issue should be based on exegesis of scripture, not on popular opinion. The elders should study the relevant material and decide what stand to take.

The big picture

Having plural eldership and open-ended deacon positions throws the door wide open for leadership roles in every local church. Large churches could have scores or even hundreds of leaders, all with frontline, real leadership roles. Even small churches could have dozens. Instead of restricting leadership to a professional clergy, anyone in such churches would see the way open to meaningful roles involving guiding other people and groups into spiritual victory. The awesome power of every-member ministry would be unleashed.

When leadership becomes the goal of many members in the church, motivation to excel spiritually rises to heights never imagined in churches where people see themselves as passive receivers. Paul saw people aspiring to leadership (properly understood, as servant leadership) as a good thing (1 Timothy 3:1).

---

[75]For a male-only position see Mark Driscoll and Gerry Breshears, Vintage Church. See consideration of this subject at http://www.xenos.org/essays/role_of_women.htm.

At the same time, access to qualified leaders becomes available to all members on a regular basis because the group has more leaders (and they're not just people with the label 'leader' but well-equipped, truly spiritual leaders). Instead of expecting people to handle their lives and families on their own, or to schedule a session with a professional counselor when needed, people in this kind of church would be in position to get quality advice and help in their lives any time they needed it without going outside the normal course of body life.

A small staff of professional leaders cannot expect to understand what's going on in the lives of most people in a sizeable church. But with dozens or even hundreds in leadership, needs and problems in the members' lives are quickly recognized and dealt with. Replication of new leaders would be a constant struggle, resulting in an intensified approach to equipping. Every new Christian won into the group would have access to enriched feeding and follow up. In a word, a church led according to the New Testament pattern would be well-fed, motivated, and ready for growth.

Chapter Eighteen

Outreach in the Church

The ingrown vs. outreaching church

Nothing is more exciting than living in an outreaching church, and nothing is more dreadful and sad than living in an ingrown church. The difference between these two is greater than night and day, as anyone who has experienced both will attest.

Dynamic

In a victorious, outreaching church, people feel a tangible sense of excitement as they watch others come to Christ. The church's mission is clear, and God's blessing rests on the community as they share Jesus' love. Both those with evangelistic gifts and those gifted in nurture have their hands full as the needs of lost people and brand new believers call out to Christian hearts like the cries of baby birds to their mother.

People routinely experience the thrill of sensing God's power flowing through them as he uses them to meet desperate needs in others' lives. Prayer ministries are at a premium in an environment that draws extra fire from Satan. He can ignore peace-loving, ingrown churches in order to focus his attacks on outreaching churches. The outreaching church is always tottering on the edge of confusion and chaos as the church's expansion challenges those with administrative, healing, equipping, and leadership gifting to keep up.

An ingrown church suffers pitifully by comparison. Members of an ingrown church wonder, "What's the point?" As the sense of reality in people's spiritual walks drifts into eclipse, a quiet desperation wells up. "What's wrong with me?" people wonder. They begin to question whether they have drifted away from God. With a sigh, they may remember earlier days in their Christian journey and wonder where the zeal went. Ingrown churches lack deep unity. In the absence of clear direction, everyone has a different idea of what the church needs. Yet, outright division may not occur for the simple reason that no one has the energy to put up a fight. Squabbling and negativity are the more common results. People in the ingrown church lose their vision for our true mission. This is why the ingrown group turns features of healthy Christianity into unhealthy gimmicks.

Don't get the wrong idea. Life in an outreaching church is far from a pleasure cruise. If anything, the turbulence and spiritual attack typical in outreaching churches can lead to increased pain and suffering. But this suffering is so much more bearable than the sad apathy in ingrown groups! Once members know they are suffering for the sake of victorious expansion of Christ's kingdom, they can bear infinitely more than when they have little idea why they are suffering. We all would rather suffer battle wounds than bedsores anytime!

Learning

In an outreaching church, people are eager to learn. New Christians are loaded with questions and challenges that demand answers. Many a home Bible study has drifted for months in aimless pondering as older Christians remind one another of things they already know. Then a new Christian enters their midst. Suddenly, articulating the central truths acquires an urgency it never had among those who already believe they know the answers. How quickly a new Christian's or non-Christian's questions unmask our own lack of ability to articulate God's Word! In my experience, nothing sends older Christians scurrying to the books and Bible classes more than a good drubbing by a sharp young believer who can tell the difference between a biblical answer and a fudge job.

The ingrown church may admit the importance of learning, but when the leadership offers a class on something biblically sophisticated, no one shows up. People in an ingrown church can't remember why they should learn any more of the word than necessary for their own survival and peace of mind. But every experienced Christian worker knows the quantum leap of difference between the kind of knowledge that meets my need and knowledge that enables me to articulate that truth to another, even without consulting my books.

There are always a few, even in ingrown groups, who like to learn, but their learning often takes a strange turn. Instead of strengthening their skills at explaining needed doctrine to young Christians, these students become doctrinal wranglers. They specialize in scholastic questions of no importance, like the levels of heaven and hell and whether Mary really had a sister named Mary. Very few in outreaching churches have the luxury of wasting time on unimportant study.

Leadership development

In outreaching churches, new leadership is essential, and people's spiritual lives depend on it. Unless the church raises up new leaders, new believers will be orphaned on the street—or worse yet, will have no opportunity to hear at all because home groups are already full. People who have invested effort and heartache into reaching out to their lost friends will not tolerate an environment where those friends, now converted, can find no help in growing or any groups to meet with. They are insistent that someone step forward and lead the needed groups, even if they have to do it themselves.

An ingrown church really doesn't need more leadership and everyone knows it. While the preacher may pound the podium on the subject of lay mobilization, response is halting and dutiful. Unfortunately, halting and dutiful effort will rarely produce visionary, well-equipped leaders. In the press of daily schedule, busy people know that if they fail to equip themselves fully, no one is in any real danger. If something finally does happen, someone else will probably take charge. Most of what goes for leadership is nothing more than fussing over the inconsequential anyway. Who wants to serve again on some committee trying to figure out what color to paint the classrooms? Most ministry in the ingrown church is chrome-polishing. The ship may be slowly sinking, but at least it's going to go down with nice shiny chrome!

In a word, when outreach goes out of the church, the fizz goes out with it. I'm not suggesting that evangelism is the only important feature in a healthy church, or that all churches that have evangelism are healthy. I am suggesting that churches without evangelism are unhealthy by definition, and that such churches will never get healthy without correcting that central deficiency. The Bible is very clear on this point, as we shall see.

An Important Distinction

An outreaching church is one that reaches out to the lost millions who do not know Christ. Thousands of churches today in America are intent on growth primarily at the expense of other, weaker evangelical churches. They forfeit many of the sweetest rewards of outreach.

The new people coming into the church are not brand new Christians full of questions and honest needs. They are often dissatisfied believers who have many preconceptions about how the church should be. Too often, those who move from one evangelical church to another are the ones who most seek to satisfy themselves. Their old church "didn't meet their needs," or they were too immature to resolve personal conflict. Any large influx of such people may present more of a menace to a church's health than a blessing. This is probably less likely when Christians move in from another city, or when people return who have been out of church for a long time. But while reaching lost sheep is a good work, it isn't on the same level as reaching the truly lost.

While no one feels right about turning away any who come, whether Christian or not, our goal must be clear if we expect to reap the blessings of an outreaching church: only authentic conversions of lost people can fully galvanize a church community into action. Competing with other churches only takes the focus away from the lost and onto issues that will more likely lead to a slick Madison Avenue institution rather than a vigorous outreaching movement. A critical failure of the church growth movement was that they often did not carefully distinguish between transfer and conversion growth.[76]

As a leader in a number of different churches, I have led outreaching groups and ingrown groups. In fact, the same group can go through ingrown and outreaching phases in its history, and I've been in both. The difference is staggering. Of course, I'm speaking in generalities. Most churches are neither completely outreaching nor completely ingrown. But we can describe general tendencies, and we can also recognize which direction we are heading.

Winning converts today will only come to those who long for it with all their hearts. The days of easy conversions in western culture are over, unless we see a major turning. Only churches where people cultivate a heart burning with zeal for evangelism can expect significant numbers of converts—especially converts who stick around with the intention of growing spiritually. No task is more daunting for a leader than that of turning an ingrown group outward, but it's definitely possible.

Evangelistic Motivation

Before people will share their faith, they must *want* to. Every leader knows a group needs motivation. So often, it's not that people don't know what to do, but that they either don't feel the energy to do it or have fears that hold them back. Into this situation God sends leaders—and not just the top leadership of the church, although they are in the best position. Any opinion leaders can accomplish a lot as long as the top leadership agrees with their goals.

The wrong way

All too often, leaders set out on a quest to raise people's guilt level to the point where they begin witnessing. People sink lower in their seats as the preacher rehearses the terrors of Hell and reminds members that because of their disobedience, many of their friends

---

[76]This problem is well documented in William Chadwick, Stealing Sheep: *The Church's Hidden Problems with Transfer Growth*, (Downers Grove: InterVarsity Press 2001)

and family are going to go there. Yet it doesn't seem to work. In ingrown churches the average person may not have led anyone to Christ during the past decade. Indeed, many who have grown up in evangelical churches have never led any one to Christ in their entire guilt-ridden lives.

Occasionally, evangelicals, after sustaining a litany of finger-wagging imperatives, reach a point where they have had enough. They decide, "Alright, I'm going to witness this week." How sad this situation is, and how unfortunate the poor non-Christian who happens along the path of the guilt-ridden Christian witnesser! The encounter that follows is as pathetic as it is ineffective. The Christian is often not really communicating the love of Christ. He is just trying to get the "blood off his hands."

The dutiful discussion is usually short, inappropriate, unconvincing, awkward, and perfunctory. If the non-Christian is responsive, the poor guilt-ridden witnesser nearly falls over from shock. Much more often, the two walk away from the conversation shaking their heads. The Christian is glad he "got the job done," but even gladder he doesn't have to do it again for a long, long time. The non-Christian wonders what the strange out-of-context experience he just had means. "Why are Christians so strange?" he muses. Tragically, in his heart he is less receptive than ever, and in all likelihood will remain so.

I sincerely wish, along with all who are excited about evangelism, that those motivated by guilt would stay home and keep their mouths shut. Witnessing is not supposed to be a way to ease guilt; it's supposed to be an exciting meeting of hearts and spirits, where God's love moves from Christian to non-Christian. My advice to those who feel unable to witness from any motive other than guilt? Take your time. Wait until God teaches you a different way. You will only do harm in this condition.

What Christian can honestly say he or she has never felt the slightest bit guilty about lack of witnessing? This is a prime area of satanic accusation, in large part because our enemy knows how ineffective we will be once he moves us from our proper motivational base—the love of God and others—to a guilt motivation.

Finger-wagging sermons are not the way to motivate evangelism. I'm not suggesting that the Bible doesn't contain commands to witness. In fact, outreach to the lost is at the center of what God calls us to as his body. But unless we can teach these imperatives in a spirit of grace, we will never lead our people to relish opportunities for evangelism.

An Alternative to Guilt

We need to move from a negative to a positive motivation for evangelism. Look at a successful witnessing episode recorded in John 4. We read that the Samaritan woman left Jesus and immediately went into town to tell the people there that the Messiah might very well be sitting outside their city. This led eventually to a major spiritual awakening in that city, according to verse 39. But don't miss the most interesting phrase in the account in verse 28. John says, "Then, leaving her water jar, the woman went back to the town." How strange! She had walked all the way to the well to get water. Yet when she went back into town she forgot her pot! I'm sure John must have been struck by this fact or he wouldn't have recorded it.

Why did she leave her pot? It's an unmistakable and eloquent statement of pure spontaneity! No one needed to tell her the townspeople might perish in hell. No one needed to remind her of all the commands to witness, or of how disappointed God would be at the judgment seat of Christ if she failed to witness. This was a witnessing episode born of the raw excitement of discovery! No wonder it was so successful. The enthusiasm of the new believer is hard to resist. Even if people don't believe, they feel the need to find out what's so exciting. This explains why new Christians are so often successful at bringing friends to hear the gospel.

This excitement is what we need to tap if we are to have motivated, witnessing churches. Meeting Christ as a new Christian is one kind of excitement. Older Christians should be just as excited about seeing others come to Christ. They need to reawaken their awe about God's grace regularly.

In all eagerly witnessing groups I've been in, people witness for the same reason: they think it's fun! They love the adventure of entering into spiritual conversations with people. They like the feeling that they're engaged in meaningful spiritual battle. They like to share their experiences with each other and pray for each other. They especially feel excited when people they've been praying for during past months finally show up at a meeting and hear the word of God. Churches need to get their people reading quality books on personal evangelism like Hybels and Mittlberg's *Becoming a Contagious Christian,* which does a good job explaining all aspects of evangelism. All the creativity of church leaders should go toward helping members discover the joy of sharing their faith.

The Role of Leaders

Vision

We need a vision for the outreaching church similar to what we've been discussing. Once we settle on that vision as the only way to go, once we see it as the most wonderful of all futures, and the one thing we cannot live without, God will show us how to get there. After all, he wants that future for us as well. Though it won't be a goal we can achieve in a few weeks or perhaps even in a few months, the goal of living in an outreaching church is attainable for *any* church.

Leaders need to give vision to their people. Those who agonize before God in prayer and study his word can get God's picture for their church in a living way; a way that begins to burn in the heart. Getting a clear sense of vision is not easy. It can be a struggle that might last some time. We will discuss how to develop and propagate vision in a later chapter.

Prayer

Well-led churches mobilize their people for prayer, and prayer can ignite outreach. Smaller prayer meetings are ideal for praying by name for people with whom those in the group are sharing. There, leaders can encourage efforts and console failure. Anyone who has experience in evangelism knows that far more efforts are going to end in failure than in success (in terms of conversion). That's why leaders must cultivate a culture where people learn to feel good about sowing seed, whether or not the ground is good. This is not how people view things by nature; only well-taught and counseled believers adopt this view.

At one point, my middle-aged men's group was in a state of utter defeat in outreach. We not only hadn't won anyone in recent memory, we didn't even have any ideas. The trail was so cold that nobody had any realistic opportunities for friendship evangelism.

The first thing I did was call on them to face the problem. We had a long discussion about our difficulties and agreed that unless we could get some outreach going, we might as well disband our group; we would be doomed. I had a plan. I suggested we begin with prayer. I asked every guy in the group to name a person or two that we could pray for. We went around our study table, collecting names. Some had three names, some had to struggle to think of one. That's all. We agreed to pray over those names every week. We agreed that if an opportunity came up to talk with one of the people we were praying for, we would take it—not necessarily to share the gospel, but maybe to take an interest in what was happening in the other person's life. If the conversation turned spiritual, so be it.

Each week, we went around and asked each brother whether anything had happened—a conversation of some kind, a crossing of paths, anything. The first week or two, people didn't have much to share. I just said, "Fine, let's pray for them again." We also studied personal evangelism while we waited.

Within three or four weeks, we began to get action. Conversations occurred, and thanksgiving mingled in greater proportion to pleas. Within three or four months, we had multiple male and female guests attending our home church and asking questions about God. Later, several received Christ.

Interestingly, few of our guests were from our original prayer list. But that's not unusual. God sent in a harvest that eventually led to duplicating that group, and I believe regular prayer was the key. God probably steps us into unexpected opportunities just to make the point that people are being reached not by our effort but by his power.

Today, I attend a prayer group every week in a younger home church where we are enjoying ongoing success. This home church has roughly doubled and planted a new home church every year for the past ten years. Although our current group is not the fastest growing group I've seen, I do notice that most weeks, the majority of people in that meeting have concrete stories to tell of efforts to share their faith.

We get our full share of refusals from people we witness to, but we also get successes, and God is regularly answering our prayers. Few weeks go by without a new person or several relatively new people coming to our meetings. People have come to expect that. Every meeting matters when several in the group are moving toward a decision for Christ. In a home church culture like this, members feel eager to contribute their stories. Nobody wants to be left out of the action.

I'm working with a younger crowd these days, where first-time guests are more numerous than they were in my middle-aged group. But the principle is the same. Those reaching out to family-aged people have to be prepared to exert more patience and careful work. But it's even more exciting when older groups at last see someone respond to the gospel and begin to walk with God.

Practical ideas

Leaders also need to help with the practical parts of evangelism. They should show up with ideas for how to set about the task. These practical ideas will contain some mistakes, but that doesn't matter. Far better to try some new ideas and fail rather than wringing our hands, waiting for success to come upon us like the flu.

When I was in one adult home church that lacked successful outreach, we developed a scheme we called *Conversation and Cuisine*, involving a dinner party with topical discussion afterward on a secular subject like animals rights, or crime. Using this we were able to jump-start outreach that had stalled for months.[77]

---

[77]You can read more about this idea, along with other topics and materials at http://www.xenos.org/justforfun/cc1.htm.

On another occasion, a student men's Christian house canvassed their neighborhood around Halloween passing out invitations to a BYOP party (bring your own pumpkin). Their invitation promised a judged contest and a prize for the winner. Multiple student neighbors came out to the party and the guys were able to meet a bunch of their neighbors and establish rapport.

Another church had several ladies join a belly dancing class where they met and won other women to Jesus.

Service evangelism holds special promise today because Americans are demonstrating a growing desire to make some kind of difference with the poor. If Christians arrange to paint the home of a poor family, for instance, and invite non-Christian friends to come and help, they get to spend a whole weekend working together doing something good—a perfect opportunity for sharing.

Examples like these would be easy to multiply. Any group that sets its heart on outreach can come up with creative ideas for how to engage with non-Christians and get the process rolling.

Equipping

Leaders realize that their people aren't going to do something they feel incompetent to do. Training is motivational in itself. People who invest time and effort into training want to use that training. Through classes and a network of discipleship relationships leaders can push information and ideas out to people, resulting in motivation. Wise churches put together quality classes on how to share your faith and get one of their finest inspirational teachers to lead them.

Encouragement

Finally, once people start to act, good leaders know how to encourage them to further action. Healthy churches celebrate not only conversions, but also every effort at sharing the faith. Instead of focusing too much on results, they counsel those who experience rejection to see that sharing their faith was a victory, regardless of the outcome. Maybe their role was to move a person from negative ten to negative five in his or her attitude toward the gospel. People need to see that the majority of those they talk to will ultimately say "no."

When people think they should always win people they share with, it poisons their ability to frequently and spontaneously share. They become too afraid of saying the wrong thing. Instead, they should realize that by sowing seed abundantly, they have the best chance of running into a responsive person.

The Evangelistic Community

Many today also envision the believer working alone or perhaps with one friend. In other words, evangelism is mainly up to individuals.

Thank God for individual initiative in evangelism! Any motivated Spirit-filled Christian can go out and speak for God with good results. Surely, the New Testament bears witness to fearless, caring individuals who went out and won others for Christ. Andrew is a favorite example. He brings someone to Christ almost every time he appears in the Gospels. Philip the evangelist stands out as another strong example of individual evangelistic victory (Acts 8).

On the other hand, the New Testament presents an additional picture not contained in this image: the picture of the outreaching *church*. Many of the evangelistic imperatives in Scripture were originally addressed to local churches, though we often tend to read them individualistically (e.g. Colossians 4:5-6; Philippians 2:14-16).

Francis Schaeffer argued persuasively in his book *The Mark of the Christian* according to John 13:34-35; 17:21 and 23, the unity and love Christians express to each other in the body of Christ is compelling evidence of the truthfulness of Christianity. Since this evidence is more subjective than objective, people have to *feel* and *see* it; it can't be explained with words. This whole line of teaching points to the need for an evangelistic community rather than merely witnessing individuals. When churches take *koinonia* seriously, enhanced evangelism is one of the great blessings they receive.

The atmosphere produced by a group of Christians who love each other "fervently, from the heart" will often do a great deal to convince the non-Christian to respond to Christ. How often I have seen with my own eyes a hardened non-Christian, full of critical comments and resistance, melt into openness after attending a warm and authentic meeting in somebody's home.

Corporate evangelism can draw on a number of other advantages:

- Since we have diverse gifts in the body of Christ (1 Corinthians 12:12), corporate evangelism makes it possible to expose guests to people whose gifts compliment those of the one who originally invited them.
- If we bring non-Christian guests to a number of Christian meetings that have been crafted to appeal to non-Christians, they will hear a much more complete and convincing presentation of the gospel than I could give during the five minutes we might talk in the hallway at work or school. Well-reasoned presentations of pre-evangelistic or evangelistic material are effective, especially when we put our best communicators up to speak.
- If I reach someone on my own, he will have to make a second decision to get involved in Christian fellowship. But if I reach him through corporate evangelism, he will already be accustomed to attending Christian meetings and will have already overcome the common fear of going to a new group of strangers.
- Experts state that members' attitudes toward their own church is the single most important factor in determining a church's ability to grow. When members in a local church are enthusiastic about what God is doing through the church, guests sense this and are attracted. We have to work on our group's attitude at meetings. In our church, we encourage people to verbally agree with others' prayers and sharing like they did in the New Testament church to openly express engagement.[78]

---

[78]In 1 Corinthians 14:16 Paul says that one reason for not speaking in tongues unless they are interpreted is that people won't know when to say the "amen" at the giving of thanks. In other words, they verbally affirmed each other's prayers by saying "amen," which means "yes" or "truly." Jesus also spoke of agreeing in prayer (Matthew 18:19). When young Christians pray something worthwhile and the group softly agrees aloud, this encourages the one praying. Silence tends to discourage prayer. But another reason is that when a whole group is engaged this way, outsiders sense their enthusiasm, which is attractive.

The big picture

Outreach-oriented communities win people who don't know God and teach them how to walk with him and minister to others. Churches with good, outward looking ethos are "intent on one purpose": seeing God glorified in the nations (Philippians 2:2). Groups with a New Testament ethos are patient, persistent churches where people go out of their way to make friends with non-Christians and boldly declare God's word. Any group that continually relies on God in prayer and seeks out opportunities to share will eventually see people come to faith. That will revitalize the group as the natural flow of spiritual ministry finds a healthy outlet.

Chapter Nineteen

Church Finance

The Bible has a lot to say about money. According to some experts, Jesus spoke more on money than any other subject.[79] Paul and the other New Testament authors teach on it extensively as well. Much of this teaching has to do with the individual's handling of his or her own money, but even more has to do with the use of money in the church.

A local church's use of money powerfully demonstrates its ethos. In some groups, they use money to glorify God, win people to Jesus, and relieve suffering, but other churches bring public contempt onto the name of God and rob their own people. Churches powerfully affect the spirituality of their own people through their faithfulness or lack thereof in the use of money.

Money is nothing but a symbol of human life—work, creativity, and often privilege. As such, it has great power to transport human work from one venue to another. Like our lives and the whole world, our money is the personal possession of God (Ps. 24:1), but he lets us hold it and use it for him as stewards. For Christians who live a life of self-sacrificial love, it would be unthinkable that our giving-out would fail to include our money. God calls christians to be sacrificial givers.

---

[79]Jesus taught more on money than anything else according to Gene Getz, *Rich in Every Way: Everything God says about money and possessions*, (Howard Books, 2004).

Giving to the church

For a number of reasons, the Bible teaches that we should pool our financial gifts together in the church.

First, this is the New Testament example. In Acts 4:32 we read, "All the believers were united in heart and mind. And they felt that what they owned was not their own, so they shared everything they had." Moreover, "There were no needy people among them, because those who owned land or houses would sell them and bring the money to the apostles to give to those in need" (v. 34-35). We see Paul orchestrating a massive collection for the poor in Judea through the churches in Greece (1 Corinthians 16:1-4; 2 Corinthians 8-9, see also Acts 11:27-30).

Secondly, Jesus taught that gifts should be given anonymously (Matthew 6:3-4), and this argues for indirect giving most of the time. Rather than handing money to those in need, believers normally should give their gifts to the church leadership and have it indirectly given to others.

Thirdly, the church has its own expenses, and these require that members entrust significant sums to the group.

Finally, by collecting the group's money and pooling it together, the church is able to meet large needs over lengthy periods. The church leadership can serve as a clearinghouse for needs, collecting information in a way no individual could.

Things the church does with money

The way a group distributes its funds demonstrates its priorities more than its words do. When churches can't find money for missions, ministry to the poor, or equipping ministries, it's usually because they wasted too much on foolish expenses. Scripture gives us considerable guidance on what funding priorities should be.

Paying workers

Although most Christian workers should be "tent makers," (who work at secular jobs and do ministry as volunteers) churches are free to pay key workers so they can forsake secular employment and serve part or full-time in ministry. Jesus established this principle when he said, "Those who work deserve to be fed" (Matthew 10:10 NLT). Paul quoted this when teaching that at least some elders should be paid (1 Th. 5:17-18). He calls on those who are taught to share with those who teach (Galatians 6:6).

Although paying leaders is legitimate, over-paying them is bad stewardship and a negative testimony to the world. Non-Christians are already suspicious that churches exist only to get people's money. So when leaders drive up in super-luxury cars and live in mansions, we give them little reason to reconsider. Wealthy leaders are also a bad example to the church, suggesting people should live for money. Leaders cannot expect their people to be any more sacrificial than they are.

Operational expenses

Churches can cut expenses by using volunteer workers most of the time. But sizeable churches begin to need accountants, secretaries, janitors, and other staffers. Leaders should pay attention to which staffers are doing substantive work and which have more to do with image and frills. As churches grow, they need to have the strength and integrity to terminate ministries and positions that are no longer demonstrating usefulness in pursuit of the main mission.

We saw that "sacred cows" are ministries that used to serve some purpose, but which now are mainly kept going because it would hurt someone's feelings to cut them. Good leaders have enough strength to kill the sacred cow. Inability to do this accounts for why churches end up saddled with immense expense that seems to do nothing of lasting value to the church. Bureaucracy tends to grow with a life of its own; bureaucrats often blame their ineffectiveness on lack of funding. Only rigorous and honest annual re-evaluation can keep bureaucracy from growing like a cancer that takes over the church.

On the other hand, ministries like equipping don't issue in immediate results, but they are very important. The leadership of the church has to decide what is important based on biblical emphases and see that adequate money is reserved for those ministries they deem important for the mission of the church.

Facilities

Large churches can make a good case for buying or building a facility, although they are wise to put this off as long as possible. Rented or leased facilities are cheaper, and using them allows the church to grow into a facility.

Remember, a facility is like a glass. You refill it as often as you want. One severe limitation on churches in America is the belief that meetings have to happen on Sunday morning. Because most church people think Sunday morning is a spiritual time, their buildings sit empty the rest of the week. In our church, we have six large meetings at other times during the week to supplement the six on Sunday mornings. That doubles the value of our facilities. Two other large meetings gather in rented buildings in different parts of town saving more money. Since these are all different groups of people, the cost per meeting is significantly reduced.

Through frugality and non-showy building methods, big churches can keep their financial focus on needed ministry rather than on unnecessary building extravagance. People are drawn to God through his word empowered by the Holy Spirit, not by fancy sculptures and plush d cor. Some churches conclude that having bowling lanes or nice gyms will draw people to the church. Recent studies show the opposite is true.[80] These are wasteful features suited more to pleasing members than winning the lost.

Ministry to the poor

The Bible uses strong language to condemn Christians who see poor people nearby and do nothing to help. In Matthew 25:31-46, Jesus describes a judgment where people are sent to hell because they did not care for "the least of these my brethren." He considered that as bad as not helping Jesus himself. John says, "We know love by this, that He laid down His life for us; and we ought to lay down our lives for the brethren. But whoever has the world's goods, and

---

[80]"Our research uncovered the gym fallacy. Many pastors hear from their members that building a gym will help attract the unchurched in their community. We, however, found the exact opposite to be true." Thom S. Rainer, and Sam S. Ranier, *Essential Church?: Reclaiming a Generation of Dropouts*, (B&H Books 2008) 63.

sees his brother in need and closes his heart against him, how does the love of God abide in him?" (1 John 3:16-17).

Affluent churches should devote a significant portion of their budget to ministry to the poor. And these ministries should include community development, not just handout programs that result in dependency and further poverty. We devote a later chapter to ministering to the poor. For now it's enough to note that God calls on us to make this a priority in our budgets.

World missions

Jesus' call to make disciples of all nations is still unfulfilled. Many areas in the world today have no viable Christian witness of any kind. These same areas are often among the most poverty-stricken. Churches in the west should get serious about making a difference in un-reached lands. Penetrating these fields is tough work. It means sending people to those areas to learn their languages and cultures. Then, years of investment might result in reaching a core of people who can in turn reach others.

Missions should be a visible, significant part of every church's budget. Some new churches may be so strapped that they have to work their way up to this, like we did. But it should definitely be a goal. Our church devotes a third of our giving today to missions, which includes our inner city ministry in the U. S. We had to work up to that figure over a couple of decades, and we're still increasing both the dollars and the percentage devoted to missions each year. Some churches are much stronger than ours, giving half or more of their dollars to missions. Since world missions is so important to the health of the church, we will devote a later chapter to that.

Accountability and transparency

In the handling of church funds, Paul says he always takes "precaution so that no one will discredit us in our administration of this generous gift; for we have regard for what is honorable, not only in the sight of the Lord, but also in the sight of men" (2 Corinthians 8:20-21). Paul is arguing that we should not only handle money devoted to God honorably and with integrity, but that *we should also be able and ready to prove that we have done so.* This is a good example of a church structure based on principle. His collection of up to eight people to travel with the offering to Judea was the wineskin he felt was appropriate. We don't have to use that wineskin, but we do need to honor the principle he teaches.

Because of the first amendment to the U. S. Constitution (that the government will not pass laws involving religion) American churches are free from normal requirements for disclosure like those applying to businesses. Churches can keep their books secret, and even the government cannot audit them if they refuse.

Unfortunately, this well-intentioned law has resulted in the church being the most unaccountable institution in America. Churches have become the perfect venue for criminals and con-men to ply their trade while remaining unaccountable and even remaining tax exempt! Paul's standard—being able and ready to prove where the money goes—is long-forgotten in many modern churches.

The American legal situation does not, however, prevent churches from disclosing their finances voluntarily. I believe every legitimate church should hold its books completely open to the public. Why not? What secrets do we need to keep? If everything is as we say, we should have no problem with anyone, even enemies, looking at our books in detail. In our church, members or non-members are free to examine our accounting books to any level of detail they desire (except how much individuals give to the church). Such complete accountability and transparency certifies to everyone that we have nothing to hide.

We also put out an annual report on the state of the church. These reports remind people of ministry accomplishments, admit failures, and give summaries of our finances. We present the report at a large, public meeting each year, and follow up with a more detailed report which runs on our website.[81] We also propose new expansion at these meetings, and people can question the speakers or disagree with their direction.

---

[81] Recent examples of these reports can be viewed at http://www.xenos.org/aboutxenos/reports.htm.

If more churches committed to practices like these and more Christians insisted on it from any ministry they were willing to support, we wouldn't have the scandalous behavior in American churches' use of money that we see today. Christ's body should be zealous to protect God's reputation, and total accountability and transparency are the best ways to do so.

Regular auditing by respected outside firms is also a helpful seal of legitimacy especially for large churches. Big multi-million dollar budgets become too complicated for normal people to analyze, so getting audited puts a team of professionals on the job. A group in America called the "Evangelical Council for Financial Accountability" certifies that its member organizations observe the highest and most honorable practices. Interestingly, complete public disclosure of members' books is not one of those practices. Joining this organization is another option.[82]

Small churches have to be careful with money also. In some small churches, the temptation is to treat the church's till like a 'ma and pa shop.' Leaders may feel free to reach into the collection money and take some for use on a trip, for instance. This is wrong. The time to begin building the habits of discipline, careful record-keeping, and accountability is when you are small. Then you won't have to learn a different way later.

Spiritual and financial leadership

In the New Testament, those who led the church in spiritual matters were also entrusted with the church's finances (Acts 4:34-35). This is probably another structure based on theological principle, and should still be followed today. Some churches divide the spiritual and financial leadership of the church into different entities, such as different boards or different voting groups. But if we can't trust the spiritual leaders we have chosen, why would we trust others? This is not to say we should trust spiritual leaders to

---

[82] http://www.ecfa.org. While this group seems like a good idea, several recent cases of financial scandal involved member organizations! Our church hasn't joined because they require audits too often in our view. The cost of an audit can exceed $20,000.00, and with all the pressing needs we face, we don't believe it would be good stewardship to spend that much every year or two. We usually get audited every five to ten years.

the extent where they become unaccountable. But where the church spends its money determines in large part the direction of the church, and these are spiritual decisions that should be made by a group of qualified spiritual leaders.

The big picture

How people in a local church view money and stewardship is crucial. We made the mistake of leaving this part out of our early teaching, and the result was a devastating weakness in our church that nearly brought us down. When our group reached a point where we had thousands attending, but had never taught clearly on responsible giving, we were nearly choked to death! As we reached a point where we had to turn away hundreds of people because we couldn't afford space for them or their children, we realized we had erred dangerously on this whole issue.

We knew our people didn't give much, but in the early days that seemed reasonable because they were mostly students with little income. Later, it became clear that even after joining the work world, the giving remained low. When the government began requiring churches to keep records of giving for tax purposes, we learned that even a third of our leaders gave nothing at all! We began requiring giving for leaders and taught more strongly on the subject in public meetings, which resulted in suspicion on the part of many members. The resulting battle cost us over a thousand members. It never would have happened if we had taught clearly on this from the beginning. Today we recognize that refusal to give is not a minor error but a powerful statement of carnality or ignorance.

Every church's use of money is a crucial part of its witness to the watching world, as well as to its own members. Through the handling of God's resources, we teach people in the church what the heart of God is like. Much prayer and deliberation should go into how we handle this precious stewardship in accordance with biblical priorities and principles.

Chapter Twenty

Church Discipline

Perhaps nowhere do modern churches find themselves at greater distance from the New Testament picture than in the area of church discipline. In the early church, people loved one another too much to watch passively as others destroyed their lives. Instead, they vigorously intervened to plead with those caught up in destructive sin.

This intervention might be as mild as admonition (*noutheteo*) which suggests directive correction in the sense of counseling. Or it could be a more forceful demand for change, such as reproving or rebuking (*elegxo* or *epitimao*), which carry the idea of confronting someone with their wrongdoing and warning them. In extreme cases, early Christians loved each other enough to remove people from Christian fellowship altogether, rather than allow them to continue soothing themselves with relationships in the church while pursuing a destructive lifestyle. There in the world, deprived of the support of Christian fellowship, the person caught up in serious sin had the best chance of coming to repentance.

Shock and awe

When confronted with this plain and oft-repeated teaching in the New Testament, modern Christians often recoil in horror, and I was no exception. The first time I had to become involved in serious discipline, I couldn't believe my ears.

My friend and his girlfriend were hosting high school students at her place on weekend nights for all-night movie sleepovers. Around one in the morning, the two of them would walk upstairs and go to bed—in the same room! Everyone knew this was happening, but the students didn't see any problem with it. When I complained, the couple pointed out that "nothing bad was going on." We couldn't talk them out of what they were doing, and they were offended that we were even trying.

When I went to an older Christian and related the story, he told me we had to demand change or turn the couple out of our fellowship. I stared for long seconds, blinking in unbelief. Finally, I said, "If they're having a problem, how is it going to help to kick them out? They'd be in way more temptation out in the world!"

But he opened the Bible and showed me the relevant passages. I gradually realized that we either had to begin ignoring New Testament teaching or do the right thing. Since that time, nearly forty years ago, I've been involved in many cases of church discipline at all levels. I've seen it change lives dramatically. Even those removed from the church often reach the end of their ropes and return with a new perspective.

The stakes

Discipline doesn't always work, but it always has a positive effect on the church, and the alternative should be unthinkable. Are we ready to form groups where everyone knows that half the people in the group are living double lives including even gross sin, and nobody seems to care? When those same hypocritical people lift their hands in praise and share super-spiritual testimonies, serious believers feel their flesh crawl. The whole act of *koinonia* now becomes a foolish charade, a dance of falsehood that will sicken spiritually sensitive people while it grosses out non-Christian guests.

Are we ready to see our churches overtaken by immorality? When everyone in the room knows the dating couple on the couch are going to sleep together tonight and nobody seems to care, the motivation to resist temptation is shredded. Weak Christians simply cannot maintain their walks in this environment. Paul challenged the Corinthians, who were not disciplining a member living in open immorality: "Don't you realize that this sin is like a little yeast that spreads through the whole batch of dough?" (1 Corinthians 5:6 NLT). Lax responses to this kind of sin make two statements to the church: "Anything goes," and Nothing matters." It says to the whole group that sin is inconsequential and that sincerely following God is optional. It also affirms individuality—that our private lives are none of the church's business.

God is not going to exert his spiritual power to bless a group of people who have formed a conspiracy of silence designed to accommodate evil in their midst. If we want to go soft on discipline, we can plan to lose our effectiveness both inside and outside the church. Serious believers will be demoralized: What's the point of continuing the struggle when there seems to be no difference in the group's view of those who do and who don't?

In the group where I work, the overwhelming majority of students have recently come to faith. Their background is raw, relativistic, and habituated. If we didn't take a strong stand on things like sexual immorality or intoxication, we would be overwhelmed with sin in a matter of months. Indeed, it sometimes seems like we're being overwhelmed even with a strong stand (but nothing like the 80 percent fornication rate among evangelical young people documented earlier by Regnerus!).[83]

We've had house churches where the leaders refused to discipline when they should, and the results have always been pitiful. The poison of spiritual apathy and double-living spreads like wildfire in these groups, just as Paul said it would. Such groups follow one of two paths: repentance and a return to faithful discipline, or withering down to spiritual death.

Assumptions behind discipline

The modern liberal church, the emergent church, and even much of the evangelical church have largely abandoned the practice of discipline in the church for all practical purposes. Many modern

---

[83]Mark Regnerus, "The Case for Early Marriage," *Christianity Today*,
http://www.christianitytoday.com/ct/2009/august/16.22.html, posted 7/31/2009.

Christians are horrified at the thought, believing that practicing discipline would mean they couldn't win anyone into the church, and further, that it would be unloving. I've had a number of leaders tell me with baffled grimaces, "That's rejection!"

The non-Christian world is even more horrified. Secular people today believe it's arrogant to criticize other people's moral choices. As Christians, we agree with our culture that admonition based on nothing more than personal opinion would be presumptuous and arrogant. However, with the Word of God, we have a basis for correcting each other, and such correction, when practiced in a spirit of grace and acceptance, will have life-transforming power. Key assumptions underlie the correctness of church discipline.

Dynamics of sin

Communities that discipline appropriately accept that all people sin on a regular basis. This includes self-righteous believers who bellow about the wickedness of sin and imply that only false Christian backsliders go on sinning. These hard-liners have re-defined sin so narrowly that they seriously believe either that they don't sin, or that they sin only rarely. The only way they could reach that conclusion would be to eliminate all sins of thought, attitude, and omission from their definition. To seriously face passages like Romans 14:23 ("whatever is not from faith is sin") or James 4:17 ("Therefore, to one who knows the right thing to do and does not do it, to him it is sin") and project a picture that Christians who sin are in big trouble or not even believers is pure foolishness and hypocrisy. Christians who pretend sin is not commonplace even among true Christians have not understood what sin is, or are simply lying.

In a biblical, disciplinary church, people understand that all of us are in sin much of the time (James 3:2). But not all sin is alike. Unlike the Pharisees, who could see no difference between failure to tithe their spice boxes on one hand and failure to show love, justice, and mercy on the other, we realize some things constitute "the weightier provisions of the law" (Matthew 23:23). Yes, all sin is alike in that any sin would disqualify us from acceptance by a holy God apart from forgiveness. But all sin is not alike in the damage it does to the one sinning and to others in the area.

Discipline is usually unnecessary and inappropriate for minor problems that are so commonplace that God has to bring deliverance to believers at his own pace. Any effort to rush this process through criticizing people has little or no benefit and leads to a critical atmosphere in the church that breaks down community. The New Testament repeatedly teaches that we should be "showing tolerance for one another in love" (Ephesians 4:2). By far, for most sin we see in the body of Christ, we simply forbear, forgive, and ignore.

But that approach wouldn't be loving for other types of sin. Some sins are so damaging to the one committing them and to others that we need to intervene. This distinction may seem confusing. How do we decide? Where do we turn to learn what we should or should not confront? The basis for decision is this: What would be best for the one in sin and for the group?

In most cases, the answer is that forgiving and ignoring people's weaknesses is best because the sin involved is too trivial or unavoidable to worry about (like someone getting more heated than he should or saying something that seems boastful). At most, a comment once in awhile might be in order. This is why I will argue that students shouldn't be hassled about the way they talk or other slovenly or questionable aspects of their lives. They will naturally grow out of most of these problems if they are growing spiritually. In other cases, it becomes clear that the stakes are too high for that approach.

To summarize this point: discipline is not an effort to eliminate sin in the church—a forlorn project that would never work and shouldn't even be attempted. Instead, discipline is an effort to prevent significant damage in people's lives. It's an effort to replace sorrow and misery with happiness and purpose. Faulty definitions of sin lead to an atmosphere of picky legalism, while the biblical picture is of grace and caring love.

Love

Discipline is not rejection. According to God's word, discipline is an indispensable component of true love. God loves us, and he disciplines each and every one of us (Hebrews 12:6). Discipline means "training" and is linked to the idea of discipleship. True discipline has nothing to do with rejecting or judging people, but rather with helping them change. In the Old Testament, where discipline took different forms, we read, "You shall not hate your fellow countryman in your heart; you may surely reprove your neighbor, but shall not incur sin because of him. You shall not take vengeance, nor bear any grudge against the sons of your people, but you shall love your neighbor as yourself; I am the Lord" (Lev. 19:17-18). Here, as in the New Testament, failure to discipline is tantamount to a lack of love.

Leaders who turn away from discipline in the church simply do not love those caught up in sin enough to run the risks involved in every act of discipline. Neither do they love their groups enough to protect them from the devastating rot that takes over non-disciplining churches.

Community

Most Christians today accept the idea that a family might discipline one of its own. But discipline in the church seems like a different proposition. Many westerners think discipline is bizarre because they have both embraced individualism and have little real community in the body of Christ.

Under individualistic thinking, what I do in the privacy of my own home is none of the church's business. Even friends who would dare to criticize and confront sin in another's life are reminded to mind their own business. But in the body of Christ, others' lives *are* our business because "we are members of one another." If people want to live isolated lives where nobody intrudes into the privacy of their sin, they shouldn't become involved in a Christian community. Community and love become myths and dead letters any time we make our lives out of bounds to others in the group.

Lack of true community explains much of the lack of discipline in the church today. Ironically, failure to discipline also puts good community out of reach as we'll see. This whole teaching makes no sense in a group of disengaged modern pleasure seekers. How would we even know if someone had a problem? Such groups have never built the personal relationships between members that enable people to know what is going on in others' lives.

We've noticed multiple cases in recent years where couples in our church fall into fornication. Then they leave our church and begin attending an area mega-church where they know singles are free to fornicate and even live together, and nobody asks or cares about what they are doing. This is probably one of the big attractions some people feel to a church that is little more than a huge public worship where people are strangers to each other—the freedom to sin without anyone knowing or asking questions.

In a group where people take the New Testament vision for the church seriously, the opposite is true. I attend a home church of about thirty people where most of us know each other's problems. Members open up to each other, because that fits the atmosphere of supportive relationships in the group. The group has de-emphasized the values of privacy and confidentiality (without removing them in appropriate cases) while extolling the values of openness and transparency.

People in groups like this not only know each other's struggles, they know who is serious and who is faking it. The intimacy in a group of this kind is too great for anything major to fly under the radar for long. Those who are not trying are subject to loving discipline. And guess what? Their lives tend to change.

It's hardly surprising that people feel awkward about disciplining one another in a relationally disengaged group, but that's not an excuse; it's an admission of guilt.

Truth

One of the key reasons people in our world today reject the notion of discipline has to do with epistemology. To postmoderns, we have no universal standard for right and wrong, and even if there were such a thing, how could we ever know it? Since everything is interpretation and perception, we cannot know normative, objective truth. Anyone who thinks he knows how someone else should change his life is being arrogant, because he's just putting his own values over those of others.

This is not the position found in scripture.

Key passages

Jesus

Jesus initiated the idea of a disciplining church in Matthew 18:

> If your brother sins, go and show him his fault in private; if he listens to you, you have won your brother. But if he does not listen to you, take one or two more with you, so that by the mouth of two or three witnesses every fact may be confirmed. If he refuses to listen to them, tell it to the church; and if he refuses to listen even to the church, let him be to you as a Gentile and a tax collector (Matthew 18:15-17).

Jesus gave a three-stage scenario for confrontation, and ultimately, if none worked, they were to remove the person from their group. In their context, pagans and tax collectors were not admitted into believers' fellowship. Later commentary by Paul and John make clear that this is what Jesus meant.

Notice that the goal of discipline is to "win your brother." In most cases, we will win our brothers well before it comes to "telling it to the church."

Paul

Paul repeatedly refers to church discipline. The best-known passage is 1 Corinthians 5. There he rebukes the Corinthian group for tolerating flagrant immorality that even non-Christian communities wouldn't permit. He insists on immediate discipline, calling on them to give the man an ultimatum: Either change his ways, or leave the church (v. 5). This passage teaches that refusing to practice church discipline is a direct violation of the will of God (vs. 2, 12).

He had earlier written that they should "not associate with people who indulge in sexual sin" (v. 9). But he now wondered if they were confused, thinking he meant they should not hang around with non-Christian immoral people. That, he says, should be unthinkable—it would mean depriving the world of the light they need. No, he meant that unrepentant immoral "so-called" Christians should be removed from fellowship, for their own, and the group's good (vs. 9-12).

In 1 Timothy 1:20 Paul says he removed two false teachers until they learned not to blaspheme. He tells Titus to remove those who create factions in the church after a second warning (Titus 3:10; see also Romans 16:17). He makes numerous calls for lesser forms of discipline (2 Corinthians 7:8-12; Galatians 6:1; Colossians 3:16; 1 Thessalonians 5:14; 2 Thessalonians 3:6-15; 1 Timothy 5:1-2; 2 Timothy 2:24-26; 3:16,-17; Titus 1:13).

John

John has a short passage in 3 John where church discipline comes up.

> I wrote to the church about this, but Diotrephes, who loves to be the leader, refuses to have anything to do with us. When I come, I will report some of the things he is doing and the evil accusations he is making against us. Not only does he refuse to welcome the traveling teachers, he also tells others not to help them. And when they do help, he puts them out of the church (vs. 9-10 NLT).

Diotrephes gives us an example of a potential problem: misuse of church discipline. He was a dominator who was using church discipline to establish his power.

Church discipline could be misused in other ways as well. Personal bitterness, legalism, rejection of unseemly members, competition, or fear, could all be faulty motives for removing people from the church. In fact, fear of abusive church discipline is one of the reasons churches are reluctant to practice it—and especially to trust their members to have a part in it.

But that's not John's solution. He plans to come to the church in question and discipline Diotrephes himself. That's the right solution.

If people get out of line in the use of discipline, they, in turn, should be corrected. This could include removal from leadership positions. Adequate accountability systems should prevent abuse almost all the time.

John also recorded Jesus' praise for the Ephesians because they *did* practice church discipline (Revelations 2:2), as well as Jesus' rebuke to the church at Pergamum because they *weren't* practicing it (Revelations 2:14). He called on them to "Repent of your sin" (v. 16), and he rebuked the church at Thyatira for the same thing (v. 20). Practicing church discipline is not optional, according to Jesus.

Lesser types of discipline

According to Jesus, anyone who learns someone has a sin problem should confront the person privately. This is not a matter for church leaders any more than other members. But if the first "reproof" doesn't work (in that the person either doesn't agree that there is a problem, or refuses to consider change), others come into the process. This might be a good time to involve an older Christian whom the one in sin respects. Having two or three fellow Christians sit you down and carefully reprove you in love is a powerful force for persuasion.

We saw earlier that Paul thought all believers are "able also to admonish one another" (Romans 15:14). When members come to complain to leaders about others in the group who are in sin, those leaders do well to send them back to admonish those they believe are in sin, rather than fostering a "tattle-tale" ethos, where the leaders solve the problem for them. When believers complain to leaders and the leaders do the admonishing, those leaders perpetuate immaturity in their members. The members are supposed to be learning how to work with people, and that includes admonition. By coaching and insisting that Christians take the first try at correcting problems, leaders impart field training on how to sensitively but firmly call others to change. We should only excuse very young Christians from taking such responsibility. For young believers, the best experience is going with an older believer to see how reproof in love works.

Approaching a fellow believer about a sin problem should be

something all Christians do from time to time. Paul urges, "Brethren, even if anyone is caught in any trespass, you who are spiritual, restore such a one in a spirit of gentleness; each one looking to yourself, so that you too will not be tempted" (Galatians 6:1). Christians who learn how to gently appeal to others, using compelling reasons, positive ideas for how to change, and vision for the better life change will bring, gain valuable relational skills that will enhance the rest of their lives.

Admonition and reproof don't always work. Sometimes people are simply unwilling to change, and this may have nothing to do with how you spoke or what you said. People are free-choosing beings, not machines, so we shouldn't feel too disappointed when people refuse to listen to even a carefully-worded appeal.

But what next? That depends. With minor issues, perhaps nothing. We can pray for the person and wait for God's Spirit to bring in more conviction. Maybe we'll bring the issue up again sometime. But in some cases the sin involved is serious enough to do substantial damage to that person or to others. In these cases, the church has to be willing to take things to the next level.

Extreme discipline

Removal from Christian fellowship is extreme discipline that should be reserved for severe cases. This step is to be taken only when all else fails.

When is it appropriate?

Extreme cases are those where people are involved in damaging sin and usually that sin is part of a lifestyle of disregard for God's will, not just a fall from grace.

Paul points to the kinds of sin calling for removal from fellowship in 1 Corinthians 5:11: "I wrote to you not to associate with any so-called brother if he is an immoral person, or covetous, or an idolater, or a reviler, or a drunkard, or a swindler."

At the head of the list is "sexual immorality." All kinds of sexual misbehavior could be included in this term. "Covetous" people are apparently engaged in extreme materialism or greed—and perhaps urging their views on others. "Idol worship" was the main religious alternative to following Jesus, and could imply other forms of non-Christian religion or false teaching as well. Paul says elsewhere that he removed false teachers from fellowship (1 Timothy 1:20). "Revilers" are those who verbally attack others in the church and are probably linked to those who foment division (Titus 3:10). "Swindlers" would be those who steal, con, or in other ways defraud and cheat people. 2 Thessalonians 3:6-15 indicates that those who refuse to work and instead bum money and food from others are in this category. Some churches hold that unrighteous divorce could amount to swindling by breaking the marriage vows.

Since the sins mentioned in the various passages about removal from fellowship never match those in other discussions, we must assume these lists are representative, not exhaustive. Therefore, other sins could also call for extreme discipline. For instance, physical assaults, child abuse, spousal physical abuse, or disruption of meetings are not mentioned but could probably also be considered serious enough to call for removal because of the danger these behaviors pose to members.

Everyone comes

Both Jesus and Paul make it clear that the whole community is to be involved in this form of discipline (1 Corinthians 5:4 "when you are assembled"). Excluding a person from fellowship in the body of Christ is painful, both for the one excluded and for the church. But real love requires the willingness to do the right thing for people even if it hurts. This form of discipline involves adding social pressure to pleas and persuasion.

The errant brother or sister should be called to meet with the church to hear their admonition and their ultimatum. Unless the person is willing to repent convincingly, he or she will not be allowed to come to gatherings of the church. At a meeting of this kind, all the person's friends should speak their protests, and the person should be able to respond. After a full discussion, the church has to decide whether to relent and leave the errant one in fellowship or call on him or her to leave. Jesus says the key to this decision is whether the group believes the person "refuses to listen even to the church" (Matthew 18:17).

Why does the Bible call on everyone to be there for such a confrontation, instead of letting the leaders handle it? One reason is that the whole community learns something at such meetings. An experience like this reminds everyone from the youngest Christians to the oldest that God's will matters and that sin destroys lives.

Groups who have had to discipline a member in this way are marked by the experience in a positive way. Leaders repeatedly report that morale and seriousness for the things of God rise noticeably after such meetings. Younger believers come away realizing, "So, they're not kidding." I have personally talked to a number of believers who said they attended a disciplinary meeting while in secret sin of their own and decided then and there that things had to change.

Some complain that a corporate confrontation would create fear, and fear is not a good motive for leaving off sin. But Paul doesn't seem to agree. He says in 1 Timothy 5:20 that elders who continue in sin should be rebuked "in the presence of all, so that the rest also will be fearful of sinning." Obviously, fear isn't the best motive for moving away from sin, but going on in sin could be even worse if the sin is damaging. We're not always in a position to wait for perfect motives when it comes to life change in key areas.

A meeting like this is a chance to explain to the whole group why real love is disciplinary and what the Bible teaches on this subject. By making it clear that everyone's voice matters in this decision, even young believers come to understand the importance of their roles in the church.

Another reason for bringing everyone together is that the combined voice of the group caries more weight than that of only a person or two. People in sin are usually deceived and can dismiss the admonition of close friends, or even a whole leadership team, thinking that those people just have an attitude problem or personal animosity. But dismissing the word of one's entire group of friends is harder to rationalize. When the whole community confronts a sinful believer, chances are good that he or she might break and repent and the matter can be laid to rest with forgiveness and reconciliation. If not, then at least the person will remember how all his or her friends agreed with what happened. That makes it harder for Satan to convince him that there was nothing wrong with him.

Disciplinary meetings are for believers only, and usually just those who know the people involved. This suggests that house churches or other smaller groups are the right venue for such meetings, maybe at a special time when non-Christian guests won't be confronted with family business they cannot understand or appreciate.

Deciding

When the Corinthians removed one of their own, Paul later said, "Sufficient for such a one is this punishment which was inflicted by the majority" (2 Corinthians 2:6). Apparently, they determined somehow that the majority of those present believed removal was appropriate. Perhaps they voted, or it may have been an emerging consensus that was obvious. I've seen both approaches work well. Of course, if the leaders call for a show of hands, they have to honor whatever decision the group makes.

In most churches, the top leadership needs to be involved in making an important decision like this. In ours, home churches need agreement from the elders before they call a group discipline meeting. This is a safeguard against improper discipline.

After discipline

The point of removal from fellowship is to create a situation where the person is no longer able to enjoy sin while at the same time drawing relational support from the church. This is why Paul and Jesus call people to not associate with them after removal, even in non-fellowship situations. Paul says "not even to eat with such a one" (1 Corinthians 5:11b). Those who oppose the idea of church discipline like to call this "shunning." But the point is not to shun the person. In another passage Paul says, "Yet do not regard him as an enemy, but admonish him as a brother" (1 Thess 3:16). So, people can talk to the removed member, and should not project hostility if they run into the person.

On the other hand, going out to fool around with someone under discipline would be counter-productive and in fact unloving. If the person needs discipline, then allowing him or her to continue enjoying fellowship and closeness with believers would only tend to make the discipline less effective. If a removed brother wanted to meet and talk, that's fine, but the talk should include where he stands with regard to his problem and whether he is ready to change his mind.

Restoration

Extreme discipline works to change lives in a high percentage of cases, provided the community from which he or she was removed is warm, loving, and deep. I would estimate that a majority of those removed from our church end up returning, usually with a whole new outlook. Even several leaders in our church remember the key turning point in their lives as the time when fellow believers finally drew the line through this kind of discipline. Until this happened, they never took their problems seriously.

Even in cases where people never return, the church itself receives blessing. Instead of "a little leaven leavening the whole lump," the church learns a key lesson: that living for God is a serious matter, and not a game of "let's pretend."

Criteria

Different groups have different criteria for returning to fellowship, and different decision-making processes. Usually, the leadership has to agree that the person is ready to return. Since the goal of the whole process is to have the person return with a changed heart, this decision is important. In our church, home church leaders are empowered to receive back someone under discipline at their own discretion. But we also teach them what to look for.

In the biblical case mentioned earlier, Paul later says the Corinthians should receive the disciplined man back because the discipline was "sufficient" (2 Corinthians 2:5) and there was a danger that the man would be "overwhelmed by excessive sorrow" (2 Corinthians 2:7). We can reasonably conclude that the man had demonstrated repentance, as indicated by his sorrow. Although many commentators think this is a different man, I think it was more likely the same man mentioned in 1 Corinthians.[84]

Leaders often engage in a running dialog with someone who wants to return to fellowship. They may want to counsel the person, and they definitely want to understand what has changed in the person's outlook and actions. They may prescribe an ongoing plan of restoration that could include some accountability, counseling, or other agreements.

The last time I had a friend come back after a two-year excursion into the world, I asked him to come to our prayer meeting and explain to the home church what had happened. He was nervous about that, but he came and had a wonderful, warm, welcoming talk with the group where tears were shed. It got him started on the right foot—transparency, humility, and honesty. Today he leads a home church.

Cases like that are very encouraging to the church. They realize that by taking a firm stand they did the right thing and rescued a brother from a highly destructive way of life. By refusing to be a "soft" church, they showed real love.

---

[84]This debate turns on whether 2 Corinthians 2:3-4 and 7:1-13 refer to Paul's second lost letter to the Corinthians, or whether he is referring to 1 Corinthians in these passages. If the latter, then the only lost letter was the one written before 1 Corinthians (1 Corinthians 5:9). I believe the burden of evidence is on the theory that yet another letter was written between First and Second Corinthians, since we have no definite evidence that such a letter ever existed. The only arguments for a fourth letter stem from commentators' sense that references to the severe letter don't fit 1 Corinthians. I think they could fit, and I see no compelling reason why Paul's "painful letter" could not refer to 1 Corinthians. Most of the case for denying this possibility rests on language about the man under church discipline in Chapter 2, arguing that it could not be the same man referred to in 1 Corinthians 5 and in fact refers to a different episode that came up after Paul wrote 1 Corinthians and before he wrote a now-lost letter. Other critics claim the "painful letter" has been partially or fully spliced into 2 Corinthians at chapters 10-13. The discussion is too complicated to unfold here, but I would simply point out that even advocates admit their scenarios are only tentative and rest on some speculation. I find it unconvincing on multiple grounds, not least of which is the history of higher critical source division that originally gave rise to this view. These source divisions are based on the thinnest subjective impressions and have no documentary basis. For examples of commentators arguing for a second lost letter see Paul Barnett, The Message of 2 Corinthians: Power in weakness, in The Bible speaks today, (Leicester, England; Downers Grove, Ill., USA: Inter-Varsity Press, 1988). Also Ralph P. Martin, 2 Corinthians, Word Biblical Commentary, Vol. 40 which gives a full discussion of the history of source division and criticism of 2 Corinthians in his introduction. For a view similar to mine, see Donald Guthrie, "2 Corinthians" in *New Testament Introduction*, (Downer's Grove: IVP Academic, 1990).

Leaders and discipline

Leaders in the body of Christ are subject to discipline just like others in the church, and even more than others. James' statement that teachers "receive stricter judgment" (3:1) probably refers to a higher standard that leaders should be held to. In 1 Timothy 5:19, Paul puts the burden of proof on members when an elder and a member contradict. However, when two or more members agree that an elder is in sin, he gets the same discipline as anyone else (1 Timothy 5:20).

Removal from leadership is often appropriate whenever leaders fail to live up to the leadership requirements we saw earlier, but that should normally be after a warning and a chance to correct the problem. Only cases of totally discrediting sin would call for immediate and unquestioning removal.

Remember, church leaders are public figures. That means they stand under a different standard than others (James 3:1). When a leader is removed for moral reasons, the church should be frankly informed of the reasons (perhaps minus the gory details). I know of some remarkable cases where leadership colleagues agreed to a confidentiality policy when removing a fellow-leader, only to bitterly regret it later when the removed leader had more credibility with people than he would if they had told the truth. Paul's call for public disclosure upon removal of a leader is a wise provision we ignore at our own peril.

During my time as a Christian I've seen several situations where a beloved leader fell into serious sin and his colleagues would not remove him from leadership or only secretly reduced his duties. This failure to discipline is usually at least partly due to self-serving reasons (the ministry would suffer too much if the leader's sin became public). People in decision-making positions may not even realize their thinking is being influenced wrongly because they are so used to being loyal to the leader in question. But when the truth later comes out (usually after further serious sin) and people find out that the organization knew about the problem earlier and took half measures, the disgrace becomes very discrediting. The Catholic

Church recently became a public demonstration of how wrong it is to overlook serious sin in its pedophilia scandal.

The temptation to take it easy on prominent leaders must have been behind the strong language Paul used with Timothy when discussing the need to discipline elders: "I solemnly charge you in the presence of God and of Christ Jesus and of His chosen angels, to maintain these principles without bias, doing nothing in a spirit of partiality (1 Timothy 5:21).

The big picture

Discipline is love. Discipline is integrity. Discipline leads to health in the church. While most of our interactions should be positive and formal discipline is the exception, we should care enough about our people to discipline them when necessary, just like the early church did. We should also be willing to submit to discipline ourselves. If you build in an ethos of loving discipline, your vision of a community with high motivation and spiritual living can shift from fantasy to reality.

A local church's willingness or refusal to discipline its own members determines whether it will be a "soft" group. Soft, undisciplined groups lose their ability to accomplish God's mission. They come to believe that sins of omission and low-commitment are the norm, and even accept the presence of flagrant sin with a helpless feeling. Real, exciting spirituality in the body of Christ seems like an unrealistic dream. Consumer Christianity takes over.

The leadership in groups like these often tries to keep attention focused on the front stage (with shows, sermons, and media) as people in the group carefully avert their gaze from each other— everyone knows they are faking it, but nobody wants to look at that. Leaders of undisciplined groups know they have to do everything because they can't count on their people for anything. In groups that go soft, leaders even create their people's excuses for them, constantly talking about how you can't expect too much from people today.

Soft groups usually can't operate a successful network of home groups because the groups have no good way to deal with the problem people that ruin the experience for everyone. Undisciplined groups might see some successful evangelism, but will quickly lose those people. Only well-disciplined groups are effective at ongoing follow up and discipleship of new converts.

Only deeply held biblical convictions will give a modern western church the courage to practice church discipline faithfully. This is a quintessential example of how a group's theology determines the quality of their lives together. Because so many judgment calls are involved, weak groups can always convince themselves that they are okay, even though they are incredibly soft by biblical standards. Strong, loving groups, on the other hand, are filled with people who enjoy the happiness of good community and the significance that comes from accomplishing God's will (John 4:34).

Chapter Twenty-One

Student Ministry

The western church today is facing an unprecedented crisis involving our own kids. Although Jesus said, "Let the children alone, and do not hinder them from coming to me; for the kingdom of heaven belongs to such as these (Matthew 19:14)," children in evangelical churches are losing all vitality and interest in their faith. Josh McDowell's recent book title, *The Last Christian Generation*, warns that the loss among students is so severe that we could well be the last generation of Christians in the west. Whether that is true remains to be seen, but the massive recent "National Study of Youth and Religion" showed incredible apathy in young people's version of "faith." Dean explains:

> Time and time again in our interviews, we met young people who called themselves Christians, who grew up with Christian parents, who were regular participants in Christian congregations, yet who had no readily accessible faith vocabulary, few recognizable faith practices, and little ability to reflect on their lives religiously.[85]

---

[85]Kenda Creasy Dean, *Almost Christian, 16*. Not pulling any punches, she points out, "The problem does not seem to be that churches are teaching young people badly, but that we are doing an exceedingly good job of teaching youth what we really believe: namely, that Christianity is not a big deal, that God requires little, and the church is a helpful social institution filled with nice people focused primarily on 'folks like us'—which, of course, begs the question of whether we are really the church at all." 11, 12.

That may not be what church people want to hear, but the problem is real. The data on this is convincing.[86] Thom Rainer says over 70 percent leave the church around the time they go to college and most never return. McDowell says it's closer to 90 percent. Rainer says,

> The average church is losing the young generation, and those young adults are not returning... Perhaps most startling is the gravity of how many exit the church and the pace at which this exodus is occurring. Each generation that passes loses more than the previous generation. Shock does not begin to describe how we felt after reading the research results. The church is losing the generational battle. Not only are we losing our nation to the ways of the world, but we are not winning our own children in Christian families. Multitudes are dropping out of church.[87]

His explanation for this exodus is exactly right in my opinion:

> The most glaring issue of estrangement for eighteen- to twenty-two-year-olds is the interminable gap between their personal beliefs and their church's stated beliefs... Only 53 percent of all young adult churchgoers state that they are in line with the beliefs of their church. To be blunt, God has *converted* our children, but we have failed to *disciple* them.[88]

It would be easy to write a soothing chapter on how these problems aren't that bad, and we're really doing alright after all. We could always claim that the kids will be back when they grow up, and a few probably will. But on the whole, such a chapter would be

---

[86]This is true, notwithstanding Bradey Wright's efforts to show that church young people are doing fine. His faulty conclusions result from his dependence on the National Social Survey's category of "affiliation"—a nearly meaningless category that would suggest over 80 percent of Americans are Christians. Bradey Wright, *Christians Are Hate-Filled Hypocrites ...and Other Lies You've Been Told*. (Bethany House, 2010).

[87]Thom S. Rainer, *Essential Church : Reclaiming a Generation of Dropouts*, (Nashville: B&H Publishing, 2009) 8, 14. His findings are based on a nationwide, scientifically controlled survey.

[88]Thom S. Rainer, *Essential Church*, 30.

a big lie. The truth is this: The western church is facing a crisis today unlike anything in memory.

The good news is that it doesn't have to be this way.

One of the biggest questions facing serious Christians today is who to believe when it comes to student ministry. Some of the "experts" writing on this subject today have failed to show the ability to win significant numbers of non-Christian students or to deliver student Christians into adulthood as fired-up, zealous Christian servants. Christian readers need to carefully distinguish between theorists with no valid fruit and those leaders who actually know what they are talking about.[89] If we limited who we consider credible to speak on this subject to people who have actually lead successful student ministries, including reaching significant numbers of non-Christian students and delivering good numbers of qualified, motivated students into adult ministry, our reading lists could be reduced by ninety percent.

I have wrestled with this issue in recent years as I watched my own church's student component dwindle almost to the vanishing point, just like those in most western churches. But today this situation has turned around amazingly. Through a concerted effort of the whole church, we went from a few dozen students in the nineties to two thousand today. The majority of them are converts who did not grow up in our church.

We, too, have lost some of our own kids, but the overwhelming majority are fired up for God and reaching large numbers of their non-Christian peers. Instead of straining to join their peers' world,

---

[89] I'm not going to go into detail on this point for the sake of peace. Suffice it to say that our studies of student ministries nationwide indicate that most of those attending (over 90 percent) are only the children of church members, and even these are far less numerous than they should be based on the size of the churches in question. Probably the biggest fraud today (that deserves to be named) is the emergent church movement with its claims that postmodern young people will only respond to gimmicky, strange worship experiences and postmodern theology that denies objective truth. These groups are the weakest ones we have studied. The idea that secular student-aged people would respond to walking around with candles chanting is absurd according to the students I work with. I think the fact that emergent groups fail a pragmatic test [i.e. that they are unsuccessful at reaching postmodern young people] is important, because they advance a pragmatic definition for truth ("what works for me"). These groups are usually mostly disgruntled church kids trying to do something 'cool.' Groups we have seen that are actually penetrating secular student culture today are those with a strong ministry of the word (understood as the authoritative word of God) and good discipleship.

these kids are intent on giving up worldly advantage in order to live for God. We have planted scores of student home churches, mostly led by highly committed, well-trained students.

None of this has been easy. Student ministry today is tough. We're swimming directly upstream against a very fast current when we call young people to forsake the sensuality and materialism of the world and live for Christ. Half-measures will never work in this environment. Unless the western church wakes up to the emergency facing her, the future looks dreadful.

Positive vision

What if most kids in the local church and even more of their formerly non-Christian peers sold themselves out for lives of Christian service? What if they not only continued successfully in school, but added hundreds of hours of Christian class work in addition, just so they could teach and lead more effectively? What if 90 percent of them either spent time each week being personally discipled or discipling others? What if they were doing all this, not in their own Christian schools or home schooling, but in the midst of hard-core, secular high school and university life?

All of this is possible. I know it is, because we see it every day in the ministry where I work. Keeping up with the demands of these students for training and expansion takes everything we have to give. I can look around at our student facility on campus at The Ohio State University any afternoon of the week and see dozens of them meeting together with Bibles and books open, or bent over their tables in prayer. A steady stream of conversion stories flows into the student email group—several every week. I have them calling and emailing me for advice about complicated ministry situations daily. I see a joy and excitement in their faces; these kids are thrilled that they can build up the body of Christ.

Any church that sees a student awakening like this can expect a positive future. Less than one person in twenty move away from Columbus after college. The reason? They want to stay and continue to build their ministries in our church—now contributing to adult ministry in growing numbers.

Why isn't this scenario more common in today's western church? Consider these changes that could lead to successful student ministry:

Raise the value placed on student ministry: Western churches place more value on winning adults. You see this from their budgetary expenditures, staffing priorities, and insistence that student ministry fit in with what the main body of the church is already doing. Adults send their own kids away to college, heedless of whether they will be engaged in quality fellowship there. "Oh, I'm sure there are Christians there," says the worldy-minded parent who hasn't spent a single minute researching the Christian scene at the coveted school. Rainer reports,

> "Most churches do not have a college and career ministry for young adults between the ages of eighteen and twenty-two. And the reason is not because these churches are located outside of college towns. Ten percent of the population in the United States is between the ages of eighteen and twenty-four. That's more than thirty million student-age people!"[90]

Doesn't this reveal a lack of value placed on student ministry? Church leaders tell me they don't push for a college-aged ministry because most of their students plan to go away to college. But should we accept this American assumption as normative for the church? Why don't church leaders, especially in large cities, challenge their students to consider staying in town so they can continue to be equipped and build their ministries? Too often, this is a nonsense question because the students have no ministry to continue building. At the same time, church leaders don't want to anger their members by suggesting that something is more important than career.

---

[90]Thom and Sam Rainer, *Essential Church*, 81. Barna says, "The most potent data...is that a majority of twentysomethings – 61% of today's young adults – had been churched at one point during their teen years but they are now spiritually disengaged (i.e., not actively attending church, reading the Bible, or praying). George Barna, "Most Twentysomethings Put Christianity on the Shelf Following Spiritually Active Teen Years," September 11, 2006.

If a church truly raised their estimate of student ministry's importance, they might end up with a situation like mine: I'm the senior pastor in my church, and the chairman of our board of elders. I've served in this church longer than any other person, and my income from the church is equal to the highest level we pay. But my main focus today is on student ministry. How often have you seen that? I have never seen it, and I study many churches. It doesn't happen because most churches would never consider releasing their top leader from working with adults in order to immerse himself into student work. If you want success in student ministry, you have to be prepared to release your best leaders into that field.

Mobilized Adults:
Our success with students begins with our adult membership. Adults in Xenos really believe in the value of reaching and discipling students. They almost always find a way to fund any need we present. They have sent not only me, but also some of their other top leaders into this field. This would be rare in other churches.

Instead, the usual practice is to hire green seminarians for youth ministry at less than a quarter of what their lead pastor makes. Maybe this is partly because they are young, and seem to be more culturally close to students. But whenever they are successful at student ministry the next step is normally to graduate up into adult ministry, usually with a big raise. Other churches leave almost all student ministries to volunteers.

Our crisis
In the '90s, our elders commissioned a group of us to study what had gone wrong with student ministry in our church. In the '70s Xenos had started as a student movement. But by the '90s our stake in high school and college ministry had dwindled from several hundred to a few dozen students.

When we studied the situation, we agreed that the number one priority for our church for the next few years should be student ministry. The elders commissioned me along with some others to find a student harvest before it was too late. The church moved student ministry spending to the front burner. They committed to give us whatever we needed to get the job done, and every group put student outreach on their prayer lists. Later, they reinforced us with additional adult workers. At one point, most of our elders were working in student ministry (some have now returned to adult ministry). Today we have are approaching two thousand high school and college students in our ministry. When adults place high value on reaching the young, good things can happen.

Why would some churches place a low value on reaching and discipling students? I can't be sure. If a church expects to grow by bringing in professionals, building buildings, or running good programs, then reaching and developing students doesn't matter. On the other hand, groups who believe the key to success is developing their own workers usually realize that nobody is more likely to become a quality servant of God than a well-discipled student. Possibly, increased income for the church could have something to do with the low value placed on reaching students. Adding adults adds to the budget. Adding students *detracts* from the budget. Probably churches that under-value student ministry either are unaware or don't care that most people who convert to Christianity do so during their teen years.[91]

Students have their whole lives ahead of them. They are in position to marry someone who shares their desire to serve God. For this reason alone, many of them will escape the trap of "unequally yoked" marriages (where one spouse is eager for the things of God and the other is reluctant). Students have the time to undergo extensive equipping. We believe the students we work with today will be here ten and twenty years from now—still bearing fruit, still winning others, still leading (just like those we worked with twenty years ago).

That makes student ministry a highly strategic and important

---

[91]"Starbuck noted that the average age of a person experiencing a religious conversion was 15.6 years. Other studies have produced similar results; as recently as 1979, Virgil Gillespie wrote that the average age of conversion in America is 16 years." January (Web-only) Larry Poston, "CT Classic: The Adult Gospel" January, 2002, Vol. 46.

effort in the church. Our adult members have concluded that this ministry is so important to the future of our church that almost any sacrifice is justified.

In many churches, people view their students (especially the older ones) as a nuisance rather than an asset. When students show up looking like hoodlums and freaks, many adult congregations feel annoyed. Their raw language and disrespectful behavior inspires outright contempt in the minds of many church people.

Age Appropriateness

To reach and disciple large numbers of students, leadership has to correctly match their approach to the students' age. According to my observations, most churches use curriculum and programs that are below the intellectual level of secondary and college students. The material is over-simplified and uninteresting compared to the complex material they study at school. I don't remember ever being challenged intellectually at church when I was a teenager, and I'm afraid this may be often be true today as well. I believe students are smart and completely able to handle any material adults can.

Purpose

If we want to win and develop students, we need to intentionally train them and link them up with significant ministry. If we ask ourselves "How often are students in western churches personally discipled over a several-year period?" the answer is usually, "Never." We should be asking other questions as well. Has church leadership designed training specifically for students? Have students been trained to lead their own groups? Are students in western churches just as competent in using the word and teaching as adults? Do adults come alongside students to help them win their peers at school? Do adults host student groups in their homes for years without interruption? Does the church publicly honor students' accomplishments in ministry? In the church I attended as a young teen, I remember students being publicly praised for becoming the valedictorian of their class or for being accepted to Harvard, but never for doing anything in ministry.

Students want purpose in their lives. As the church, we either show them real purpose in serving God with their lives, or they will find purpose elsewhere. If we don't want students who live for excelling in career and worldly prestige, we have to give them an alternative.

Showing Respect

Students want to be treated and viewed like adults. Maybe they aren't exactly adults yet, but they want to be treated that way. I think we should try to go along with that. I have seen youth groups where students get ordered around, publicly rebuked, or controlled in ways the leaders would never try with fellow adults. The resulting resentment from students is predictable.

I meet with a number of students every week, and I actually treat and view them as adults. They insult me and joke around with me as if I were one of their peers. They know they don't have to launch into some kind of special behavior when I'm around. At the same time, they know I view them as being capable of transforming the world. They know I think the work they do is some of the best Christian work going on in our city. The way they share their faith, devote themselves to following up with new believers, counsel and help fellow believers, and do quality discipleship—it measures up with any work going on in our church or other churches. Even when they make mistakes, they're usually teachable. They also know I admire their heroic stand against temptation, which is often more intense at their age than at any other time in life.

Discipleship

No group in the church is more receptive to personal disciple making than students. They appreciate someone spending time with them, and are willing to study and work to become well-equipped workers. Many churches devote little to nothing to this project, which I find baffling. If we only have a short time to prepare students for the power of the world in high school and college, why wouldn't we be earnest to see most of them discipled as much as possible? After all, these include our own children.

Instead, we often find the galling belief that students must be controlled or entertained rather than discipled. Entertainment is light fare that won't really equip people to withstand the world or to excel in ministry. The idea that entertainment could hold students in loyalty to God constitutes a low view of students (not to mention an underestimation of the world's appeal). Consider these findings from Thom Ranier's nationwide survey of evangelical churches:

> While most students are participating in church activities, relatively few have actual responsibilities in their church... The church that teaches and disciples all teens to think outwardly has a much better chance of retaining them inwardly... Activity alone is not adequate. Participation did not help keep college students in the church. This group must be given responsibilities and leadership. Most important, the church should be obedient about teaching them one of its essential functions: reaching outward into the community and the world through giving, service, and missions.[92]

Cultural tolerance

If we want to reach significant numbers of students, we will have to let meetings get outside church culture and into contemporary culture. Just as missionaries work within other cultures without calling on them to adopt western culture, we have to work within student culture. We cannot call on them to adopt a church culture radically different than their own; that would be attaching cultural baggage to the gospel (see 1 Corinthians 9:19-23).

In traditional cultures, teenage rebellion is virtually unknown. Think about that. Teenagers accept their rites of passage and their village's belief systems without question. Yet in the west, teenagers frequently rebel against their parents' beliefs and practices. Nowhere is this more evident than in the evangelical and fundamentalist

---

[92]Thom S. Rainer and Sam S. Rainer, *Essential Church?* 85, 86, 87.

church. Today, experts say the overwhelming majority of youth in evangelical churches are disgruntled or simply don't care. Why this difference?

People sense it has something to do with media, and that's true. Media in the west facilitates rapid distribution of new styles, ideas, and beliefs. Unlike traditional villages, western culture changes rapidly. Most traditional cultures are the same as they have been for centuries. The parents' culture and their kids' culture are the same. Our culture changes so rapidly that parents and kids find themselves in very different worlds.

My hippie culture was nothing like my parents' post World War II culture. My kids' punk rock and indie rock culture are nothing like mine. This is a setting waiting for friction. Styles of dress, hairstyles, views on education, musical taste, and views about society, God, and the church are all different. What music should we play when driving together? What am I supposed to say when my son comes home with a Mohawk and wearing chains and silver studs? Many of the students I work with identify with hip-hop culture, wearing the sagging pants, using strange expressions, and reciting lengthy profane raps they all seem to know by heart.

Christians sometimes wring their hands over situations like these and bluster against the vileness of western culture today. They often demand that kids not listen to what's happening culturally, hoping to keep them from being influenced by their own culture. In fact, this has been the church's strategy during every major cultural shift for the past hundred years. My grandmother's church viewed the advent of brassieres as scandalous—I guess they considered wearing bras to be a tawdry attempt to show off one's breasts. Today that sounds funny, but not then. I'm afraid some of our current efforts to oppose cultural features will sound just as funny in a few years.

Instead, we should embrace the New Testament position on culture: "Each of you should continue to live in whatever situation the Lord has placed you, and remain as you were when God first called you... For instance, a man who was circumcised before he became a believer should not try to reverse it. And the man who was uncircumcised when he became a believer should not be circumcised now" (1 Corinthians 7:17-18 NLT). The New Testament Jews had terrific difficulty accepting that Greco-Romans didn't need to change their culture when following Jesus. Their culture was raw, sinful, and godless. How could Paul say they shouldn't change?

They did have to change some things, but Jesus is trans-cultural. People should mainly follow him within their own culture. They are not to form a Christian sub-culture. To do so would compromise their ability to win others from that culture, just as it has today.

We should, however, teach students to engage in a vigorous critique of their culture and its lostness. They should be able to articulate what is wrong with the way their friends live and why they aren't going there. But the critique is in the area of values and moral issues, not with their music, cinema, dress, or language. Christians should be counter-cultural when it comes to beliefs, values, and moral qualities, but pro-cultural on externals.

Responding to materialistic values

Studies show that the millennial generation is more responsive to their parents than previous generations. Most say their parents are their best friends. They are eager to please their parent or parents and feel no urge to rebel. They find it difficult to imagine refusing their parents' requests. They are the best educated and most numerous generation ever.[93] This could be a great opportunity to develop the most powerful generation of Christian workers ever.

Unfortunately, Christian parents may not be taking advantage of this chance to promote spiritual living. Increasingly during the past decade, parents, including Christian parents, seem more intent on turning their kids into successful worldlings than vital Christians. Those of us in youth work today are repeatedly seeing something we used to see only from non-Christian parents: Christian parents pushing their kids toward academic and sports achievements even at

---

[93]While Boomers numbered 78 million, Millennials number 95 million. Eric Greenberg and Karl Weber, *Generation We: How Millennial Youth are Taking Over America and Changing the World*, (Emeryville, CA: Pachatusan, 2008) Chapter 2.

the direct expense of their spiritual lives. This is part of a well-documented cultural shift in America during the past decade or so.[94] So the people of God are resisting the externals of their kids' culture (like dirty music), but they have not recognized the problems with their own culture, especially careerism.

Student workers today regularly see situations where kids who were responding well to the things of God suddenly don't have time for fellowship. The reason? They have gone out for several sports, music lessons, and some extra "enrichment" camps or groups, are pushing for a 4.0 grade average in advanced placement courses (hoping to get a college scholarship), and have to stay home and study. There isn't much time left over for the people of God.

Sadly, some Christian parents are the ones pushing for this frantic quest for worldly success. At other times, the parents aren't pushing for advancement in the world, but they see it happening and have no problem with it. We hear too few Christian parents saying kids should moderate their pursuit of worldly success in favor of excelling spiritually. In fact, that concept draws baffled stares from an increasing number of Christian parents. "What, so Christian kids are supposed to grow up and be ditch-diggers?" Such black-and-white thinking signals a dishonest effort to spin the discussion into extremes.

Both Christian and secular sociologists have demonstrated that the new urgency for kids' success is damaging to kids. The kids succeed, but they are not happy. Affluent, driven kids have more

---

[94]Christian leaders and parents owe it to themselves to read this literature. Unfortunately, I found few Christian titles on this subject, which is indicative of the relative silence with which Christians have answered this shift. The only title I've seen is the recent: Ann Kroeker, *Not So Fast: Slow-Down Solutions for Frenzied Families*, (David C. Cook publishers, 2009). Her perspective focuses on what is good for the family, more than the spiritual imperative. From a secular perspective, see Madeline Levine, *The Price of Privilege: How Parental Pressure and Material Advantage Are Creating a Generation of Disconnected and Unhappy Kids*, (San Francisco: HarperCollins, 2006). Alexandra Robbins, *The Overachievers: The Secret Lives of Driven Kids*, (New York: Hyperion Books, 2006), Denise Clark Pope, *Doing School: How We Are Creating a Generation of Stressed-Out, Materialistic, and Miseducated Students*, (New Haven, CT: Yale University Press, 2003), Susan Gregory Thomas, *Buy, Buy Baby: How Consumer Culture Manipulates Parents and Harms Young Minds*, (New York: Houghton Mifflin,2007), Alissa Quart, *Hothouse Kids: The Dilemma of the Gifted Child*, (New York: Penguin, 2007), Mihaly Csikszentmihalyi, "If we are so rich, why aren't we happy?" *American Psychologist* 1999; Vol. 54:821–827, and Susan Gilbert, "For some children, it's an after-school pressure cooker," *New York Times*, 1999 August 3:F7.

angst, use drugs more, commit suicide more, and report less happiness than lower performing kids. One study convincingly shows that these driven "hot house kids" are even worse off psychologically than were a control group of inner city kids.[95] While even secular news analysts and books are raising the alarm on the dramatic trend toward encouraging kids' constant non-stop pursuit of worldly goals, the Christian world has been largely silent on this issue.

The strange paradox is that American Christians are anti-cultural when it comes to cultural expressions opposed to the American dream, but they have no critique of mainstream "straight" culture, intent on the pursuit of materialistic success. But when you think about it, Satan uses obsession with success in the world to compromise Christians' walks more than any other thing.

We should be calling our kids to devote time and mental energy to the things of God and pursuing progress in sports and career with whatever time is left over. Students who take this approach in our ministry are plenty successful, earning bachelors and graduate degrees and landing good jobs. The question of whether they got a consistent 3.8 or higher in high school or whether they won the championship in soccer never comes up in later life. But the spiritual life and relationships they develop become the center pieces of their lives.

Even marriage has to take a back seat to material success in today's evangelical churches. Sociologist Mark Regnerus points out that evangelicals "advise our children to finish their education, to launch their careers, and to become financially independent" before marrying. As a result, Christian young people marry late, just like secular people, and almost like secular culture, 80 percent of evangelical young people fall into sexual immorality before marriage (compared to 90 percent for non-Christians).[96] Here again, some

---

[95]From the previous footnote, Madeline Levine's and Allissa Quart's books amply demonstrate this point.

[96]Mark Regnerus, "The Case for Early Marriage," *Christianity Today*, http://www.christianitytoday.com/ct/2009/august/16.22.html, posted 7/31/2009. He adds, "many young adults consider it immature or humiliating to rely on others for financial or even social support. They would rather deal with sexual guilt—if they sense any at all—than consider marrying before they think they are ready." See also his main work on this, *Forbidden Fruit: Sex and Religion in the Lives of American Teenagers*, (New York: Oxford, 2007)

Christian adults seem to value progress in the world over spiritual progress.

Negative vision

Before going on, let's consider a different vision for our kids. In this vision, our kids go on to become successful doctors, lawyers, and executives. They live in spectacular houses where their children can visit them when they have custody. They probably suffer from drinking problems, loneliness, obesity, and all the other things that afflict wealthy, successful non-Christians in our society, but they have plenty of money to pay for their therapists. They no longer play soccer, so that turned out to be a waste of time. They remember something about God but tend to feel all religions are good if their followers find them comforting.

Take your pick. As parents, nobody has the influence you do. How will you use that influence? Are you like me, feeling that I would do anything to avoid this fate? Any Christian who thinks this negative vision is unlikely simply has not faced the facts, according to authorities in the field, about what is happening to *most* Christian young people today.

Eleven suggestions for change

This isn't a book about student ministry, so I will briefly suggest a few practical ideas for upgrading student ministry in your church, based on our experience and the teaching of scripture.

Initial leadership

To build a vigorous youth movement, you'll need to send in a leader. You need a leader who has a clear vision to convert a group of semi-disinterested students into a vital self-multiplying ministry. The leader should have demonstrated the ability to lead before this— not someone fresh out of seminary who has never led a group. He or she needs to believe that working with students is the ultimate thing to do, not just a stepping-stone to greater things, career-wise. Your leader needs to view student ministry as his or her future for the next ten years or longer. Student ministry is a long-term project if you take a biblical approach, and even after several years of work only a couple of disciples would be coming online, ready to lead their peers.

The task of initiating a movement among young people won't be possible on a volunteer basis unless the beginning group is extremely small. Even then, if the group grows, it will become a time consuming endeavor. The church has to recognize the need and find the funding.

Empty nesters (like me) can do this work with university students (although high school work is a bit of a stretch for me these days). Young people are responsive to older people as long as they don't act or think old. Young leaders without children can also do this work. But those with their own kids at home will have difficulty, especially with the university crowd. I go to work at about noon and come home at midnight or later most nights (and my wife is on campus with me). That wouldn't work if I still had kids to father at home.

Your main leader will need help from volunteer leaders. You need at least one leader of each gender, even for a small group. Larger groups may need several adult leaders. If the group gets big, these may become part-time paid positions. In very large group, several may be full time.

Plan on two or three years before you see significant fruit being borne. Raising up qualified opinion leaders among the young takes time, and you will not see major fruit until young people begin leading their own peers.

Preach the word

God works through his word, empowered by the Holy Spirit. Entertainment or cool activities are not what attract and win over the hearts and minds of students. Any thought that students are too restless to sit under substantive Bible preaching is flat wrong. Our hundreds of students sit happily under 30-40 minute expository Bible lectures in high school, and 45-55 minute lectures in college. After each lecture, we open the floor for comments and questions for another fifteen minutes. After this comes group prayer, where maybe a dozen or more students pray and the leader closes.

Students love these meetings; especially non-Christians and the recently converted. They take notes, come up afterward with questions, and refer to the teachings in subsequent weeks. Low estimates of what students are willing to learn is deadly to a successful movement. We find that students will match anything adults can do in terms of devotion to learning. I shoot slightly *over* students' heads; I would rather confuse some students than bore any. Make sure you are teaching the Bible, not topical teachings that don't cause kids to learn the scriptures. Those lectures may be fun, but won't changed lives in a lasting way.

As you teach the word, you have to make a case for what real New Testament-style church life should be. Developing inner convictions and goal orientation begins as God convicts people from his word.

Forget the church's schedule

Most churches like to do their meetings on Sunday morning— a generally poor time for student ministry. Students operate socially at night. They don't want to be viewed as church kids and usually won't invite their popular friends to Sunday morning meetings. The biggest reason for scheduling student meetings on Sunday morning is for the convenience of families. But here again, we are valuing the rest of the family more than the students. Find times that students like. Sunday evening is often good, because school activities tend not to fall on that night. You'll need another time slot when you organize home groups.

The same goes for other church activities. Think about this story:

A large church in downtown Columbus was dwindling almost to nothing as the neighborhood changed. Their youth group was down to half a dozen apathetic kids. They approached me (I was a college student at the time), saying they had heard that our group was good at getting student groups going. Would we come and help revitalize their youth group? I didn't think it was a good opportunity because I had other things going. But I had a friend who was interested and he could bring his girlfriend and another guy. I hooked them up with the church and they went down weekly to take over the leadership of this forlorn group.

They began teaching the word and making friends with the kids. By the third week, they saw their first non-Christian guest. Others appeared soon after. Some of the kids who had quit coming to the group heard things were going on and returned. After working through fall quarter, the group was catching fire, sometimes with twenty five or more kids attending.

In mid-November, the woman who had invited us approached the leader. She told him that beginning in two weeks, the group wouldn't be able to meet for the following six weeks because of rehearsals for the Christmas cantata.

He stared at her aghast. "You must be kidding! I thought you invited us here to revitalize this group. Can't you see something is happening here?!"

"Yes," she said. "You guys have done a wonderful job, and we want you to continue in January. But the church expects the high school group to perform for the cantata, and I'm afraid there's nothing we can do about it."

Of course, all the newer students were lost during those weeks. Furious, my friend swore he would never minister in the traditional church again. I hope their cantata was good, because it might have cost them the souls of their own kids. Their youth group rolled over and died after that.

Get out of the church building

Students don't want to feel like they're doing their parents' thing. They want to do their own thing.[97] Even if some are willing to do their parents' thing, they won't put their hearts into it until they see it as their own. Meeting at a church building won't necessarily kill your group, but it will be better if they have their own space that doesn't seem like a church.

Home meetings should be fine for smaller groups. Find homeowners who aren't uptight about their homes and see this as a

---

[97] The simple church movement argues for having teens and all ages together for house church meetings. This may be okay at times, but it ignores the psychologically inevitable desire to separate from the family's ego-mass. Young people from the mid-teens until the mid-twenties need to feel they are off with their own—doing their own groups, without Mom and Dad looking over their shoulders.

valid ministry. There will be sacrifice. I urge homeowners to arrange to have the group there even when they are on vacation. Our church provides a small sum to high school groups to have their hosts' carpets cleaned or to replace anything they break.

If your beginning group is larger or becomes larger, look for a place you can lease or buy. Plan to deck it out completely for student meetings. Have students do this, or at least give input. Avoid filling the place with pictures of Jesus and crosses. It should look like a cool place to hang out, not a church or a schoolroom. The coffee house idea works well, or you could set up the space as a forum, with seats in the round.[98] Meeting in a Starbucks or a pizza place works for small groups.

Carpet is better than hard floors for acoustics. You want to be able to hear people talk during participatory meetings, and hard floors echo too much.

I learned a lesson during my first year as a walking Christian. I was going to a traditional church with my parents because the court required it as part of my probation. They had a three to four person Sunday school class for college students. I wasn't impressed by the students there: all were kids of church members and seemed rather disinterested. They were also nerdy.

The leader, however was a different story. He was an MD who had previously been in Campus Crusade. He had a real burden for reaching college kids and a good personality. I liked him. One day after the meeting he asked me if I would meet him for coffee before the next meeting. When we met at a nearby restaurant, he pitched me on showing him how to get this group moving. He had somehow picked me out as a leader. He said he was sure I could bring people and be an influence, partly because I had only recently come to Christ.

I was reluctant. "Hmm. I don't know," I mused. "I just don't see my friends coming to something like this."

"What needs to change?" he pleaded, explaining that he was ready to do whatever was needed.

---

[98] You can see teachings at the Xenos facility at Ohio State University on Youtube. Search under 4thstreetsudycenter.

"Well, first of all, I think we'd have to get out of the church." I stared at him as he processed that.

"Like where?" he asked.

"Like here," I gestured to the pancake house. "They have a smoking section here, and a lot of my friends would like that. It's a neutral place, and it's near the church. Guys could come to church with their families and walk a block down to this place for the meeting. We could just pull a few tables together, have breakfast, and talk."

To make a long story shorter, he agreed and we began meeting at the restaurant. I got a couple of guys to come out, and even a couple of the church kids got people out. Within six weeks we were having excellent discussions with a dozen students. I dared to get somewhat excited about it.

Then after meeting one week, the good doctor asked me to stay and talk. He struggled, trying to figure out how to break the news. "I've got bad news, Dennis." He went on to explain that the elders had discussed what we were doing and they were uncomfortable with it. They didn't like that people were smoking at our meetings (this was in 1969, before the worry about second-hand smoke arrived; it was strictly moral). Further, they didn't like us meeting outside the church building. They wanted us to return to the college classroom.

Just like my other friend, I stared in dumbfounded amazement. "Did you tell them what's happening here?" I demanded.

"I did. I pleaded with them for over an hour, trying to convince them that this was the wrong decision."

I could see he was miserable. "Well, we'll just tell them no," I offered. "What are they going to do about it? We don't need their permission; we can do what we want."

He explained that they were his elders, and he had to respect their rulings. He was actually near tears and couldn't be more apologetic. I tried to understand his position, but I couldn't. I eventually walked out, shaking my head. The class moved back into the church and within two weeks it was back to me and the three nerds. They were just as angry as I was.

I pondered this incident often during the months that followed. It was clear to me that these church people 1) didn't care about their students reaching their friends, 2) had a strange hang-up on their building, and 3) were high-control and legalistic. They would rather have a dead-end Sunday school class than a growing college group of excited converts, especially if it meant people were going to smoke. Of course, all the smokers who were coming had been smoking for years, and none of the three church kids ever smoked, so I couldn't see why they were upset even about this.

Forget about the church building, and put first things first.

Make friends

Some leaders go into student groups with a very top-down leadership model in mind. That might be necessary at times, but the goal is to move to collaborative leadership, which means leaders have to make friends with key students. Students can usually be talked into hanging out, especially if you meet at a restaurant and buy lunch or dinner. There, exploration into the kid's life can begin, and a leader will know how to work his way up to proposing reading something together, usually after a few hangouts. The process of creating vision can begin.

Cast vision

When students' imaginations are awakened to the possibility that this could become something more than a church group, things begin to happen. They need to see their role as something that matters. When students get a vision for becoming leaders in something exciting, they begin to exert effort and creativity toward the goal. It helps to have stories of cases where such things have happened before. There are historical cases of youth movements, and maybe the leader has seen something him or herself that he or she can share with students.

Avoid picking

When making friends with students, they have to feel like they can be themselves around you. Leaders who regularly correct students for inappropriate language, or smoking, or who preach too much about what they shouldn't be doing may get their way, at least while they're in the vicinity. But kids will feel that they have to pretend to be something they are not while around that leader. The leader becomes an authority figure, but not a friend. You can forget about getting far with them in this setting. Of course, if they are having sex or doing drugs that's a different story. You can't look the other way when it comes to serious sin or you lose moral authority. Don't pick at their behavior on minor things. Instead, show that you like them, believe in them, and enjoy being with them.

Teach discipleship

Students can become good disciples, and they can make disciples. If anything, college students make disciples more easily and comprehensively than do most adults (fewer high school students are capable of doing this). Once students get the vision for multiplication through personal mentoring, they will devote themselves and see major change. I'm continually amazed at how determined and consistent students can be when working at discipling others. As people meet together for edification, you will have more and more opinion leaders with transformed minds.

Read our book, *Organic Disciplemaking*, and Robert Coleman's classic, *The Masterplan of Evangelism* with your students to help impart this vision.

Keep the bar high

Students may be sloppy on the externals like language and sloth, but they can become truly spiritually zealous. You can teach them to spend time regularly in the word, and they like to pray. Don't settle for a group that claps their hands, sings some songs, and lives like the world the rest of the week. Students like to be challenged, and they don't want to be patronized. Groups with a low bar feel like Sunday school classes and they fail to win students' loyalty and commitment.

Extol models

Students like attention. Don't spend your attention or that of the group on those who cut up and cause distraction. Those people should be ignored or removed. Instead, have those who are serious and zealous get in front of the group. They can do student teachings, testimonies, etc. Public roles are for those who are truly going for it spiritually. Be careful to distinguish between big talkers and actual doers. Call others' attention to how well key students are doing. In our ministry, people aren't qualified to teach at a home church meeting until they have won at least one disciple.

Students who progress well can be brought into the leadership council of the group. By recognizing student leaders, you make the strongest statement possible about what matters in spiritual things. Recognition signals to the whole group what matters most in people's spiritual lives. You want leadership to seem attainable and realistic, but never false. Their peers should genuinely respect student leaders.

Practice discipline

Student groups cannot develop apart from discipline. Particularly as groups begin to grow through conversion, some will show up with no intention other than serving self and using others. You have to firmly oppose fighting, sexual immorality, and drug use. Don't be afraid to lose students; more will come in their place.

Plant home groups

A self-replicating home group strategy works better with students than with any other age group in America. Students get excited about leading their own groups and work hard to grow and plant new groups.[99]

---

[99] See our approach to this in Dennis McCallum, "Urban Home Church Planting at Xenos" http://www.xenos.org/classes/leadership/urbanhousechurchplanting.htm.

The big picture

When a local church taps into the power of student ministry, they will see a steady injection of life into the whole church. Student groups have astonishing ability to grow. They have far less trouble bringing friends out to Bible studies than adults do. Over the long haul, these young people will become the best workers in your church.

Chapter Twenty-Two

Ministry to the Poor

Both through teaching and example, the New Testament shows that God's people should be intensely active in relieving poverty. We see that local churches in the New Testament period ministered not only to their own poor (Acts 4:32-34), but also to distant regions where they knew people were in poverty (2 Corinthians 8, 9; Acts 11:27-30). Proverbs warns, "He who shuts his ear to the cry of the poor will also cry himself and not be answered" (Proverbs 21:16), and a real, loving community will not shut its ears to the cry of millions in desperate need.

When Paul checked the accuracy of his message with the leaders in Jerusalem, he said, "They only asked us to remember the poor— the very thing I also was eager to do" (Galatians 2:10). Jesus powerfully argued that God expects us to care for the poor (Matthew 25:31-46). Every local church should assess its situation and devise strategies for ministry to both Christian and non-Christian poor people, beginning with fellow Christians (Galatians 6:10). This includes poor people worldwide, but we will consider ministry to the poor in other countries in our next chapter.

Relief or community development?

Poor people live on the edge where hunger and other perils are never far. When stressing situations come, immediate relief is essential. This is a good time to hand out food, clothing, and other goods rather than money, which too easily goes astray.

But handing out help is not the lasting answer to poverty. Poverty happens for reasons, including spiritual reasons. Alcoholism, drug addiction, crime, family breakup, and child neglect are all problems that require spiritual change, not just relief, and this kind of change isn't easy. Poor people need Christians who will go to them and form relationships in which they impart God's love and life-changing power. This won't happen at a distance. Merely throwing money at the problem doesn't help in the long run.

If we really care about the poor, we have to be willing to take on the much more daunting task of *lasting economic development*. To deliver poor people in a lasting way the church must take upon itself the burden of ministering to the whole person. Real development that lasts after we're gone happens one person at a time. When churches accept the burden of holistic ministry to the poor, they realize that Christians will have to go to where the poor are, make friends, share the gospel, and minister to their physical needs at the same time. Poor people need to be won over to Christ, discipled, and taught the skills and attitudes needed to work their way out of poverty.

Although many churches have some ministry to the poor, this more demanding approach is often missing. Consider some of the pieces needed for real community development:

- **Education** – American urban and rural poor people are usually not successfully educated. Their schools are worse than suburban schools, sometimes leaving even high school graduates virtually illiterate. The drop-out rate often approaches half of all students. In our world, uneducated people are usually doomed to ongoing poverty.

- **Addiction** – An alarming percentage of inner city poor people have alcohol or drug problems that destroy any chance for normal family lives or gainful employment. Rural poor also commonly have problems with alcohol.

- **Sexual immorality** – Most kids in the inner city are born out of wedlock. Few are from intact families. Children of divorce or illegitimacy are at high risk for delinquency and school problems. They are less likely to succeed at forming families of their own. Immorality is such an accepted part of life in the inner city that very few young people will be able to resist the consensus without powerful help from outside.
- **Neglect** – Poor children are usually neglected children. Nobody reads to them or nurtures them in a family way. When these kids show up for first grade, they are already years behind their suburban counterparts. Human kindness, the ability to trust and love others, and a sense of significance are often missing in these children. They often have to be more or less 're-parented.'
- **Neighborhood ethos** – Young people in poor neighborhoods often believe that prostitution, pimping, drug dealing, robbery, and gang membership are good things. They make fun of and even assault kids who refuse to join in. Kids that start out good have a lot of opposition and pressure to face if they are to make it to adulthood intact.
- **Absence of positive role models** – If the only successful people in a social group are pimps and thugs, young people see little reason not to aspire to the same. Kids tend to imitate respected members in a social group.
- **Media influence** – Movies and TV shows make poor kids acutely aware of what they are missing. Envy and anger follow. Contemporary hip-hop glorifies violence, sex, and materialism. This may have more impact on poor kids with no positive alternative models to follow.

Anyone who honestly faces this web of causality realizes we have our work cut out for us if we think we can do anything to help in any lasting way.

Our story

People in our church have always believed that God's will for the church includes ministry to the poor. But for the first seventeen years of our existence, not much happened. We assumed that proliferating house churches would gradually spread into the poor parts of town, resulting in a ministry with the needy. But by 1987 it became clear that this was never going to happen. Birds of a feather stick together, and our house churches were only proliferating in the university campus and other mainly white, middle class neighborhoods.

We realized we would have to be more intentional in initiating a meaningful ministry to the poor. We felt that if we were going to invest time and treasure into the project, we wanted a ministry that would alleviate poverty permanently, through development. Whether our project has succeeded is still uncertain, but it has borne some good fruit.

We decided to begin by focusing on children in a desperate, gang-infested inner-city area. In this government project, gangs claim most kids by the time they are teenagers, and even grade school kids carry drugs for the gangs because they can avoid prosecution. To reach kids so young that the gangs weren't interested in them, we had to begin with preschool-aged kids.

We hired one of our members as director and gave him a small budget to get going. We also began talking about the project regularly with our church. We devoted fifty thousand dollars to the first year of operation, which seemed like a fortune to us in 1987. Following the advice of African American Christian leaders, John Perkins and Tony Evans, we collaborated with an African American church near that area and went into the government housing projects to meet people and begin forming relationships. Soon we had a Bible study going in the projects for kids.

After talking with parents in the area, we determined that the most helpful project would be an after-school program. Inner-city kids are usually alone from the time they get out of school until mom comes home from work or other activities. They need help with their homework, which they often don't understand. (Poor education is one of the best predictors of lifelong poverty). We bought two vacant crack houses and refurbished them as a place to operate. Later, we leased an adjacent vacant storefront. Between 3:30 and 7:30 our volunteers served as the kids' proxy parents. We were also able to contribute to their nutrition and continue developing friendships.

We developed a tutoring program, set up like a Big Brother/Big Sisters, so older Christians from our church could help specific kids. Tutors usually meet on Saturdays to go out and play, eat lunch, and help with their schoolwork. These relationships often go on for years, even decades.

We initiated job training, emergency relief, low-income housing, and other ideas for upgrading life in the neighborhood over the next ten years. Most of our key leaders in the ministry moved their families into the neighborhood so they could share the hardships of the ones to whom they ministered.

Inner city school

Finally, after nearly fifteen years of work, the staff and volunteers felt we needed even more exposure to kids. We began an inner city school for disadvantaged youth. The school met in a laundromat we leased and other houses we had purchased by then. It grew to include kindergarten through 6th grade. Students there now score in the 62nd percentile on the MAT (Metropolitan Achievement Test), while public schools in that neighborhood average the twenties. Kids regularly meet Christ in the school and many of their families do as well. Recently, we built a new school building and community center. We're expanding into Junior Hi next year.

Spiritual deliverance should go along with material deliverance from poverty, so we include house churches and youth groups focused on Bible study and fellowship.

Key themes

The Xenos ministry to urban poor (now called "Urban Concern") is clearly a ministry suited to a larger local church. But even small churches join in with us, and that could happen in other cities as well.

We think it's important to send in people, not just dollars. People who form relationships with the poor and serve onsite gain a perspective that they can gain no other way. Also, poor people need the love of Jesus, not just handouts. Handouts by themselves don't relieve poverty, and may actually make matters worse if continued after emergencies have passed. In the years since Urban Concern began, we have also added ministries to disadvantaged youth, free medical clinics, and others.

The big picture

When people in a local church devote time, talent, and treasure to ministering to the poor, they demonstrate that they are going beyond serving themselves. If we give out to our own people, that's fine, but not enough. God calls his body to get outside of itself and care for those in need outside the church.

Our group has been the object of suspicion in our city at times, either because we are an unconventional church meeting in homes, or because of misbehavior by our members. But our work with the poor has brought more positive appreciation from the city than anything. This ministry is often on the news or receiving awards from the city, state, and even federal governments.

We consider this work part of our testimony. As a largely white church with numerous affluent members, we think it would be a disgrace if nothing like this ministry existed. Jesus said we should live in a way that people see our good works and glorify God (Matthew 5:16).

We had to work our way up to the point where we had a significant ministry to the poor. During our early years as a student group, we could barely keep up with our own needs. But as we grew up and became more affluent, we were better able to fund a ministry like this, and the moral urgency grew as well. No longer poor students ourselves, how could we justify living directly next to poor people, and not helping? We believe all churches in America should take a hand in relief as well as the far more difficult task of development for the poor.

Inner city ministry has been a source of blessing to our people, to the people we serve, and a positive statement to our city about how Jesus changes lives. At the same time, this ministry has probably produced more frustration and anxiety than any other in our church. Any successes we win are constantly mixed with failures. Nothing is harder than ministering to the poor, and only a group with rock solid convictions about God's will can last long in this field.

Chapter Twenty-Three

Missions

The Bible is a book about God's missionary heart for lost people. From the earliest days he made it clear not only that he was pursuing a plan of rescue, but further that we get to be players in that plan. You see this in the Abrahamic covenant in Genesis 12, when God says "all the families of the earth will be blessed" through Abraham (v. 3). The early church was also a missional church. When the Holy Spirit commissioned Paul and Barnabas to take the word abroad, he called it "the work to which I have called them" (Acts 13:2). Our own country remains one of the largest mission fields in the world, but we also stand obligated to reach out to lands where people have never even heard the gospel. World outreach is a necessary ministry for any healthy church. It also is a long-term, expensive project, both in dollars and in effort. New churches might have to work their way up to success in missions, but you can start immediately.

Mobilizing

Churches first need an awareness and burden for distant lands. By raising people's awareness of the biblical mandate and the need, you set the stage for later action.

Before ever sending people overseas, it would be wise to spend several years raising missions awareness. At the suggestion of missions expert Ralph Winter, we began offering the "Perspectives on the World Christian Movement" course about every other year.

This course, offered through the U. S. Center for World Mission, is an excellent way to get people interested in missions. In addition, the *Global Prayer Digest*, published by the U.S. Center, helps families or small groups pray over the needs in other countries, explaining as you go where each country stands currently.[100]

Allowing visiting missionaries to explain their work and solicit prayer partners helps people realize what missionaries do. Nobody can speak with more passion or persuasiveness than missionaries.

Teaching on the validity of missions is also important. Today, postmodern culture views world missions as interfering with the natural beauty of other cultures in order to impose western ideas. Most people see no valid reason to go to other cultures with the gospel or anything else.

I believe we should directly confront this view. The whole critique of missions is based on the assumption that nothing is true or knowable in the objective sense. Religion is just a cultural artifact according to our culture. To suggest that one is in some way better than another is arrogant. Even Christians imbibe this view without realizing it. Teachers have to press people to think about their own views of missions. They need to face the word of God, where God strictly denounces idol worship and other religions. Christians must face the truly lost state of non-Christians and be challenged as to why we would even consider doing nothing about it.

Education can also help people realize that many cultures are living in daily suffering and bondage to fear because of their false religious beliefs. Nothing is beautiful about belief systems that result in backwardness, fear, infanticide, racism, sexism, or economic oppression.

Short-term mission trips are also an excellent way to raise awareness and burdens in people's hearts for the lost and needy in other lands. Nothing works like actually seeing the desperation of poverty and ignorance in developing countries to make people realize how affluent they are and to put a burden in their hearts to help the helpless.

---

[100]Now available as a free PDF download at http://www.global-prayer-digest.org/.

Be sure your short-term trips are well led. Short-term teams need to gather for teaching and prayer regularly during trips to make sure they are reaching the right conclusions about what they see. While doing short-term work projects is good, point out that much more is needed. To do meaningful long-term work, people have to commit to living in these cultures, learning their languages and cultures, and building relationships. Only with people on the ground long-term can we expect to make a lasting difference. Today, another option is to pay for indigenous missionaries to reach their own people. But this isn't an option in people groups where no witnessing church has yet been planted.

Supporting indigenous groups

Today, the most positive development in missions is the way indigenous churches in the developing world are taking off. Unlike the stagnating and declining western church, these groups are growing like wildfire, and that suggests that in many cases, the best thing we can do is support indigenous ministries rather than trying to start new ones.

The biggest needs are for training and funding. Indigenous missionaries are usually able to work for a tiny fraction of what westerners cost, and they may be very effective. In areas like India, the Phillipines, and Latin America, healthy national churches are producing thousands of quality missionaries who need funding. While we should not fund normal pastors of churches (because their own people should do that), we can and should fund those who go out to unreached areas to spread the gospel. Often, if they are successful in planting churches, they no longer need western financial support.

Development projects like education, infrastructure, medical help and training, etc. often contribute to the testimony of Christians in an area. Micro-lending programs are good examples of how to use western money without creating dependency. Development can also be a good way to lead into church planting. If we train indigenous missionaries in medicine or other needed development skills, they will be welcomed and find an open door for the gospel.

Supporting local Christians isn't always the answer. In numerous completely unreached areas, only pioneering missionaries can open the field; there are no local Christians. Of course, near-neighbors from similar ethnic linguistic groups are sometimes more successful than westerners at penetrating these difficult areas, but not always. Sometimes westerners may be accepted more than historic enemies from neighboring countries. In other cases, indigenous Christian groups have become corrupt and are using people for money or other things, or they no longer preach a biblical gospel. Backing groups like these would clearly be a huge mistake apart from convincing reformation.

Sending

The way today's church usually handles missions is similar to how it handles pastor selection. People feel called by God and go to missions training. They contact a missions agency and apply to be accepted as a missionary. If accepted, they begin raising support. Their own churches might offer to cover part of their expense, but usually very little. While they usually need a pastor's recommendation to be accepted by a sending agency, these are rarely withheld. Once missionaries go to the field they deal with the agencies that sent them.

This is not how the New Testament church launched missions. There, we read that when Paul and Barnabas got the call to go abroad, the other leaders heard it also (Acts 13:1-3). Then, the whole church got behind their effort, funding it, praying for it, and later sending additional workers to reinforce the endeavor. So, the local church led the way, and was involved from first to last.

When a local church sends their own teams or indigenous teams, they are already used to working together and share a common philosophy of ministry. The sending church knows their character and capabilities in ministry. When those teams engage with ministry on the field, the local church can continue to take an interest in their work, sending short-term groups to visit, helping to raise additional funding, and supporting them in prayer.

Networking

Sending agencies are good for their expertise and experience. Most are perfectly willing to enter into agreements with local churches where the church sends teams that work together and the church has ongoing input both on the field and stateside.[101] When churches take this approach, they are in a position to mobilize their congregations to take an interest in the work through short-term visits, regular airtime at church meetings, and caring for the needs of their overseas operatives.

The big picture

Just as with serving the poor, it may take a local church a number of years to reach the point where they are making a significant impact in missions. But teaching on missions and awareness-raising can begin immediately. Missions is part of the ethos you build into your group. As a new church matures, missions should become even more a focus, and that should be reflected in its budget. Good churches in America direct a quarter or more of their giving to missions; some as much as half!

Doing long-term work in foreign fields is difficult and requires patience and perseverance, especially if you go into unreached fields like those in the so-called 10/40 window.[102] Sponsoring workers in indigenous churches and sending groups can immediately result in significant fruit. In the end, God will reward those who obey his command to "Go."

---

[101] Xenos has such agreements with Worldteam, OMF, and Frontiers. The agreements govern who will go to what field (including screening procedures), field selection and research, missionary training and preparation, how teams are composed and led, field supervision, financial responsibility and budget planning, field visitation, and home assignment arrangements.

[102] The 10/40 window refers to the area between the 10 and 40 degrees north of the equator in the eastern hemisphere. This area contains over 2.5 billion of the poorest and least Christianized people on earth. Ninety percent of the unreached peoples in the world live in this area, but only ten percent of all Christian missionaries work there.

Section 4

Practical Ideas for Change

What if the Lord has spoken to you while reading this book? What if you see a vision for a more New Testament-style church and long for that? This section discusses practical ideas for how you could move in that direction.

What position do you work from?

Your strategy for moving toward the real experience of biblical church life depends on your starting point. We will consider ideas for each of four possibilities: 1) Pastors or elders who want to see their current church change to resemble more closely the New Testament picture; 2) Leaders of home groups who have a more modest goal of transforming their home groups; 3) Christians who want to be opinion leaders in their churches to spread the word; and 4) Those who want to plant new churches.

Regardless of which position you work from, read the next chapter so you can think through how change-making works. Then, read later chapters as appropriate to get ideas about how to apply your convictions to your situation.

Chapter Twenty-Four

Pastors or Elders Seeking Change

Are you a pastor or elder who wants to see your church change? Stimulating and fostering change are key leadership challenges. As a long time elder, I've had experience moving our church to change, although in fairness, I have to admit I've never had to move a church from a traditional to a New Testament paradigm. I have worked, however with other leaders on that project, and I've included some of their comments below.

Leading groups to change is difficult and can be dangerous. Careless approaches to change making usually lead to unnecessary fights, unintended change, or even a hardening of the status quo.

While authentic, deep change requires time and patience, it is definitely possible. Scattered through this chapter I have included comments from Craig, a leader in Apex church of Dayton, Ohio. Some years ago, the leaders of this large church nearing two thousand in attendance underwent a lengthy time of reflection. They reached the conclusion that God wanted them to change from a more traditional "Sunday go to church" approach to one based on deeper community through house churches and intentional discipleship. In the five years since, the group has gone from fifteen to seventy home churches. Their large, Sunday meetings have grown as well. Today they have over three thousand attending and people are more engaged, more interested in serving, and more proactive in their efforts to love the people in their city.

Leaders at Apex feel their movement toward the true experience of New Testament-style body life is still in progress. But people in the group are excited and seem to feel the church has never been healthier. If these leaders can turn around a church of thousands, then most churches in the west are capable of change.

When pastors have counseled with me about bringing in major change, my first word of advice is, "Take your time." Real change is a lengthy proposition, even for relatively small groups. If your group is large, it will take even longer. Adequate preparation is essential to success. The process of leading change begins in private as you study scripture, assess your situation, and make plans with God, just as Nehemiah did when he felt called to lead change (Nehemiah 1, 2).[103]

Study the suggestions below and pray that God will lead you. Most leaders find it best to work on paper or a computer as they think through these issues.

Defining Convictions

Before talking to people (other than your spouse), take extra time to define carefully and prayerfully exactly what you believe God wants. With God, re-read sections that struck you in this study or others, passages from the Bible, and perhaps review memories of experiences and situations you've been in where elements of real body life were evident.

Decide which parts of the picture are essential and which parts would be nice, but can wait. What exactly comes from God, and what is personal preference? Where can you compromise, and where must you refuse to do so? Put differently, if only partial success is possible, which parts are most important?

Apply your convictions

Try to imagine what it would look like if your church bought into

---

[103] Craig from Apex commented that one of first questions must be, "Why should I try to lead change here rather than simply start something new elsewhere?" This is a good question to pray about. For those who feel led to go out, a later chapter takes up ideas for planting a new church.

the vision you have. How would people be affected? How would things be better in your new picture than under the status quo? What are the risks involved in change? Why are they reasonable?

What price are you prepared to pay to bring this change about? Your answer could range from the low end—"I'll put some work into this, and give it a try, but if I can't move people, I'm not going to make a fuss over it"—to the high end—"I'm not willing to continue under the status quo. Things *must* change, and I'm prepared to go as far as needed, including getting fired or starting a fight in the church in order to see change." Are you prepared to invest several years in accomplishing this change? Or are you on a shorter schedule that requires action within months?

Considering that a high price might be necessary, are you sure that what you are going to propose is from God and not just your own idea? This is a crucial question that will keep you going through the rigors of change making. If you're not sure of the answer to this, you're not ready to create change. You need more work. Perhaps discussions with colleagues will help clarify what God wants.

Assessing

When leading change, you begin where you are and move to where you want to be. So where are you? Accurately appreciating your current situation will help you know what to do.[104]

Group type

How big is your church? Smaller churches are easier to change than big ones from the standpoint of communication, but they can be quite stubborn in their own way.

What age are the people you'll be dealing with? Generally, the older people are, the harder it is to get real change. You'll be "teaching an old dog new tricks," which isn't easy. Remember, you aren't interested in passive change, where people merely acquiesce

---

[104] Craig suggests getting input from outside your own church. Talks to observers you invite to come and give feedback could help you see an area of blindness.

when they hear you talk about changing direction. You want active change, where people embrace personal sacrifice, including changing their own actions and attitudes. Nothing less will come close to a New Testament picture.

What is the leadership structure in your church? Consider not only the formal structures, but any informal lines of influence that may be just as important or even more important. How are decisions made in your group? Who are the colleagues that must buy into what you're suggesting before it will work?

Where will the likely opposition come from? Do you see individuals or groups who may stand to lose from the change you are suggesting? Who are those who tend to oppose anything and everything?[105] By anticipating opposition, you make it possible to head it off with personal meetings and persuasion.

Spiritual assessment

How deep is the spirituality of the group? Are you frustrated by fleshly attitudes in the group? Or are most people excited about living for, and serving God? Will you need to work with a smaller group within the church who 'get it'?

How is morale? Are people discouraged? Is there dissatisfaction with the status quo? Do people feel frustrated with the progress of the church? Negative views could fuel the perceived need for change but could also sap motivation. Usually, at least in larger groups, we are dealing with a range of answers in this area, and we will have to develop different strategies for those who are well motivated versus those who feel hopeless.

What tradition are you up against? Most churches have some ways of doing things that are incompatible with the New Testament picture. Long-standing churches are harder to change than newer ones. Highly traditional denominational churches are notoriously hard to change. On the other hand, some traditions are harmless. Which traditional features can you retain without harm? Are you

---

[105] Craig: "I affectionately refer to these folks as CAVE people (Christians Against Virtually Everything). ☺".

necessarily refuting existing beliefs? If so, make sure you study these areas carefully and enact a plan like the one discussed below. For traditions that are harmless, you can point out the unchanging parts, which will comfort members.

Which parts of your vision are already present in some measure? Any positives you can see in the current situation will be useful to point out when calling for change.

What are your group's expectations? Compare what your colleagues expect to what people *should* expect. For instance, people may expect to feel close to God and loved by others with little or no time investment on their part. Some people expect to be regularly entertained and soothed through their involvement in church. They may expect a sense of community even though they also expect everyone to mind their own business and not intrude into their privacy. Or are people's expectations way too low? Have they settled for mediocrity when they should be looking for God's best? Is it a combination? How can you manage people's expectations to a realistic level? If they have improper expectations, you will have to develop a plan to reprove them, and call for a change of heart.

What is your attitude toward the church? Are you angry or frustrated? Do you feel cynical about the church's ability to change? Do you believe in your people? If so, who are the ones you believe in the most? Have you seen God work in your church in ways that make you feel he is with you and will work again? Are there problems with your relationships with other leaders or members that could cause trouble at a time like this? Do you need to work on key relationships before launching into a change program?

Have you taught a theology of the church that anticipates regular change? Long before you actually change, you should regularly argue for an ethos of adaptability and change. Stress the carnality of those who opt for control rather than change, and point out their inability to follow the Holy Spirit. Use illustrations from the book of Acts, where God had trouble getting the early Christians to change (e.g. Acts 10, 11). When change comes, well-led churches can refer to this body of teaching, which has already become part of the group's ethos.[106]

Leadership status

How much confidence does the church have in your leadership? When people view their leaders as unreliable, all the planning in the world won't make them seem trustworthy. Christian leaders are able to persuade and excite others about their vision roughly in proportion to how trustworthy people perceive them to be. People consider Christian leaders trustworthy based on their honesty, their consistency, their willingness to sacrifice themselves, and their humility. Christian leaders caught in the act of self-aggrandizement deserve to lose trust, while those who work hard at empowering others deserve confidence, according to Jesus (Mark 10:42-45).

How do your people, your staffers, and your colleagues view you? If you sense distrust, you should wait. Work on the problems in relationships and perception first. You can come back to change making later.

Time management

You need to assess your current time usage and that of your key staffers. The question is, what are you going to cut in order to apply yourself to the new directions? You can't just add in a major new initiative and new work to everything you already do. This question comes up a lot when pastors consult with me about converting their churches. They wonder where I find the time to disciple multiple young men, coach and counsel many home church leaders, teach every week publicly as well as in weekly classes.

The answer is that I have managed to delete many of the duties from my schedule that burden other pastors. I haven't married or buried anyone for several years. I don't do visitations except to

---

[106] Craig from Apex: Much of the western church has taught what I call "The Arrival Myth" a belief that there is one "right" way to do everything and our job is to discover that one right way. Once we've discovered it, our work is done... I believe we need to constantly reinforce the concept that we are all on a journey to be more like Jesus – not only in our morality and belief system, but also in our Way of life and good works. An honest awareness of this journey – and the fact that we never completely 'arrive' – tends to keep people both flexible and humble, two essential characteristics for leading and experiencing change."

people in my own home church. My time in committees and other bureaucratic functions is negligible. In a word, our top leaders have stripped off everything but the essentials. You will have to do the same if you plan to take on the daunting task of church conversion (Acts 6:1-7).

Build your case

Before you begin to agitate the church, you need to build a case for change. You may not use all the points you develop, especially with different audiences. But it's best to be thorough, which means you should work on paper with these ideas and revise your points several times before going public with them. You will need careful thought and prayer in each of the following areas:

Inadequacy of the status quo

What is wrong with the situation as it is now? Without being overly negative, name things you see that are improper and could be better. Name other things that you don't see but should be seeing. Is there a negative trajectory if you keep going like you are? What price is the church paying by staying with the status quo? Your thinking in this area is useful in thawing current belief systems and readying people for new ideas.

To balance the negatives, spend time thinking about why your people are well suited to taking on a challenge, especially when they realize God is calling for it and empowering it.

The alternative vision you are suggesting

Try to condense what God is calling the church to, including preparing clear ways to communicate that calling. What wording would be best? How will you frame your picture in a way that is appealing to the kind of people you are addressing? Work on positive descriptions for each of the components of the change and think through how to explain and persuade people that this vision is best.

The correctness of the vision based on scripture

To lead fellow Christians, you have to go to the word of God and detail your case in his words. Anticipate counter-arguments and consider how you will respond. Are you certain that God teaches this in his word? Is what you argue an emphasis in scripture, or only a minor point?

The tangible benefits people will see if the vision is realized

This part depends on a combination of common sense, scripture, and imagination. What positives can leaders anticipate? How will this be good for typical members? How might it enhance evangelism and growth? Think of problems you know of that might be eased or solved if the group goes this way. You can't be sure what the benefits will be, but don't worry about that now. Let your imagination move without limitation, and then let God show you what you should cut from the list later. When speaking to the people, however, don't over-promise. Point out that the vision is sweet enough to justify a high cost and even pain.

The urgency of the vision based on the dangers from not changing

After you detail the benefits you foresee, develop an antithesis for each point. You can juxtapose your positive vision with a negative vision, or antithesis, that will apply if your group fails to attain to the vision. This negative future should be odious to your people. They have to feel that it would be worth exerting considerable effort to avoid the fate you describe.

Illustrations, metaphors, and emotionally evocative pictures help to create emotional arousal in connection with your vision. (See how Jesus gave antithetical metaphorical pictures of the future in his description of the houses built on sand or on the rock in Matthew 7:24-27.) The antithesis is the negative picture of what a group without this feature looks like. For example:

Positive	Antithesis
Are we going to be a church where people are actively engaged in real love relationships that have a transforming effect on all?	Or are we going to be a crowd of disinterested self-seekers who really don't care?

Positive	Antithesis
If we can begin to reach non-Christians, we will feel the energy every time we meet.	Nothing we do as an all-Christian club is going to satisfy anyone.
If most people in our church developed a burden to build a personal ministry, the whole church would be active and all our needs would be met.	If most of our people see the church as a place to receive instead of give, we can expect nothing but apathy and discontent.
We as a church have always respected and followed God's word, and he has always blessed our intent to do so.	If we turn away from this clear teaching of scripture, we will be choosing to defy God's explicit call as seen in these passages.

These dangers are very important, because people fear change, and you must show them that failure to change deserves fear as well. To achieve buy-in from a substantial number of your people, they have to be convinced that there is no good alternative to what you are proposing.

Why this applies to us

To argue that the vision applies to your group, you have to show how future possibilities relate to past realities in the group. For instance, "We see x, y, and z in the New Testament church, and we realize we have the same Holy Spirit they did. We have seen something similar to this in our own ministry before, and we are already seeing some parts of this vision successfully carried out today."

Your people need to see that they have always held values that accord with the vision. As a leader, you should avoid taking a position that you and your people have been all wrong in everything you have believed and practiced until now. Such a position is very problematic. First, it's usually not true. Few groups are this mixed up. Maybe they haven't seen as clearly as they should, but what they have seen is still valid and good.

Second, it would be discrediting. Why should your people believe you now if you've been so mistaken on everything else you've taught them? Finally, if people feel you are attacking their beliefs, you are more likely to see revolt. If, on the other hand, they see that this is a further outgrowth of what they already know, they will feel obligated to help.[107]

The plausibility of the vision

One of the biggest killers of vision is people's sense that "this would be nice, but there's no way we can pull it off." As a leader, you have to convince people that what you are suggesting is doable. Think of cases in the past where your church has set about a difficult task and reached the goal. As you share theology (the power of God and his will) and experience (things you and they have seen before) you can point out why your vision is not too far-fetched. As you plead your case that "We've already seen this, so there's no reason we wouldn't see that," your listeners should be saying to themselves, "He's got a point!"

At the same time, don't dilute your vision to the point where it's banal or unremarkable. Be sure you courageously call people to follow God's full picture. People don't feel inspired by weak, watered down visions. Good visionary leading stretches people's credulity just the right amount. They should feel challenged by the immensity of your vision without feeling hopeless about attaining it.

Risk management

Be ready to respond to possible dangers or barriers others may suggest. Why are the risks reasonable and manageable? Why are the dangers from not changing far worse than any dangers under the new vision?

---

[107]Craig from Apex: "Again the analogy of a journey is so useful here... It's not that we've been wrong all along and must now double back – it's that we've never been on this part of the journey before and we must now make a choice about direction. And everything we've learned along the way is useful to inform this next choice."

Take action

When you've spent your time with God, assessed your situation, and built your case, you're ready to act. Remain patient. Real change takes more time than many are willing to invest. You don't just want superficial change in some structures or external actions. Don't settle for anything less than change that comes from people's hearts and moves all the way to continued action.

As a leader desiring change, you have probably been struggling with the issues for weeks or months. Your people have yet to grapple with them. You will have to allow them time to process the information, the value judgments, and the action steps, and that may take even longer for them than it has for you.[108]

Build convictions

Your first step is to see others develop the same convictions you have. Begin with key opinion leaders and staffers. If you are married, your spouse has no doubt been struggling along with you the whole time. For people to build convictions, they need interaction with both you as a leader and with God as they consider what you say. Ask them to pray about it, and plan on making this plea several times, each time adding more things to consider.

Write it down

I find that writing out an extended outline with explanatory text is very helpful during times of change. In a few pages, explain what you see and what you think should be done. Carefully detail the scripture involved and summarize the work you did in the previous section.

A written outline will cut down on distortions and confusion (assuming the outline is succinct and well written). Make copies for your upper level opinion leaders. Don't make copies for the rest of the church yet, because your core people may have revisions.

---

[108] A good suggestion from Craig: "Send [key people] to other church communities that may be farther down the path of a similar journey so that they can see things first hand."

Other reading

Select books that help make the case you want to argue. You could use sections of this book, related books, and other articles. It's better to have a moderate amount of reading—not hundreds of pages. Consider the credibility of the authors.

Discussion

Begin discussing what you are seeing. There may be two or three key people you need to win over in order to have good likelihood of success. Begin with them by having individual conversations. If key insiders are resistant to what you suggest, it would be better to encounter this resistance one-on-one rather than in a larger group. In a group, they may feel they have to defend their contrary position once they have taken it.

Ask them to consider what you're seeing and to do the reading you suggest. Let them know you plan to bring it to the other staffers and key members and that you need their help. Ask them to review your outline and contribute edits. Point out that when the meeting comes with the larger team, you will be depending on them to speak up.

Develop your core

If you have your top people agreeing (including your spouse), you are ready to meet with your larger team. You may decide to go to your board first. Or, depending on your judgment, you could talk to them and key others at the same time. Usually you need at least two meetings: At the first, you explain what God has been showing you and ask them to do the reading. At the second, you focus more on interaction based on the first meeting and the reading they have been doing.

During the interactive meeting, listen carefully in order to detect misgivings. Give counter-arguments and reassurances as needed, but remember who had problems. You will need to reflect on what underlying fears might be motivating resistance. Allow time for open debate and slow movement from one paradigm to another. People change their minds slowly, and not without inner conflict, so don't be thin-skinned when people resist your direction. They may even take this opportunity to launch accusations or doubts about your leadership. Such dissent becomes a real test of your stability, humility, and strength as a leader. At an interactive meeting, you should already have key leaders prepared to defend your judgment and ideas, and to redirect the topic back to the issue at hand.

If you sense ongoing doubts, suggest tabling the discussion and call on everyone to pray about what God wants. Then you can meet again later for further discussion. During these discussions, make clear that you all need to agree on the direction, because you are going to need their help to win over the rest of the church. Be prepared for several meetings if necessary.

Between group meetings, meet privately with any dissenters for personal counseling on the issue. Try to understand their worries or reservations. Be prepared to negotiate on any points that won't impair the vision. For each one ask, "What would you like to see?" Is there a way they can get what they feel is needed while also achieving the larger goals? In the end, you should be prepared to go ahead with or without the support of such dissenters. But you will clearly have fewer problems if you can win them over to at least giving it a chance.

During these discussions, you hope to see a building sense of excitement for the vision. Hopefully, you can begin to shift the discussion from what and why change is needed to how to best accomplish the change. Brainstorming ideas for catching people's imagination for the new direction can build further excitement and confidence in the feasibility of your ideas. Ask for suggestions on any changes in your written outline.

Don't worry about people in the leadership group talking to others prematurely. People are suspicious of secrecy. It won't do any harm to let people talk. Just point out that you aren't ready to go to the whole group yet, and you're just discussing possibilities for now.

Go public

When you have your leadership on your side, you're ready to go to the rest of the church. You want committed members to know what you are thinking and what you propose. Have your facts ready, and announce the change as something the leadership thinks is a good idea and would like everyone to support. This is in contrast to a democratic approach ("Do you guys agree that we should do this?"). With members, you should lead in a more directive way than with colleagues. You are calling them to see that what God teaches on these issues is not optional.

A measured approach

However, here is where leaders often err. Some of the things you hope to see in a return to a full New Testament pattern will take time to learn. If your group isn't used to meeting in smaller groups or seeing themselves as ministers, you have extensive training to do before you can expect them to be competent. This means that, although you roll out your burden, the church can expect little positive change for some time to come. You should point this out to them.

A common failed strategy for converting a church from a traditional to an organic approach goes like this: The leadership gathers the church for a big meeting and rolls out the plan. They divide people up into small groups and announce the time of their first meeting. At the new home groups, people show up not knowing what they are doing, not understanding how it works, and in a word, feeling awkward. The group flubs through their meeting, which is not likely to be very good. After a few of these, support begins to diminish. After six months, the groups have dwindled instead of growing. In the end, the whole project fails.

Instead, I suggest you explain what you have in mind to your committed people, but that your action plan for the church involve nothing more than training at first. Your training could take two forms. First, offer a class on the biblical view of the body of Christ. You might want to consider teaching this yourself. At least have one of your best teach it. This class is for interested people who want to make a difference in taking your church to the next level. You will learn who has caught the vision and who is willing to do the work. This is your chance to pick out people who can lead the change.

Secondly, you need to begin discipleship. Get your top few people to each select an ideal disciple—someone who understands the vision and is committed to help—someone they wouldn't mind leading with in the future. Each one should begin meeting at least weekly and studying scripture relevant to the body of Christ, how to minister to others, and evangelism. Your previous work gathering reading material and scripture should be helpful in providing material to go over.[109]

Unless you train leaders you believe in, the project will never work. Merely creating meeting structures without having the spiritually mature leaders who can show others the way is futile. That would be like building a beautiful racecar with all the right lines, but no engine! It's not going anywhere. Your first goal as a leader is to develop a leadership cadre you trust. This phase may last for months or even a year or longer, depending on how things go. There should be no hurry.

You also want people to get used to one-on-one or three-person meetings with study, sharing, and prayer. You hope to see this pattern spread through the church, so it should begin with your top people.

A pilot group

Finally, you are ready to begin your first small group.[110] This could run concurrently with the previous step. Whether you call it a house church, a home group, a small group, a life group, or whatever, doesn't matter. Pick a term you can live with from now on. The point is, you are forming one group, not many. *That group must include you.* The point of the pilot group is to learn together, and in a real way, to do what scripture teaches. That includes consistent efforts at evangelism. If this group doesn't reach out to the lost, other groups birthed off of it

---

[109] Craig says, "the bulk of this training should be hands-on rather than class room instruction... change can happen more quickly and more effectively (with less of a bloody trail of failure and wounds inflicted on others) if we model the kind of action we're hoping to see in real-world situations."

[110] Your church may already have a set of small groups, but you may sense that these were assembled under a different paradigm and are not suitable for the new mission. In this case, I recommend you devise a different term for your new groups and leave the original groups intact while you build a new network alongside them. Gradually, the older type groups will tend to diminish and transfer into the new type groups. Or, they may carry on as before, which shouldn't harm your effort. The point is, if your existing groups aren't good, you should not saddle your new approach with an old wineskin. Make it clear that both the approach and the wineskin for that approach are going to be different.

won't either. Doing what scripture teaches is something that you and the group have to explore and determine to do together.[111]

The pilot group should meet for a number of months. The best plan is to begin with half the number your meeting place can handle. In other words, if the house can hold forty people, begin with twenty. If only thirty, begin with fifteen. Your growth from there should be a combination of new Christians you win and select people from the larger church. You should regulate how many believers are allowed to join this first group from the church. Try to have several new Christians among the final group.

Group DNA

During the life of this pilot group, you have the chance to sow new spiritual DNA into the church; to change the ethos of the group. A pilot group is like a stem cell (placental, of course!) that allows you to begin a new chain reaction. By making sure the group is what it should be and thoroughly training the whole group, you will have the best assurance that the principles and values you inculcate will transmit to future groups. Even several generations (or cycles) down the line, people will look back to this group experience as a guide to what a group should be like.

Group DNA or ethos is so persistent that some church planters doubt that the DNA of a group can ever be changed. This is wrong, but not far wrong. The point is not that ethos *can't* be changed, but that it is *very difficult* to change. You should strongly prefer establishing good ethos to begin with.

Here is the crucial sticking point when trying to convert a group from one type to another: So much of what you hope to see is subjectively defined—based on experience, outlook, values, and interpretations that cannot be explained on paper. Only being in a group like this will make it probable that people will develop something similar in the future. In our forty years of experience

---

[111] Craig from Apex raises an important point: "I think it is also important that pilot group members understand from the beginning that this will be a group with a short life expectancy and that when the group is disbanded those who have participated in it will be expected to become leaders of new groups that the pilot group will spawn."

planting and replicating house churches, we have learned that the founding group has an amazing impact on future generations. Questionable original groups tend to plant questionable daughter groups, while strong originating groups (strongly led, deep, well-discipled, close, and outreaching) seem to produce whole families of strong daughter groups.

If you can't fashion a group that fits your understanding of the New Testament church, your project has failed. There is no point continuing if you cannot develop a pilot group that is sufficiently close to the ideals you are advancing. The group is not going to be perfect, but it should be pretty good. Any amount of effort is justified on this part. Taking much longer than expected or even changing the people in the group would be better than going out to replicate something you didn't want in the first place. As the leader, you should reserve the right to veto going ahead further until you are relatively satisfied.

Everyone else

During the time of equipping and running your pilot group, others in the church may decide to start their own groups spontaneously. Don't resist this, because God may be leading them, and they may surprise you with something very good. However, you should point out that you might call on them to reorganize later if they want to be a part of the network you are building.

Likewise, don't view the pilot group and events within it secretively. You can be open with the rest of the church about what is going on and the need to continue waiting and preparing while you are making progress. Especially if things go well in the pilot group, encourage the members of the group to share how good it is with other people in the church. This will build expectancy and positive motivation. Secrecy creates suspicion.

Replication

Aside from learning how to practice community, discipleship, group evangelism, and all the other needed functions of a spiritually vital house church or small group, the pilot group should also fill the house where you meet with new people. They should also develop two leadership teams. When all these things happen, the time to plant your first group approaches. As the senior leader, you and the rest of the leadership team have to decide when the pilot group has served its purpose.

Your first partition will open the door for additional recruits from the larger church as well as for adding more non-Christian converts. You can continue this process of group duplication until all of the willing people in your church belong to small groups. Don't worry about getting everyone into a group quickly. Far more important is that the ones who are in groups want to be there for the right reasons. For everyone else, the church can go on as it was before, and you can offer the preparatory activities we will discuss later.

Fast-tracking

You could also choose a fast-track option for your first group replication. In this plan, you have a dozen couples or mature singles gathered to begin your pilot group. When you are satisfied that they all see what you have in mind (and hopefully have experienced successful evangelistic outreach) you replicate the group after the fashion of a bursting pod. When pods burst open, they scatter their seeds everywhere at once. Likewise, in this approach, each mature couple or single goes out and originates their own group. They can invite people from the church to join, but be sure they don't merely fill their new group with church members. They need to also add a significant percentage of converts and lost sheep (people who haven't been in church for years) if they are to maintain the needed ethos in their groups.

Before trying a pod-style replication, you should plan out and negotiate who is going to invite whom to their groups. This could prevent an unseemly scramble to invite key people. I also believe that, at most, you should attempt only one pod-type replication. This kind of replication is too rapid to give good results except possibly in a situation where you have brought well-trained leaders and staffers have been brought together in a pilot group.

While spreading small groups or home churches more rapidly

through a fast-track approach may enhance the sense of excitement in the church, the risks are considerable. For one thing, unless you are actually attending a group and partaking in the life of the group, you have no way to know what the ethos and tone are. You can ask people what's happening in the group, but the subjective elements that go into true health in a home church or small group cannot be detected accurately unless you see with your own eyes. Overly rapid multiplication of groups is a good way to completely lose track of what is going on.[112] I would recommend using the slower, partition-style replication unless your church is quite large and you have high confidence in the people you're sending out.[113]

Matching quantity and quality

Each time a group duplicates, you must be satisfied that the new leadership team has shown the marks of true Christian leadership and character (like that detailed in Appendix 2 on the character traits for deacons). If leaders like that aren't ready, the group should wait and make up the deficiency. This is a way of stressing discipleship just as you stress outreach. Quantitative growth without qualitative growth isn't good enough, and it eventually leads to shallow groups that later implode. Likewise, growing quality and depth in groups without evangelism isn't good enough either. These groups become Bible clubs with no plausible future. You should have a basic rule that all groups have to work on outreach as well as building up the saints, just as we saw in Ephesians 4:11-16.

---

[112] Recent claims by "simple" house church enthusiasts in the U.S, that the more rapid groups plant the better, are unverified and probably false. Rapid planting is sometimes necessary under revival conditions when large numbers of new converts come into the church in a short time, but this is not an ideal, and it will cause problems. It could lead to the complete breakdown of the project. Just because groups are multiplying rapidly in India or other Asian countries doesn't mean that will work here. Remember, they are replicating rapidly based entirely on conversion. That is normally not the case in the west. When you hear or read theorists claiming that faster is better, you must find a way to verify their claims in actual practice in western culture. (See footnote 35).

[113] Craig from Apex says, "Retrospectively, I would never allow a person or couple to start a new house church without first having been a vital part of an existing house church for some period of time (maybe 6 months). I just don't believe that leaders can create something active, revolutionary and redemptive in the world if they have never personally been a part of it and experienced the ecstasy of being a part of seeing a life transformed and the agony of dealing with disharmony or being a part of a life (at 3:00 a.m.) that is struggling with the wounds they have brought to their new faith in Jesus. There is no way to simulate this in a classroom." I couldn't agree more.

Replicating groups is relatively easy in the early stages, because people can simply invite friends from the church. It will become much harder when there are no longer unincorporated people left to recruit. From that point on, all recruits must come from the world. Also, most churches have an existing group of mature Christians who can easily become leaders. But after these are gone, all leaders must be raised up from immaturity and worldliness—a much more difficult proposition.

Because early duplication is relatively easy, you could see groups doubling and planting in six months or a year. Within a few years, a couple of groups could become dozens. But be sure to manage your people's expectations by pointing out that the rapid planting you see now will be much harder when you have access only to non-Christians for further growth. The ease of replication while your church converts from a legacy to an organic approach poses dangers. People's understanding of how hard it is to plant new house churches could become distorted. People too accustomed to easy home church replication may lack the toughness and tenacity needed to lead real growth by conversion and discipleship.

Change tension

Under this kind of approach, some people in the church could be waiting for months or years before getting into a home group. This can be a good thing. As people wait for their chance to join in, hopefully they will be hearing from others that it's awesome, fun, fruitful, and fulfilling. Because most of your opinion leaders are part of the new network, others in the church will want to join in.

A certain tension may build in the church, and that's not bad. Tension and frustration cause people to feel privileged when they finally get to join a home group. Make it clear that you want everyone to join in but they must be patient; the process cannot be rushed without hurting the quality of what you are doing. You can even lay down conditions for who gets to join, such as a willingness to work hard on the goals of the group, and having completed an introductory class and some outside reading. The result should be that your groups will fill up with eager, grateful people who understand what body life is and what a home group is for.[114]

Because groups could grow through merely incorporating other church members, you may need to regulate how many people can join a group from the larger church. For instance, you might say that only half of all growth in small groups can be from adding existing members from the church. Of course there is no limit to how many non-Christians can join.[115]

During one transition event in our church, the waiting list to get into a home group contained hundreds of names and the waiting time grew to about a year and a half! We pointed out that certain things could hasten or retard the process. For instance, having a newly converted Christian who wanted to join with you would hasten the process. Those with newly converted friends could move toward the front of the line. People who pursued further equipping and were known for serving strongly in the church could also be moved forward. On the other hand, those who were do-nothings or malcontents were not desirable, and home group leaders could refuse to take them. As the enthusiasm for home groups increased, the attitude and motivation in our entire fellowship soared.

The point in being selective is that people should view belonging to a home church as a privilege, not a right. People join a home group for what they have to contribute, not for what they can get out of it.

By taking a patient, gradual approach to converting a legacy church over to organic principles, you avoid the confusion and demoralization that so often come when leaders try to impose change on the whole church at once.

---

[114] Another good point from Craig: "This may be a good place for a parallel track that is conducted out of the traditional part of the gathering that begins to build some of the kinds of skills and experiences that will be common once these folks join a house church. Specifically I'm thinking about outreach groups for evangelism and good works that are done from time to time in larger groups with people not yet in house churches. It will be important not only to get people out of the walls of the church to do these important Kingdom activities, but also to provide time back within the walls to discuss the experiences together. In this way the things being done in house churches and in the traditional part of the church have some congruence."

[115] Joel Comiskey reports on South Shore Community Church in Bridgewater, MA where they practice this approach on an ongoing basis. Every small group has to win converts before they can plant a new group. Joel Comiskey, Cell Church Solutions: Transforming the Church in North America, (CCS Publishing, 2005) 90.

Feedback

People need regular news on how the conversion process is going, especially notices of any successes. At least monthly, you should update the entire congregation on how the conversion is going, including milestones reached. Personal testimonials from people who feel their lives changing are powerful. Home group leaders should share how challenging, fun, and fulfilling they think their roles are. Newsletters and email notices can help here. New classes, book reviews, and reading suggestions keep the issues alive and on the radar screen for your people.

At key stages, additional meetings for the whole church are in order. Return to the issue some weeks or months later, and review what the results of the change have been. This is especially important when the results have been good. Use this as an opportunity to remind your people how something that earlier seemed worrisome is now working out very well, and that they should remember this in the future.[116]

Plan on years

Transitioning a large church could be a five year project or even longer. Smaller churches could do it in a couple or three years—and by completing the transition, I mean *most* of your people have transitioned, not all. If a majority of your people understand and practice New Testament-style church life, they will control the ethos of the group, and the others will gradually follow.

I know many churches in America are impatient and have little stomach for lengthy tasks. But if you try to force a conversion of this kind through in months instead of years, you're going to get something very superficial that festers and collapses before long. It will not build on itself unless you lay a very deep foundation. That foundation is made up of deeply held beliefs with accompanying

---

[116] From Craig: "We make time in our regional meetings, where leaders from about 12 house churches get together on a monthly basis, for leaders to share stories of transformation that are taking place in their house churches so that we can all be encouraged by the work of God. We also have time to share concerns or difficulties that emerge from the house churches so that the other leaders can share practical experience about how they may have resolved a similar issue in their house church. I often refer to this process as cross-pollination."

scriptural backing, and personal discipleship that has transformed people's character and ministry capability.[117]

Anticipate losses

All authorities agree that change in the church is always an occasion for losses. A far-reaching change like the one we are contemplating may mean significant losses. If the change is important, you have to be willing to lose people. When you try to please everyone, you can't set a strong direction. That ends up pleasing no one. What are the chances that everyone is going to agree on the new direction you're mapping out?

You should try to win over as many as possible, but even if you fail to win the support of some, this change is important enough to pursue anyway. In cases like this, be aware that a struggle is inevitable, and it could be costly. The things you are prepared to lose people over are the things that matter to you. Be prepared to withstand the punishment disgruntled members may dish out, in the knowledge that many will come around in the end if the change is as helpful as you predict.[118]

The big picture

Upper level leaders who successfully transition a church from one philosophy of ministry to another have accomplished a major feat of leadership. While such accomplishments are not common or easy, churches like Apex are succeeding in such transitions and yours can, too. Think how much more enjoyable ministry will be when you don't have nagging doubts about whether you are doing

---

[117] Craig agrees: "What we're really talking about here is a building program – not for the construction of a physical edifice, but for the building up of the body of Christ to DO the work of the ministry. Many of the principles of successful edifice building programs can apply, however. Perhaps most important is the clear and continual communication of a shared vision followed by real visual evidence of progress."

[118] I liked this suggestion from Craig: "Here is where it can be helpful to have strong, healthy relationships with other churches in your geographic area. Actively helping people who don't buy-in to the new vision to find a welcoming church community that meets them where they are in their spiritual journey can really help to keep the 'punishment from disgruntled members' to a minimum. Being a good shepherd can mean helping the sheep find other pastures that may be more appropriate for them at this time. Taking a loving and active role in this process of changing pastures, rather than just letting them wander off on their own, is a sign of real unconditional love that keeps people from walking away from God, because they feel betrayed by the church."

the right thing. Imagine how much more gratifying church life is going to be for everyone when they all truly sense that people's lives are being changed in powerful ways and the church is no longer merely warehousing immature Christians.

Chapter Twenty-Five

Home Group Leaders and Average Members Seeking Change

People leading a home church, small group, or other type of group within a larger network or local church face a challenge similar to that faced by pastors—it may be easier to change a small group than changing a whole church, but not really easy.

Depending on the nature of the change you envision, you may need to check with higher leadership in the church to see if they have objections to what you are considering. If you are seeking change that wouldn't concern higher leadership, this might not be necessary.

My group

During a period about twenty years ago, our church experimented with low-involvement home groups on the theory that family-aged people don't have time to gather often and therefore need a different standard. My own group was used to a weekly schedule, but I didn't mind trying the experiment because in addition to being a father with young kids at home, I was also doing some high school ministry on the side. The shift to an every-other week schedule for home church included some mixing in of new people from other groups undergoing reorganization.

Some months into the new arrangement, our adult group had a frank discussion where I and others expressed dissatisfaction with the new approach. Several of us felt we were drifting apart as friends compared to what we had experienced under a more high-commitment approach. We realized that missing one meeting meant being out of fellowship for a month! Even with auxiliary men's and women's groups, we simply didn't feel we were getting the level of relational closeness needed to authentically engage with each other's lives in the way prescribed in the New Testament. We also felt our group wasn't accomplishing anything. Others didn't agree. They felt the group was fine and didn't want to commit more time.

We studied New Testament teaching on the church like that in the first few chapters of this book, which I felt would make the case for why we needed a shift in our understanding and practice. Maybe some were convinced; I'm not sure. But the same picture remained: some of us wanted a more high investment group while others loudly proclaimed their unwillingness to move in that direction.

After talking with other opinion leaders in the group (most of whom agreed with my wife and me) we announced that we were moving to an every-week home church meeting. When the others complained, I simply said, "Look, if you don't want to come every week don't come! We're going to be here regardless." That drew funny looks around the room, but nobody could think of anything negative to say. Finally, someone suggested, "I wonder if we're going to be viewed as uncommitted if we don't show up."

I shrugged my shoulders. "This isn't a legalistic thing. We realize people may be in different situations. But clearly some are going to be less committed and others more; that's not a case for judging one another. Let's just extend the freedom to choose our own level of involvement."

We later also established two different men's groups—one based on a more hard-core commitment to be trained to become Christian workers, and one geared more to fellowship. The expectations were different for each.

As we moved ahead under this plan, I noticed that fewer and fewer members were opting for the low-involvement approach. One couple that wanted lower involvement migrated to another group in the church. Most just ended up taking their involvement to a higher level than they had planned. Eventually, the whole group naturally gravitated to a high-investment approach like that described in Acts and the entire New Testament.

Elements of change

I've talked to other group leaders who had the same idea but weren't able to effect a change like the one I just described. Why the difference?

For one thing, I had several compatriots who felt the same way I did, so there was a nucleus for change. As I mentioned in the previous chapter, change doesn't come to everyone at once. It spreads out like little waves when a pebble goes into the water.

Second, we were determined to go ahead with what we believed was right whether the others joined in with us or not. In fact, we expended little effort trying to convince the reluctant to join in with us because we felt it would be better to have only those who wanted to be there. If others were coming under pressure or with little understanding of what they were doing, they would probably be a damper on the meeting. In leading this kind of change, you can't be overly worried about whether everyone joins in or not. Just go. Some will follow, and those who don't will probably be happier with the path they choose than they would be if they acted merely because of social pressure. If people are really unhappy, offer to help them migrate to a different group more in line with their views.

In the end, virtually all of the original members ended up joining in because they kept hearing about cool discussions and studies that happened on weeks they weren't there, and they didn't want to miss out. When we tried to set up a two-tiered men's group, all our guys wanted to be in the high-investment group. Nobody wanted to be in the "easy" group. When we pointed out the contradiction between wanting a high-investment men's group and low investment home church, one by one they announced that they had changed their minds about the low-investment approach to both groups.

So, on a smaller scale, the approach to change in a home group is similar to the approach described in the previous chapter for a whole church. First came talks with key like-minded members about what we were feeling and why. Then came thawing the status quo and teaching on New Testament principles. Finally, we moved with those who bought into the plan, and gradually the others changed as well.

The change I described here was relatively simple. More difficult changes, like moving your home group from an inward, non-evangelizing group to one with successful outreach will be considerably harder, as described in the chapter on outreach. But leaders shouldn't let the difficulty of a task deter them from moving ahead. Change will eventually come in most cases if leaders are prayerful, consistent, and determined. In cases where change doesn't come, godly leaders may have to consider disbanding the group and moving to a new ministry environment where people are more willing to follow God.

Seeking change as an opinion leader

People can foster change in their churches even when they have no recognized role as leaders. Every church has experienced shifts in interests and outlook based primarily on the agitation of enthusiastic members. Members who have a major influence in our church have usually adopted the following pattern.

Seek out leaders

Some key changes in our church have been the result of a member approaching me or one of our other leaders with some new idea or perspective. Often, the easiest thing to do is share some good reading in an upbeat way. These days, I get far more reading recommendations than I can possibly respond to, so people need some salesmanship in order to get me to read a new piece.

- People who want me to read and consider something new are far more likely to succeed if they show up with the book or paper they have in mind and give or lend me a copy, instead of expecting me to remember their recommendation and find it myself.
- I've read several titles because someone I liked gave me a copy with a note inside pointing out how this dovetailed with some of my own teaching, or perhaps challenged my teaching, and how the person felt sure I would enjoy it or could use it in my ministry.

- The enthusiasm of the person making the referral makes a difference. When I can see the person is excited, that pricks my curiosity.
- My perception of the reliability and wisdom of the one making a recommendation affects my willingness to read. I am more inclined to read things recommended by "doers" in our group than those recommended by people I perceive as theology hobbyists.
- When several different people mention the same title, I become more likely to read it. I feel I need to read books that are circulating around the church so I know what people are into. I don't like the feeling that everyone else has read something, but I haven't.
- Recommendations should be positive. The observation that "this piece shows where we have completely missed the boat," may get me to read some, but with a negative attitude. I may just scan it over to get a feeling for what it argues but never seriously engage with it. When I perceive someone as hostile, it makes me suspicious of what they recommend, and that's not a good way to win me over.
- People who tell me they want to know my impression or opinion of what the author says are more likely to hear back from me, especially if they can briefly explain why it matters.
- I appreciate it when people give me a book or article, observing that they know I'm busy but are convinced I'll be glad I read this.
- It may take follow up, such as asking whether I got a chance to read the piece, but I don't like being put under law to read. Effective opinion leaders check in at several-month intervals, but without disapproval. They just reiterate that they think I'll like it and are interested in my take on it. In a couple of cases, a person was able to explain further how it would be useful or challenging,

and I decided after all to read something I had already
discarded.

- Several people have gotten my attention by getting my
wife's attention.

Getting me or one of the other top leaders in our church to read
a well-argued book or paper on a subject would be a major
accomplishment for anyone who wanted to influence our community.
Obviously, there is no rule that I have to agree with something in
order for it to succeed in our church. On the other hand, getting me
on board would probably be a helpful step. On several occasions I've
read and liked books recommended by members, and I was able to
get other leaders to read the same book. A number have become
incorporated into training materials and ended up having major
impact in the church.

On other occasions, I haven't felt particularly drawn to things
people have given me. That could happen in your situation also. One
lesser goal would be to at least gain tacit approval for the idea you
are promoting—in other words, the leadership isn't going to help
drive it, but they won't resist it either. This could be a significant
accomplishment. Often leaders won't help promote an idea, not
because they think it's wrong, but simply because they don't see it as
a priority at this time or don't feel it's attainable. Still, that leaves
you and others free to pursue righteous goals for body life in at least
your part of the church.

If the leadership of your church is against what you want to see,
your idea is in real trouble. You can try further discussions and even
debate. When Paul says, "Let two or three prophets speak, and let
the others pass judgment" (1 Corinthians 14:29), he is suggesting
that the whole church should get involved in debating truth. I've had
more than one experience where a sharp member was able to
significantly shift my view after several talks, including good-natured
arguments. In some cases, inability to agree with your church
leadership on philosophy of ministry could be a reason to find a
different church, or plant a new one yourself. Either of these would
be better than ongoing fighting with your church's leaders.

Model

Leaders may not feel they have time to turn aside from what they're already striving to do to pursue some new emphasis. But if some members begin doing something together that bears positive fruit in the church, nearly all leaders will give that idea a second look.

When I heard recently that a couple of adult home churches were taking an interest in developing a relationship with an urban middle school, I thought, "That's nice." But when I heard several months later that among other service efforts, they also had a Bible study where over thirty students had met Christ, my perspective shifted quickly: this was hot! Similarly, when I heard some of our adult groups were engaging in service work with a certain refugee group in our city, I naturally approved, but said nothing. Later, when I saw up to eighty of those people sitting in Bible studies and heard that many had received Christ, I began publicly pointing to the groups involved as a model we should follow.

The same has happened with numerous ministries in our church. Most pastors are looking for ideas that move believers closer to God, deeper into commitment, and especially into effective evangelism. If you and some like-minded friends begin a group that bears positive fruit in the church, people will eventually take notice—especially if you aren't self-righteous about it, implying you're better than everyone else.

The principle here is that actions speak louder than words. When others in the church begin to hear that the new convert in their midst met Christ through an *ad hoc* home group that you got going, they'll mark that. When they meet a second and a third person also reached in that group, you'll have their undivided attention. When church leaders see that the most spiritually alive, eager to help, and enthusiastic people in the church seem to come from this new group, you'll get a second look. If, on the other hand, your group sees itself as an embodied refutation of the rest of the church, even positive fruit will be discounted.

Years ago, I met a woman who said she had gained introduction to our church through a "mom's playgroup." I had to ask her what that was, because I had never heard the expression before. It turned out some women in our church were organizing times when mothers of young children in a neighborhood would bring their kids together to play while the moms had coffee and discussed something— sometimes a spiritual book they were reading. At the least, visiting moms met young mothers from our church who explained how they loved it and how unusual it was, etc. I guess several of these play groups sprang up spontaneously through word of mouth as an outreach idea.

By the time I met a second and then a third family who came into our church through this ministry, I began asking around. I found out who had the idea and went to her and other leaders on staff, expressing excitement about what she had started. I pointed out that if two or three groups were good, two or three dozen would be even better. We began promoting the idea, supplying materials, and offering training. As groups proliferated, the leaders met occasionally to share ideas about what was working.

I don't know how many people have been won to Christ through the mom's playgroups, but I think the ministry has been a very positive presence in our church. I had nothing to do with the origin of this ministry, but I did step in and agitate for it at a certain point, and that helped propel it forward. These women didn't wait for me to get involved. They just started with their idea, and let their deeds do the talking.

The big picture

Let's face it: ideas are a dime a dozen. Why should your idea command loyalty and priority in such a busy world? Sure, the idea may be good, but leaders know there are hundreds of good ideas we don't have time for. On the other hand, when someone shows that an idea is biblical and wins over leaders' minds and hearts through solid, well-reasoned reading, they make it highly likely that action will follow. If people take the initiative to build their ideas into working, fruit-bearing ministries that bless the church, they have a highly persuasive argument for spreading them to the rest of the church.

Earlier, I suggested that leaders are not the only source of a group's ethos. A local church is a community of people, and ideas flow in all directions. Members can influence a group's ethos just as leaders can. Looking back over the history of our own church, I see numerous points where members changed our view and our ethos (usually by adding new values to what we already had). God puts it on every member in the body of Christ to make his or her contribution, including suggesting new directions. To be that kind of person, be sure to spend plenty of time in prayer and careful reflection. Be sure to bring your ideas in a positive way. And, if possible, combine your words or literature with deeds.

Chapter Twenty-Six

Planting a New Church

One good way to establish a New Testament-style church is by starting from scratch. According to the New Testament, nobody needs permission from anyone to plant a new church. Jesus simply called it "whenever two or three of you are gathered in my name" (Matthew 18:20). People need no special reason or justification for a new church plant. Planting a new group doesn't necessarily imply that none of the churches in the area are good enough. The simple fact is that Christians have the freedom to gather wherever and whenever they want, and any gathering constitutes an expression of the body of Christ.

We have biblical examples of churches sending people out to plant churches, but never of forbidding church planting or giving permission to plant a church. On the contrary, the example in Acts is that everywhere people went, they preached the word and planted new churches (Acts 11:19-20). All theories claiming that existing churches must commission or give permission for new church plants are without biblical backing (although being sent by a church is also good and biblical).

Establishing group DNA

Experts constantly point out how difficult it can be to change the DNA of existing churches. Without doubt, DNA tends to be enduring, and often goes all the way back to a group's founding, especially if the group had an early period of success that lodged values deeply into people's outlook. That's why one of the best ways to establish quality ethos in a group is to start the group from scratch.

Elements of a successful church plant

I've led in four church plants, including the one I'm in now. I also was involved in starting an additional dozen or so home groups from scratch that I could have developed into independent churches if I had wanted to. But since they were in our area, I just incorporated them into our larger work. In each case, I started with a handful of people, perhaps three to six. This original group was either friends of mine or friends of a friend who were willing to come together to hear a Bible study and to "hang out." In nearly every case one or more of the people in the original meeting were non Christians, but Christians also attended.

I don't think it's difficult to reach this point, but going forward to the point where you have a viable, growing group of dozens with up and coming new leaders and mostly new converts is another matter. Nothing is easy about that part. Even a person with strong leadership gifting will be tested severely on the way to a tipping point where the church begins to have a life of its own. Perhaps the biggest barrier to reaching such a tipping point is the church planter's own impatience. Greed for numerical growth more than for quality growth can take over. It's a very dangerous time, because here is where a faulty ethos might develop.

I'm not going to write a book about church planting, because others have planted way more than I have. But I do believe it is a good way to go, and if my current church disappeared tomorrow, I would probably follow the same path again. Instead of writing a book, I'm just going to list some things that strike me as important to seek or to avoid and leave the details up to your creativity and the leading of the Holy Spirit.

Positive elements

Biblical authority

Through teaching and arguing, you must get even the smallest group to buy into biblical inspiration in the fullest sense. Since everything you build in the future will be based on scripture, there is simply no way around this issue. People need help understanding the basis and backing for biblical authority. They need to know the extent of its authority, including its sufficiency and how to understand it (hermeneutics). You can usually pursue this goal at the same time you are pursuing other goals. Your people must come to believe that God works through his word, activated by the Holy Spirit.

Prayer ministry

Early in the life of a new group, you should establish a time to pray together as believers, without non-Christians present. By guiding a time of prayer with interested fellow believers, you guide the developing outlook of the group. The things you stress at times of prayer tend to become the values for the group. You also get a feeling for what is on other people's hearts, whether positive or negative. Spiritual disclosure is unavoidable at regular times of prayer. These discoveries will show you what instruction, correction, or encouragement you need.

Evangelism

In my experience, people who are excited about what God is teaching them through his word begin bringing friends. In most cases, you don't need to say anything. Among those new friends, some will be existing Christians and some will be non-Christians. I like to focus on the non-Christian guests. I feel I can help them feel comfortable and answer their questions.

In some cases where evangelism doesn't naturally begin happening, you will need to bring it up in teaching and conversations. Asking people what their friends and family think about their involvement in the group usually gives you an idea of whether your people have said anything at all to their connections. It may become necessary to actively resist growth in the group through transfers. Any group that doesn't develop an evangelistic ministry within the first months of its existence is stillborn. It cannot succeed, and gathering more and more Christians together will only mask this sad fact.

I've been involved in a few cases where this happened. I simply called the group's attention to the fact that no non-Christians were visiting the group and began a discussion on what people thought about that. As people gave their opinions, my own view was often quite a bit stronger than theirs. I just made clear that I would not be able to continue with the group unless we could get a hearing from some non-Christians. As much as I liked the believers attending, I didn't feel it was good for me or for them to operate a group that was ingrown.

Since in most of these cases I lived in a distant neighborhood or was working with people far younger or older than I was, I couldn't do the evangelism myself, so I depended on the group to come through. I offered training on how to reach out, and even personal coaching and assistance (where I went with them to a social event to meet their friends). I pointed out that I had to be convinced that they were putting in effort—I was more than willing to persevere as long as I believed people were trying. I have also called on groups not to invite any more Christians to the group until we found our way to successful evangelism.

Such moves could cause some angry reactions, and that may be exactly what the group needs. I've been in groups where a number of members stormed off after one or two talks along these lines and never came back. That's probably all to the good. I've seen groups turn around at this point because the leader simply wouldn't accept anything less than true engagement with non-Christians and authentic outreach.

If people are trying (you can usually tell from their stories at prayer meeting) you can try some in-between events, like dinner party discussions, or neutral outings.

In some other cases, I eventually lost hope that the group was going to get outside of its Christian cocoon. In such cases, I simply announced that I wouldn't be able to attend any longer, and that I was being called away to other work. I was usually able to suggest ongoing ways they could be fed, including continuing to meet as a group without me, or going to an area Bible teaching church. I always leave on a friendly note in these situations, because leaving with a denunciation wouldn't do any good.

I strongly believe it would be worth several tries with different launches to get some non-Christians coming into the group rather than go on struggling with an ingrown group. Unless you successfully address this issue, you are building fatal DNA into the group. If your group can't reach non-Christians now, you have no reason to think they will be able to later. You have to face the facts.

Directive leadership

As the previous section suggests, I believe (along with many experts) that a newly planted group needs directive leadership. Any notion that a leaderless group will spontaneously grow itself is naïve and foolish. If you have heard contemporary claims to the contrary, I suggest you check on the truthfulness of those claims very carefully. I have seen leaderless groups assemble spontaneously, but they never go anywhere and soon disintegrate unless someone takes a directive leadership role.

I prefer a collaborative leadership style most of the time, but a newly planted group is not the place for that. Collaborative leadership comes later. You don't come to a new group and ask, "So, what would you guys like to study?" or "How often or how long do you think we should meet?" Instead, you explain what you are going to be doing and invite people to come along. Successful church planters know how to begin strong and gradually draw others into the task of co-leadership. But they have to grow into that role—not simply be thrown in to a pseudo-leadership role for the sake of egalitarian ideals. Don't pass teaching responsibilities around in the group. People can take initiative and contribute through serving in various ways (like snacks or set up), but while the group is in its formative stage, you need a clear voice of directive leadership. If you're planting a church with a team of workers, I suggest one be given the point role, and that the others whole-heartedly accept the arrangement. Paul and his missionary band are the biblical model for church planting, and there was never any doubt who was in charge there. Planting a church is different than operating and developing a church. Directive leadership is essential at this stage.

Christian love

If you begin meeting with some people, even if it's only one or two, you have the opportunity to unleash the life-changing power of God's love. Study good sources on how to build friendships, and get into the inside of the people you work with.[119] This is often difficult, but if you expect to succeed, you have to invest until you love your people from the heart.

You will be building two levels of relationship in even a small group—those who you love on a more casual level and those you love deeply and intimately. The latter relationships are usually those that grow into disciple making relationships.

Disciple making

If your church plant succeeds, you will need multiple, qualified leaders in order to keep from having a man-centered, show-style church. If you wait until success comes, you're too late! Good church planting should include personal discipling of promising young Christians from the beginning. If you're unclear on this part, study my earlier book, *Organic Disciplemaking*, or some of the other quality books on the subject.[120]

---

[119] For my best, see Dennis McCallum and Gary DeLashmutt, *Spiritual Relationships that Last* (Columbus OH: Xenos Books, 1997) chapters 1-4. Also see Dennis McCallum and Jessica Lowery, *Organic Disciplemaking*, Chapter 4.

[120] Some of these have gone out of print, but all can be found on Amazon. Robert E. Coleman, *The Master Plan of Evangelism*, (Grand Rapids: Baker Book House Company, 1963) is still the best (after our own of course!). Christopher Adsit, *Personal Disciple Making: A Step by Step Guide for Leading a Christian from New Birth to Maturity*, (Nashville: Thomas Nelson Publishers, 1988). Joel Comiskey, *Cell Church Solutions: Transforming the Church in North America*, (Morneo Valley, CA: CCS Publishing, 2005). This explanation of cell church theory as it relates to the special conditions in North American culture makes an excellent case for why cell churches will work anywhere. Disciple making plays a key part in multiplying cell groups in this model, and this book includes

Boundaries

A group that's too loose and that tries to please everyone usually ends up pleasing no one. Groups where anything goes are usually boring or chaotic. They seem to lack direction, and people annoy each other. In the vacuum of true leadership, power struggles develop. Alternatively, people will simply disengage. In either case, directionless groups are eventually abhorrent to their members. As a leader trying to establish group ethos, you have to define for the group what is and is not acceptable in this group. Further, you have to be ready to enforce your limits to acceptable behavior by un-inviting certain people to future meetings. The group needs boundaries.

Some of these boundaries might be on moral issues, as discussed in the chapter on church discipline (this is for believers, not for visiting non-Christians). But more boundaries than those may be necessary while establishing group ethos. Different churches operate on different visions and ministry philosophies that may be quite incompatible. Sometimes you may need to draw limits to how far you are willing to bend in the direction of a different vision.

While planting one group in a small town outside Columbus, I had several new Christians and non-Christians attending, along with a few established believers. One week, a Christian young man brought his mentor—an older man from an area church. This man had a number of points to share, all of which had a legalistic and

---

helpful chapters on making disciples, training, and coaching. Leroy Eims, *The Lost Art of Disciple Making*, (Colorado Springs: Navpress, 1978). An excellent introduction to the idea of disciple making, this book includes a few study guides in the back that could be used in a cooperative study with disciples. However, he only covers the early phases of disciple making. Rowland Forman, Jeff Jones, and Bruce Miller, *The Leadership Baton: An Intentional Strategy For Developing Leaders In Your Church*, (Grand Rapids, MI.: Zondervan, 2004). This is a plan for equipping from the excellent Fellowship Bible Churches originated by Gene Getz. Alice, Fryling, ed., *Disciplemakers' Handbook: Helping People Grow in Christ*, (Downers Grove Ill: InterVarsity Press, 1989). Walter A.Hendrichsen, *Disciples are Made, Not Born*, (Colorado Springs: Cook Communications, 1974). Bill Hull, *The Disciple making Pastor*. (Grand Rapids: Baker Book House Co., 1988) and *Jesus Christ Disciplemaker*, (Grand Rapids: Baker Books, 1984, 2004). Gary W. Kuhne, *The Dynamics of Discipleship Training: Being and Producing Spiritual Leaders*, (Grand Rapids: Zondervan Publishing House, 1978). Waylon B. Moore, *Multiplying Disciples: The New Testament Method for Church Growth*, (Tampa: Missions Unlimited, 1981). Greg. Ogden, *Transforming Discipleship: Making Disciples a Few at a Time*, (Downers Grove: InterVarsity Press, 2003). Jim Petersen, *Lifestyle Discipleship: The Challenge of Following Jesus in Today's World*, (Colorado Springs: Navpress, 1993).

hell-fire flavor. I opposed his tone during the meeting, making clear that he was coming from a perspective I didn't share. Then I followed up after the meeting by confronting him directly and immediately before he could further frighten the young non-Christian he was thumping his Bible at.

I asked him to step aside with me, and frankly told him his approach was incompatible with what we were doing and that he was not welcome to return. He was furious, and insisted on his rights as a Bible believer to attend and to share as the Spirit led him. I eventually had to point out that I could call the police and prosecute him as a trespasser if he further disrupted our meetings before he finally stormed off. We also lost the young man who brought the older guy. But this summary dismissal was necessary and correct. The other people who overheard the altercation were naturally curious, and I simply explained to them what anti-cultural fundamentalism was and why I wasn't willing to have it take root in the group. The man was also way too old to be part of a student group. They learned an important lesson about what matters through the experience.

I have had to do similar things with others who were importing a brand of Christianity I simply was not willing to accommodate. Such alien visions disrupt the successful establishment of healthy group ethos. Later, after a group has its own DNA, they will deal with strange characters more naturally, and such people will pose less threat.

Consistency

Planting a new church cannot be done in spurts. Once a group begins to meet, they must meet consistently. People have to know that the gathering is going to happen and it's going to happen at the same time and place whether they come or not. Calling the group off because some will be on vacation is a mistake. People will suggest calling off your group meeting and going to a concert or other activity; don't listen. Just explain that you will be there as always and the teaching will go on. People may decide to do other things, but not you.

New groups go through ups and downs that can shake group morale. Your steadiness and unflagging commitment will help stabilize the group.

Youth

You could start a middle-aged church, but in American culture I would suggest starting with younger people. While I have had success gathering groups of middle-agers, groups without any younger component usually run into trouble. A common problem is that middle-aged people are happy to come to a group and hear an interesting teaching or discussion, but they are too often unwilling to commit time and effort to the larger tasks of becoming equipped and developing their own ministry. This is not true everywhere. In some cultures, middle-aged people would be ideal for planting a new group.

In America, younger people are more idealistic and have fewer prior commitments than family-aged people. They are easier to win over to the idea of hard work to become equipped and they like the idea of leading. They also have the opportunity to marry other committed Christians, as we discussed in the chapter on youth work.

Negative elements

In addition to striving for positive elements, you will want to avoid or resist certain negative elements that are sure to rear their heads.

Traditionalism

In western culture, the traditional church has extensive history and influence. People, even non-Christians, have certain things they expect to see in a church. Whether these things have anything to do with what scripture teaches is another question.

In planting a new church, you have the ultimate opportunity to sow DNA that isn't traditional. But this won't happen automatically. Only strong, proactive leadership will prevent people from importing unhelpful concepts from traditional Christianity. Think carefully about what you are going to do and not do. Include thinking about seemingly inconsequential things, like where and when you meet, the role and type of music, and other possibly symbolic things like the kind of language used during meetings or the way people dress. Remember, once traditional features slip in, you may never be able to get rid of them.

Transfers

In my opinion, the best possible church plant would be made up of nothing but me, any team I have along, and non-Christians or brand new converts. This would truly be a blank slate, and although such a group would have significant problems, you could set the tone you wanted from the start.

More realistically, every group in the west has to handle Christians transferring in from other churches—especially as word gets around that there's a cool new group in the area. These people could pose a threat to the health of your group.

First, some may bring in alien visions of the Christian life and of the church, as discussed earlier. You have to explain to such people that this group is different than what they are used to, and they need to decide whether to adopt the new paradigm or go to a different church.

In addition, the sheer existence of too many transfers endangers the group because they all share a church perspective instead of a secular one. This could make secular people feel uncomfortable. Too many transfers make it likely that more transfers will come and less likely that non-Christians will be attracted to the group.

Transfers can learn a different perspective in a process of mental and spiritual overhaul, but this process normally takes months or years. Therefore, the inflow of transfers should be slow enough that they don't take over the ethos of the group.

Transfers from liberal (non-Bible believing) churches or the Catholic or Orthodox church are in a completely different category. These are not really transfers in most cases and should be viewed as secular. Their churches normally don't teach on the need for personal conversion and related material. In my opinion, people from these backgrounds are always welcome in any number possible. They pose no threat to the group.

Divided counsel

In a well-formed church, it's normal and even healthy to have different viewpoints represented on non-essential issues. These issues could be doctrine or practice—such as ministry philosophy or style. But in a newly planted group, you need more uniformity. The cost of too much diversity of views in these areas is confusion and possibly failure to establish a good, clear ethos. Look for like-minded people to join in the project of church planting, and take time in advance to make sure you are all coming from the same place.

Super-spirituality

Super-spirituality, a term coined by Francis Schaeffer, represents an imbalance toward the subjective, the experiential, and the inward in spiritual matters. To super-spiritual Christians, humans can't do anything, and God does everything. The idea of planning or doing something purposeful because it makes sense is odious under this view. Super-spiritual Christians usually deprecate the usefulness of human leaders and tend to favor anarchy.

Super-spirituality is particularly likely in newer groups containing young Christians or transfers. The problem is that super-spiritual groups depart from both example and teaching in the New Testament. Such groups are establishing an ethos that will likely have to be over-thrown if the group is to go further than being a small splinter group. Super-spiritual Christians see no reason to study or work hard at ministry. Why figure out what is needed when God is going to do everything anyway? As a church planter, you should develop clear teaching and coaching materials that oppose super-spirituality and teach in its place a healthy balance between God's part and humans' part in ministry.

The big picture

Traditional church planting books often call on planters to contact existing Christians in an area and to convince them to come to the new church plant. The goal is often to get fifty or even a hundred Christians out to the first meeting. I obviously think this approach is mistaken, and in fact will guarantee the group begins in the same traditional model that is failing in so many ways today. A meeting formed this way will be mostly filled with existing Christians from day one, and that is going to determine the ethos more than anything. The stage-centered model will create a logic in people's mind that effectively overthrows the every-member model found in the New Testament. Paul certainly never planted churches this way.

Instead, with a more patient approach, you could build a group that is secular in tone and familiar with non-Christian perspectives from day one. You would have plenty of time to nurture disciples as the group grows, and they can increasingly take part in the work. Your church might not grow as fast as the other kind, especially at first. But you will reach more non-Christians this way, and you will be building depth at the same time you build size in the group. Over the long haul, a church plant based on conversions and discipleship will lead to a strong, New Testament ethos that you can develop into a full-sized, healthy local expression of the church.

Chapter Twenty-Seven

The Key to a Quality Church

Are you part of a team trying to upgrade an existing church? Are you considering starting a new one? If so, what do you hang your hope on? What will make your church awesome?

Possible answers abound on all sides. We see great church organizations today that draw thousands to Broadway-caliber stage productions. Others have world-famous charismatic preachers. These are the most famous churches in the modern west, so it's not surprising when people conclude that these things might be the key to success in the church. We see liberal groups, super-conservative groups, highly emotional groups, leaderless groups. Some groups count on developing a sense of family coziness. We have no shortage of suggestions on how to develop a successful church.

What do you think makes a church awesome?

May I suggest, your church will be awesome when God empowers what you are doing. No gimmicks, strategies, or "styles" will substitute for the raw power of the Spirit of God moving people's hearts toward him and away from sin, selfishness, and worldliness. Methods, structures, publicity, and fancy shows may not be wrong, but they are no substitute for the mighty hand of God working through his body.

I've seen God apparently get behind some pretty strange things and people. Sometimes those same apparent movements of God later evaporate into thin air or turn into something so ugly they bring shame onto the name of Jesus. Providing the test of real spiritual fruit, Jesus said, "I chose you, and appointed you that you would go and bear fruit, and that your fruit would remain" (John 15:16). Fruit that *remains*—that's the mark of a successful ministry. Some things that look highly successful initially later turn out to be wood, hay, and stubble.

The most fatal error

We could also ask the same question a different way: What might prevent God from moving through our group as much as he wants to? If you're like me, you realize the most likely barrier is your own fleshly state of mind when approaching ministry. When we think and operate in the flesh, we come up with all the wrong answers time after time. Think about some of the common marks of fleshly thinking about ministry:

- In the flesh, we tend to assess situations using a process of projection: we imagine what might be appealing or repulsive to non-Christians or Christians and build the church accordingly. The governing principle is what would please the people. This is what Paul called man-pleasing: "For am I now seeking the favor of men, or of God? Or am I striving to please men? If I were still trying to please men, I would not be a bond-servant of Christ" (Galatians 1:10). Of course we shouldn't try to find the least pleasing approaches possible. But pleasing people is not the goal of Christian ministry.
- Fleshly-minded ministers operate primarily on pragmatism—an outlook that judges all things by what results they produce. The pragmatist doesn't wonder, "Is it true?" or "Is it right?" but, "Will it work?" In this mindset, theology grows out of whatever practices garner the most results in terms of numbers, dollars, or fame. It's a difficult area, because results *do matter*. God has put us here to bear fruit, as Jesus said. But faithfulness to God, not results, is the primary goal (1 Corinthians

4:1). We shouldn't get our theology from studying what is advantageous; we should get it from scripture. Influencers for God feel the tension, the trial of faith when we see God call us to do or teach something that we know pragmatically will not please people. Under pragmatism, leaders stop teaching about the reality of hell or that gay sex or heterosexual fornication are sins because postmodern people don't want to hear that.

- People operating in the flesh can't find time to pray and aren't depending on God. The human side has crowded God out. Pressure tactics and manipulation become common when we feel we have to make something happen, and fear begins to govern instead of faith.
- In the flesh, we are constantly reading our own press clippings—mentally, if not actually. The fleshly worker has one eye on the galleries at all times. Competition and even dishonesty become common as we seek to posture as successful.
- Fleshliness breeds instability. When things are going well, our egos swell with pride. When we are "out of season" and things go poorly, we become inconsolable and desperate.
- When we operate in the flesh, outward, quantifiable results matter more than inward, spiritual results that may not show to the outside world. Numbers, dollars, and buildings trump everything else.

In a word, to the fleshly-minded Christian worker, the New Testament's picture of a church with every-member ministry is too extreme, too unrealistic, and pointless because nobody would listen to such a picture anyway. In our unbelief, we begin shaving God's picture of the church down to something "doable" even in the flesh, knowing all the while that we are disobeying what he says.

Look back over the chapters in this book. Which of the principles we have discussed can be safely dismissed? How far can we cut down our understanding of Jesus' body before we end up with something unrecognizable from a biblical perspective? If we are trusting God to provide the power in our ministry, wouldn't we be better off following the full teaching of scripture to the best of our ability?

We, as humans, have no control over when God moves in waves of revival. However, we do have a lot of say in what happens between those times. If we construct a church made up of people with good theology, who are well-equipped, who understand what we hope to see and why, and who are motivated to move in that direction, and hungry to build their own ministries, the pieces are in place for God to move mightily when he is ready. I believe that in his mercy, God often withholds revival from local groups until they are ready to handle the challenges revival will bring. Repeatedly, I have seen that when we have quality leaders and members ready, God supplies the increase—often in mysterious and unexpected ways. But if we don't have people ready, what would we do with several hundred more people anyway?

Consider this point from the late Francis Schaeffer:

> The *central* problem of our age is not liberalism or modernism, nor the old Roman Catholicism or the new Roman Catholicism, nor the threat of communism, nor even the threat of rationalism and the monolithic consensus which surrounds us. All these are dangerous but not the primary threat. The real problem is this: the church of the Lord Jesus Christ, individually or corporately, tending to do the Lord's work in the power of the flesh rather than of the Spirit. The central problem is always in the midst of the people of God, not in the circumstances surrounding them.[121]

Any group that purposely distorts the teaching of scripture because they imagine that doing so will make them more acceptable

---

[121] Francis Schaeffer, *No Little People*. In *The Complete Works of Francis Schaeffer*, Vol. 3, (Wheaton, Crossway Books, 1985) 29.

to modern people is headed down spiritually. God will not honor that approach.

No church is perfect or even close to perfection. Perfectionism actually works *against* successful church development. We live in a real world where a spiritual war is raging. We have to be willing to work with what we have and seek improvement. We can trust that God will eventually work in power if we take the scary step of honoring his word.

Appendix 1

Character Qualifications for Elders

Above reproach (1 Timothy 3:2; Titus 1:6,7)	*Anepilempton* (1 Timothy 3:2) means unaccusable. *Anegkleton* (Titus 1:6) is similar—unreprovable. In other words, elders are not to be guilty of any flagrant sin that people could use against them.
Husband of one wife (1 Timothy 3:2; Titus 1:6)	*Mais gunaikos andros* literally means a "one-woman man" (in Greek, the words for "man" and "woman" were the same as "husband" and "wife," so context determines which is intended). This expression probably isn't referring to polygamy (which was not common in the Roman empire), but rather to the idea that sexual morality is an established lifestyle. The idea is that the prospective elder is involved with no more than one woman *now*. Some wrongly think this expression means that the person has never been involved with more than one woman. That means divorcees or those who ran around earlier are out. But all of the character requirements refer to the person's *present life*, not to earlier sin. Peter flagrantly denied Christ and Paul murdered, but both were qualified to serve as elders. Instead, this requirement prohibits flirting, pornography habits, inappropriate "counseling" of the opposite sex, or other signs that the elder lacks sexual self-control.

Must exercise self-control (1 Timothy 3:2)	*Nephalion* means "restrained" and can refer to being self-controlled in a number of areas, including the use of alcohol (hence, some translations read "sober"). But heavy drinking is addressed later, so this probably means "restrained" in the sense of not lunging, being a blabbermouth, jumping to unwarranted conclusions, or other careless behaviors.
Must live wisely (1 Timothy 3:2; Titus 1:8 NLT)	The word *sophrona* can mean "thoughtful" or "sane." It suggests the person is mentally healthy (Mark 5:15; 2 Corinthians 5:13), has an honest evaluation of himself that is neither arrogant nor insecure (Romans 12:3), and has the ability to be reasonable, sensible, and able to keep one's head under stress (Titus 2:6; 1 Peter 4:7).
Must be respectable (1 Timothy 3:2)	The word *kosmion* means "well-ordered." It suggests orderliness and stability (see 1 Timothy 2:9; 1 Peter 3:4). People who are falling apart or slovenly in their life habits would be disqualified.
Hospitable (1 Timothy 3:2; Titus 1:8)	The word *philoxenos* can mean "hospitable," but that may be a weak translation. The word literally means "loving strangers," which goes well beyond merely hosting people in your home. This word suggests elders should be outreaching to those outside the church, including having a heart for evangelism.
Not addicted to wine (1 Timothy 3:3; Titus 1:7, NASB)	*Me paroinon* means "not a drunk." Elders are allowed to drink in moderation, but must not have a drinking problem. The same would go for drug dependency.

Not self-willed (Titus 1:7 NASB)	*Me autheda* can mean "arrogant" or "overbearing, as a result of stubbornness or self-will." Peter links this negative trait with rebelliousness in 2 Peter 2:10 (see also Titus 1:6). Paul uses it to refer to usurping rightful authority in 1 Timothy 2:12. Elders should demonstrate the ability to defer to others at times. Those who always have to have their way or they will punish those around them are not mature enough to be elders. Deferring to others means actively getting behind the others' way and helping it to succeed. Elders should be able to apologize when they are in the wrong.
Not quick-tempered (Titus 1:7)	*Me orgilon* means "not inclined to anger" or "not hot-tempered." Elders have their patience tried often and anyone who has not gained control of his temper will discredit himself. When leaders misrepresent God by making him seem more angry than he really is, it's a serious matter as Moses learned (Num. 20; James 1:19-20; 3:1). Elders may get angry, but they should be *slow* to anger rather than having a short fuse. They should be under control, avoiding violent outbursts.
Not violent (Titus 1:7; 1 Timothy 3:3)	*Me plektes* means "not a striker." Elders should not be prone to physical or verbal abuse (i.e. slander, put-downs, etc.). They shouldn't enjoy fighting.
Gentle (1 Timothy 3:3	This word *epieike* means "gracious," or "forbearing." Elders should not be dismissive hard-liners who are unduly rigorous or legalistic in their treatment of people. They should be kind, empathetic and patient with all. People can be fragile. Elders need to consider how their words and actions will affect others. See

	2 Timothy 2:24-25; 1 Thessalonians 2:7; Galatians 6:1; Ephesians 4:3; Colossians 3:12,13; 1 Timothy 6:11; Galatians 5:22,23; James 3:17.
Not quarrelsome (1 Timothy 3:3)	*Amachon* means peaceable and not contentious. This means not looking for ways to disagree or oppose, not loving to fight or quarrel. Elders should have a positive and constructive point of view.
Free From the Love of Money (1 Timothy 3:3 Titus 1:7)	*Aphilagruron* literally means not a lover of silver. Elders cannot be greedy or materialistic. They have to value spiritual things more than money. The NLT translation of Titus 1:7, "not dishonest with money," is doubtful. Although the term could mean dishonest gain, it literally means evil gain, and should probably be translated as in the NASB: "not fond of sordid gain" (Titus 1:7). Paul's point in both passages is not that elders should avoid dishonest gain, but that they should not live for money. The church needs models who know what is important in life, and the devotion needed to become wealthy is incompatible with real spirituality. Elders should be content with what they have materially (1 Timothy 6:8). They should not be motivated by financial considerations in ministry decisions (see Acts 20:33). They realize that true love for Christ and his work can be eclipsed by greed (see Matthew 6:24; 1 Timothy 6:6-11,17-19). Our day is replete with scandals involving money-loving in the church. Mature elders should give generously to others, and should live a simple lifestyle in order to curb temptation.

Not a new convert (1 Timothy 3:6)	*Me neophuton* means "not newly planted." Elders should have been walking Christians long enough to be tested by God (see 1 Timothy 3:10). Elders should have experienced success without becoming conceited.
Having a good reputation with those outside (1 Timothy 3:7)	This expression means, "having a good testimony with those outside," meaning with non-Christians. Those we recognize as elders should be viewed as good people by non-Christians in their neighborhoods and workplaces. These people are spiritually authentic and not two-faced. They should be sensitive to what leads to good evangelism.
Loving what is good (Titus 1:8)	This straightforward term implies that elders' lifestyles should demonstrate that they enjoy God's ways (see Romans 12:2).
Just (Titus 1:8)	To be just, elders should be fair and impartial in their dealings with people (1 Timothy 5:21). People need to feel confident that their elders don't play favorites, including with their family members or friends.
Devout (Titus 1:8)	*Hosios* is one of the words sometimes translated "holy." It means to be committed to and serious about spiritual matters. Elders should be zealous for God's will. Elders' single-mindedness for God and His work provide good models for the church.
He must manage his own family well, with obedient children (1 Timothy 3:6). Having children	This expression actually means "leading his family well" rather than managing. The fact that the children are following as well as his wife, is an indication that the elders is able to lead. Arguably, the term for children here refers to younger children, as opposed to adult children.

who believe (Titus 1:6).	Should elders be responsible for the behavior of their adult children? This would have been more plausible in the ancient world, where parents had more control. It's not clear that such would be the case. But today, as then, a person's family knows them like no one else, so Paul's call to watch the family is wise. Who can resist his logic when he says, "but if a man does not know how to manage his own household, how will he take care of the church of God?" (1 Timothy 3:5). Strong Christian leaders develop strong families.
Able both to exhort in sound doctrine and to refute those who contradict (Titus 1:9). Able to teach (1 Timothy (1:2)	The translation "able to teach" is probably weak for *didastikos*, which really means "skilled at teaching." A skilled teacher is one who can cause others to learn. And learning for Christians means learning to do what the word teaches, not just to know it. In Titus, Paul adds the extra condition that elders must know the word well enough to refute those who contradict. In both passages, teaching is associated with eldership. An elder need not be gifted at teaching, but should be able to do a good job when needed. Elders are to lead based on biblical teaching, not their own opinions.

Appendix 2

Qualifications for Deacons

Paul gives twelve distinct qualifications for deacons.

1. **Dignity** **(1 Timothy 3:8)**	Paul begins this sentence with "likewise," suggesting the foregoing description regarding elders applies in principle. Dignity (*semnos*) means honorable, or having a respectable reputation.
2. **Not double tongued** **(1 Timothy 3:8)**	*Me dilogos* means not hypocritical but sincere—not saying one thing to one and something different to another, not a liar, straightforward.
3. **Not addicted to much wine** **(1 Timothy 3:8)**	This expression means the deacon avoids drinking too much. It suggests no abuse or dependence on any drug. Deacons should demonstrate freedom not to drink.
4. **Not fond of sordid gain** **(1 Timothy 3:8)**	This is the same expression used for elders, meaning not shamefully greedy. It includes unwillingness to manipulate or resort to illegitimate means for personal gain. It means deacons demonstrate a proper values system, including a willingness to give up moneymaking opportunities for the sake of the gospel. This also implies that the deacon should be giving consistently and sacrificially of his or her money.

5. Holding fast to the mystery of the faith with a clear conscience (1 Timothy 3:9)	"Holding fast to the mystery," means deacons should *know* the word of God. "With a clear conscience" means they don't just know, but also *practice* the Word. This includes having a clear conscience with regard to the service being rendered to the church (i.e. sins of omission are also wrong).
6. Tested first and beyond reproach (1 Timothy 3:10)	Deacons must have a proven ability to do the work of shepherding and service effectively and without any grounds for accusation. In other words, we don't decide that someone is a deacon, we recognize that someone already is a deacon.
7. Not malicious gossips (1 Timothy 3:11)	They demonstrate care not to exaggerate or to speak abusively about others. This implies the ability to keep a secret when appropriate. If they do share the failings of others, it would only be with those in a responsible position and for proper reasons—not for sport.
8. Temperate (1 Timothy 3:11)	*Naphalios* means, "not given to excess, self-controlled and emotionally stable." Deacons should demonstrate they are not wild or out of control.
9. Faithful in all things (1 Timothy 3:11)	This is reliability. It implies that we don't have to worry when deacons are given a job to do; they will do their best.
10. Husband of one wife (1 Timothy 3:12)	Literally a "one-woman man," this expression means there is at most one person of the other sex in the deacon's life. It means, in principle, that the deacon has his or her sexuality resolved and under control. Considering the evidence covered earlier in the Chapter 17 that deacons were both male and

	female, this verse demonstrates Paul's lack of concern for gender-neutral language or exhaustive listing of possibilities (unlike modern writers). He lets the expression using the male gender apply to both genders.
11. One who manages his own household well (1 Timothy 3:12)	Again, the word "manage" should be translated "lead" like it is elsewhere in the New Testament. The primary application is to married men, meaning that their family lives are good. In the case of the unmarried, it would imply they have close relationships and that those relationships are generally healthy and stable (such as with roommates). A pattern of broken relationships suggests an inability to get along with others (especially your own family and friends) and disqualifies a would-be deacon.
12. Not malicious gossips (1 Timothy 3:11)	The word for gossips means to hurl against and is also used for slander and hurling accusations. Talking people down for sport is highly discrediting.